THE CASTLE IN ENGLAND AND WALES
An Interpretative History

THE CASTLE IN ENGLAND AND WALES

An Interpretative History

D.J. CATHCART KING

CROOM HELM
London & Sydney

© 1988 D.J. Cathcart King
Croom Helm Ltd, Provident House,
Burrell Row, Beckenham, Kent

Croom Helm Australia, 44-50 Waterloo Road,
North Ryde, 2113, New South Wales

British Library Cataloguing in Publication Data

King, D.J. Cathcart
   The castle in England and Wales: an
   interpretative history.
   1. Castles — England — History
   I. Title
   942   DA660
   ISBN 0-7099-4829-8

First published in North America
in 1988 by
Areopagitica Press, Inc.
9999 S.W. Wilshire
Portland, Oregon 97225, USA

Library of Congress Cataloging-in-Publication Data

King, David James Cathcart.
   The castle in England and Wales: an interpretative history / D.J.
   Cathcart King.
      p. cm.
   Includes index.
   ISBN 0-918400-08-2
   1. Castles — England — History. 2. Castles — Wales — History.
3. Fortification — England — History. 4. Fortification — Wales —
History. 5. England — Antiquities. 6. Wales — Antiquities.
7. Great Britain — History, Military — Medieval period, 1066–1485.
I. Title.
DA660.K543   1988
942 — dc 19   88-926
                        CIP

Typeset by Leaper & Gard Ltd, Bristol, England
Printed and bound in Great Britain by Mackays of Chatham Ltd, Kent

Contents

Figures

Acknowledgements

Since this work formed part of the same study as my *Castellarium Anglicanum* of 1983, I must express my indebtedness to very much the same list of antiquaries; unhappily, death has removed several of these: my good friend Professor John Beeler of South Carolina, the superb medievalist Pierre Héliot, and my excellent adviser on Crusading matters, Dr R.C. (Otto) Smail of Sidney Sussex College, Cambridge. I am still indebted to Douglas Hogue, Dr A. H. A. Hogg (my partner in the enumeration of castles in Wales and the Marches), C.N. Johns, Dr Ralegh Radford, Dr Derek Renn, Jack Spurgeon, Dr Arnold Taylor and Andrew Saunders (a pair of worthy Chief Inspectors), also André Chatellain, my continuator in *Castellarium*, John Kenyon and Beric Morley. Having lost Otto Smail, I am the more dependent on His Honour Judge Perks and on Professor Leslie Alcock of Glasgow University; he it is in particular who has encouraged me to publish the present volume, and acted rather as my supervisor, as if I were returned to my post-graduate youth — a happy time.

Correction
In dealing with the timber transoms across the openings of many gunports of the fifteenth and sixteenth centuries, I had written (p. 166) 'the subject ... is one which has hardly been studied at all in English'. This was entirely unfair to Stewart Cruden, whose *The Scottish Castle* (Edinburgh and London, 1960) contains on pp. 216-17, 219, a study of the transoms (cills) and the hook-muzzled guns which were used from them.

Until Henry VIII's great programme of defence, Scotland was far in advance of England in terms of artillery fortification.

Preface

In the course of preparing a *catalogue raisonnée*, with its attendant bibliography, of the castles of England and Wales — which has appeared in print as *Castellarium Anglicanum* (Kraus-Thomson, New York, 1983) — the author acquired a considerable knowledge of the subject of medieval fortification. He had also become acquainted with foreign castellation through the meetings of Château Gaillard and the Fortress Study Group, as well as having had the honour of serving His late Majesty in the land of the Crusades.

The resulting information was offered for publication in a number of chapters, along with the catalogue and bibliography, and was (not surprisingly) refused, the publishers having already quite enough on their plates, in the shape of the two bulky volumes of *Castellarium Anglicanum*. These chapters, in fact, were accepted as part of the Great Unpublished, when Professor Leslie Alcock of Glasgow, who had read them, and reckoned them the most significant part of these labours, suggested that they deserved to appear in print.

1

The Character of a Castle

Any book on castles is likely to start with a discussion of what a castle is, and so much has been written on the matter elsewhere that it is desirable to be very brief here. *Typically, a castle was a fortified habitation*; I would use the word 'residence' if this did not suggest a gracious and comfortable dwelling, at least by the standards of its time, whereas very many castles by no means qualify for that character. Nor, for that matter, were their owners necessarily resident in their castles for much of the time, or even for any of it. Some castles, particularly among those belonging to the king or his greater subjects, were ordinarily inhabited by an officer.

It is in some ways easier to say what a castle is not. It is not a building without defences, or without defences which could have been held against a serious attack. This last expression is not capable of exact definition, and individual examples in the complete spectrum of the less powerful buildings can only be classed as weak castles or strengthened dwelling-houses by individual acts of judgment — and individual judgments vary. At least we can set aside, as something less than castles, such rustic defences against theft as homestead moats and the little stone houses of the Scottish border which are called 'bastles'.

There are other categories of medieval fortification which are not castles, because they are corporate habitations: walled towns, embanked villages, and fortified churches and convents. A work on medieval fortification should pay attention to these, but they are not castles, and in general are more weakly fortified. But this is not to say that a castle — even one atypical, by English standards — could not be owned and used by a corporate body. The Swiss cantons are notable not only for founding castles of their own but also for buying out the baronial proprietors of a multitude of others in their very densely castled country. In England the monasteries of the North Country owned a number of towers for the refuge of their tenantry against the Scots. Moreover, they owned at least two refuges for themselves from the *furor Scoticus*: Piel (Lancashire) was the refuge of Furness Abbey, a very fine example of a fourteenth-century castle; whilst Wolsty, of which only a square entrenchment survives, was licensed to Holm Cultram Abbey in 1348. One of the most splendid and regretted castles destroyed since the great Leland's pere-grination in the mid-sixteenth century was the 'Castel Quadrate' of Plymouth, the property of the corporation of the city, a powerful artillery-castle, of which virtually nothing remains today.

Commonly, however, the owner of a castle was an individual, whether king or subject, and he might well use it as his dwelling — one of his dwell-ings if he was at all wealthy. In peaceful times and in quiet regions, when the lord of the castle and his household rode away, the castle, stripped of all its furniture except the trestle tables and benches of the hall, was left to some administrative official — sheriff or bailiff, forester or constable — and a mere 'care and maintenance party'; under less happy conditions, to a constable and a fighting garrison. But the more remote castles — it is notorious that English barons held scattered estates, and the king, in particular, could not be everywhere — were occupied by such officials and their underlings most of the time, with the owner appearing, if at all, to conduct some sort of tour of inspection (perhaps combined with a hunting-season, if the castle was favourably placed for this). Inevitably, some of these were intended for other than normally residential purposes: as administrative centres, as forest castles, military strong points, or refuges for the tenantry.

Admittedly, every castle was a habitation; a place has to be inhabited to be defended; even the most austere fort of recent times contains barracks. At the same time, the ruling classes, from the king downwards, had plenty of unfortified dwellings, at least away from the border areas. It is particularly notable that the very formidable stone and earthwork Castle Acre (Norfolk) began its short life as an unfortified hall of the Norman settlement period;[1] other earthwork castles were raised on the sites of Saxon or (more rarely) Norman manor-houses. There are (or were) examples at Sulgrave (North-amptonshire)[2] and the very curious Goltho (Lincolnshire).[3] Here the princi-pal determining factor in the siting of the new castle was simply the plain convenience of occupying the same site as the old house. Many castles, indeed, stand on level, accessible sites, their lords (particularly those of small fees) having no strong positions available on their property. This is a common feature of southern England, and also of many of the tiny fees of the March of Wales.

'Life in a castle' is a subject for another book than this. There are so many factors: the increasing appetite for comfort; the increasing means to afford it; the competing needs of defence; the advances in construction; the mere question of the resources of the proprietor and the grandeur and comfort possible within the limits imposed by the available quarters.

For example, the splendours of life at Windsor under Edward III or Richard II would not have been possible under the frugal and relatively primitive Henry II, still less the comparatively barbarous Conqueror. Any king, moving from Windsor to some more martial address — Dover or Rhuddlan, Carlisle or Berwick — must necessarily have kept a less magnificent and more military sort of state. At the Castle of the Peak (Derbyshire), which was essentially a forest-castle, the small square keep would have been the temporary abode of the lord, and a wretched little affair it was. The castle's lord, down to 1254, was in fact the king; it offered him only the comforts of a hunting-lodge of the worst kind.

Some writers, including Professor Allen Brown in his widely, and rightly, praised *English Castles*,[4] insist on the magnificence of life in the more illustrious castles: the larger royal strongholds, baronial castles like Chester or Warwick or Sheriff Hutton; but this could not be matched by smaller barons or simple knights. No doubt they would have used all the colour and ostentation they could afford, but shortage of funds and also probably of space would have set limits on what they could manage. Still less scope for grandeur was available to the occupants of a simple tower, such as those on the Scottish border; these, moreover, often belonged to men below the knightly rank — parsons and the like.[5]

Nor was this the bottom end of the spectrum of comfort and magnificence. We may suppose that most earthwork castles had timber buildings, and that at least the smaller examples of these were likely to have been the work of unskilled workmen. There is little concrete evidence for these statements; but Professor Alcock has conducted the excavation of Penmaen (Castle Tower) on the coast of the Gower peninsula, and recovered the plans of its inner buildings. The original hall (as I suppose it may be) was a small timber two-bay structure, likely to have been decently carpentered, but its replacement was a very dismal structure indeed; I understand its excavators alluded to it as 'the Slum' and even modern slum-dwellers would have found it very unpleasant; its floor was made of broken stones and clay, to level off the very uneven site; its plan is called 'sub-rectangular', with walls that are not straight, corners that are not angles, and ends which form some kind of a curve, but not the arc of a circle; drystone walls less than a yard or a metre high, in which the roof-timbers seem to have been imbedded — for there was no central row of posts to carry them. This regrettable structure 'reveals the architectural squalor which might be endured by the holder of one and a half knights' fees'.[6]

This was perhaps the nadir of comfort and dignity among permanent castles, but there was 'in the lowest deep a lower deep' — the temporary fortified positions of wartime. Generally these were siege-castles, built to blockade the fortresses of the other side, but there were examples like Topcliffe, intruded into a rebel area by the royalist Geoffrey Plantagenet, Bishop of Lincoln, in 1174. Any shelter these may have contained is hardly likely — since they were transient holds — to have been more elaborate than the Penmaen 'Slum', and may well have been even worse. Perhaps the generally poor performance of these fortifications may have been due to the difficulty of getting men to stay in them, for some simply disappeared, leaving the blockaded stronghold uncaptured; others again were ignominiously taken by the defenders.

The typical castle, however, was the dwelling of some figure in the feudal order. It was, therefore, a house, or at least contained one. There is no reason for the notion that life in a castle was necessarily uncomfortable by the standards of the time; we must compare like with like; if a medieval nobleman disliked living in a castle, he would only have had the alternative of living in an unfortified house of his own period, which would have had very much the same arrangements as the house inside the castle. It would have had thinner walls — a point in the castle's favour — and less precaution in the siting of windows; but its outside windows would inevitably have been kept small and high as a precaution against theft; and in the earlier period, when glass was scarce, all windows were inevitably small.

A similar error is that life in the major keep-towers was so uncomfortable that they were only used as retreats (*réduits*) in emergency — a mistake propagated by the great G.T. Clark. In fact, though the cylindrical keeps of the twelfth and thirteenth centuries certainly called for a greater effort (and a probable failure) to preserve comfort, the more primitive Norman keep was merely a lofty and massively built dwelling-house, and it was so successful in this character that a very typical feature in the history of construction of a building of this type is the suppression of an original pitched roof — an inverted V or W in section, sheltered by the heads of the walls — in favour of a flat roof, level with the wall-walks, so as to afford an extra storey. Some have had yet another floor added, as at Portchester.

Many castellans were very small men, particularly in the border areas; but yet their way of life may have been military, with a touch of ostentation.[7]

It is a long step from this to supposing that the principal reason — still less the sole reason — for possessing a castle was to advertise one's importance. It is these very small castles — which might serve to indicate that the proprietor belonged to the fringes of the upper class — which were built mainly in threatened areas, where fortification was a matter of deadly necessity. This was a vast distance from Veblen's theory of conspicuous waste. Barons, indeed, presumably had to have castles; a good case is the creation of the new barony of Audley in 1227, whereupon Henry de Audley built himself Red-Castle and apparently also Heighley. A later example of a castle built to support the power and dignity of a new barony is Raglan (Gwent), built in the mid-fifteenth century. A castle, however, was an object of use; in a later age 'carriage folk' were visibly of the upper classes, but they also possessed a more capacious, reliable and agreeable means of transport than others. A castle was not a cheap asset: if properly built, it was likely to be expensive to build; if cheaply built, it would be expensive to maintain. It could not, therefore, be a pure status symbol, like fashionable articles of dress, which the gentry would probably strive to forbid to their inferiors by law. There was no attempt to regulate castles in terms of the sumptuary laws; the Malefaunts

4

of Upton (Pembrokeshire, now part of Dyfed), holding half a knight's fee, on the fourth rung of the feudal ladder,[8] were permitted to build their tiny castle. The little motte-castles of the Welsh March and the towers of the Scottish border were often raised on even smaller holdings. They afforded little or no splendour — protection was everything.

A castle was likely to be the administrative centre of its owner's estate (or part of it), and like all but the least substantial manor-houses, it served as a court-house for the local tenants. In particular, for those awaiting trial, it could afford a secure prison. Lydford, indeed, though built as a fairly substantial castle, was essentially a rather notorious prison. (There were, of course, numerous arrangements, more or less effective, for custody of accused persons, away from any castle.) The dungeon, beloved of our young — who see one in every dark chamber of a castle in guardianship — is relatively uncommon; stocks or irons in the guardroom would serve very well; the dungeon was likely to be kept for desperadoes, or as a threat to discipline the prisoners, or extort funds from them (for life in prison tended to be expensive; not only in the Middle Ages).

Imprisonment as a *punishment* is not typical of medieval law; but there were jurisdictions which were forbidden to order sentence of death or mutilation: Courts Christian, and (after 1217) Forest Courts. It follows that bishops' castles often had considerable permanent prisons, as at Llawhaden, while those poachers whose limbs and eyes had been saved by *Carta de Foresta*, 1217, were fined and consigned to the prison chambers of the forest-castle until they paid. Often they could not pay, and could only echo the sad words carved on the walls of the prison of St Briavel's:

For I have been here a great space
And I am weary of the place.

It will be seen that there was little out of the ordinary about the peacetime character of a castle: it could provide very splendid accommodation, or very squalid; it might serve the *amour propre* of its owner; it might provide an effectual prison. More particularly, the periods of peace were much longer than those of war, even at such a dangerous place as, say, Wark on Tweed. This is probably true, even if one does not count times of alarm and precaution under the heading of 'peace'.

It is thus the contemporary fashion to dwell on the castle's peaceful functions; and this can be seen as a healthy reaction against the totally military view taken by some earlier antiquaries: for example, that the typical 'corkscrew' newel-stair always rotates clockwise in rising,[9] so as to make it impossible for an assailant to use his sword!

But castles need to be considered in military terms. As Mrs Olsen says of those of Denmark: 'After all, war is what they were meant for.'[10] Perhaps not entirely for *war*, the Middle Ages, as a violent period, had a number of emergencies which fell short of the operations of war, properly so called. Elsewhere[11] I have listed these as *disseisin, insurrection* and *foray:* ejection from one's property, confrontation with peasantry in revolt, and raiding.

As to the first of these, our ancestors spent an enormous amount of their time and energy in bickering over landed property, and going to law about it; but the invasion of a manor or similar area was futile if a castle stood there. The business would be unfinished; the intruders would experience a great deal of difficulty in getting hold of rents and profits if all the tenants knew perfectly well that their original master's steward was preparing his accounts in the shelter of the castle walls. No doubt one might capture the castle itself, but unless this was done by surprise, a matter of civilian incursion and minor bullying would 'escalate' into a business in which men would be getting killed; and even a successful seizure of the castle would not end matters: any reasonably adequate king — sensible of his duty as inspector-general of fortifications — would immediately object in a very formidable manner, as happened when Miserden was captured in a family brawl in 1230,[12] and Manorbier in another in 1324.[13] The destruction of Eynesford, apparently by factious foes, in 1312, befell under the weak Edward II, in a time of virtual civil war, and the capture of Caister, in 1469, occurred in an absolute vacuum of legality of the most disgraceful sort. The looting of the Despencer estates in 1321, which did involve the momentary occupation of the castles by the embattled Lords Marchers, belongs rather to the class of foray.

Peasants in revolt play an important part in some sorts of history; but in England they were not generally dangerous except at two periods: the years after the Norman Conquest, when the new lords appeared as upstart and tyrant foreigners, and when there were available a number of natural leaders — thegns and freemen — who were being deprived or oppressed under the new regime; and the great revolt of 1381 following the agricultural disasters of the fourteenth century, culminating in the Black Death. At both of these times there was plenty of castle-building, but at other times, no doubt, there were estates where the peasants had local grievances, and their lords found the shelter of a castle opportune.

Foray was a business shading off from simple crime to the fringe activities of an army in the field. In its turn such an army might be carrying out a programme of deliberate robbery and destruction, like Robert the Bruce in the north of England, or Edward III and the Black Prince in France; or depending on supplies drawn from foraging; or simply be thoroughly undisciplined. In this connection, it must be remembered that the paymaster is at least as potent a force for discipline as the provost-marshal — for unpaid and unfed troops inevitably become robbers, even if they do not compound their guilt by becoming stragglers or deserters.

But there was more to foray than the periphery of armies; in times of civil strife it was common practice to raid the property of the opposite faction.

The borders, the south coast and the islands were exposed to raiding, and not only in wartime. Any coastal area was exposed to piracy by 'enemies of the human race', and border thieves were numerous, and not confined to the Scottish nation.

In war, a castle's main duty consisted in the holding of territory. When a castle was captured, its lord lost his hold on his local property, and so did his sovereign. Conversely — since a castle could be an instrument of conquest as well as of defence — if an invader built a castle (or took one from the enemy), he obtained territory. The Norman Conquest is an example of the latter process; the Anglo-Saxons had no castles — which facilitated, if it did not actually make possible, their overthrow. The Normans busied themselves with building castles in all parts of the realm, particularly a number of powerful examples on the Sussex coast to make sure of a link with Normandy and a means of reconquering England, should they later be repulsed. Over much of the conquered nation, knights and minor nobles who had been granted estates — a process which was highly advanced by the time of Domesday Book in 1085–6 — were engaged in building the little earthwork castles, unknown to recorded history, that are so numerous in our shires; they were acting in self-defence, but they greatly increased the power over England of William the Bastard, now William the Conqueror. On the Welsh and Scottish borders, further precautions were needed; towards Scotland, where the frontier was doubtful and unsettled, Malcolm Canmore, king of Scots, was a possible rival for the throne of England, and it needed campaigns in the field, as well as the foundation of some powerful castles, to contain him. As to Wales, the boundary was not settled, and was never to be settled before the Edwardian Conquest. From the Norman point of view, the time of collision was very fortunate; a formidable Welsh national movement under Gruffydd ap Llywelyn, who had dispossessed a number of local dynasties, had been crushed by Harold Godwinsson himself as recently as 1063, and the shattered[14] Welsh nation could hardly conduct the conquest of the English midlands against which William fitz Osbern and others built a line of March castles to be sure of English territory. The Welsh learned the use of castles from the Anglo-Normans early in the twelfth century;[15] thereafter, English and Welsh strove for a mastery which could only be understood in terms of castles, with which the local divisions, the units of conquest and reconquest, were closely identified.[16] The Anglo-Normans had introduced the castle to Wales, but perpetual strife was no novelty to that country.

Towards Scotland, England had for some time been on the defensive, and for a century and a half from the Conquest was subjected to massive invasions by the kings of Scots, aimed at conquering the north of England. The Norman kings from time to time mounted counterattacks, and William Rufus in 1092 seized on the country later called Cumberland, annexed it to his kingdom, and built the fortress of Carlisle.[17] This effectively discouraged invasion by the bad west-coast route; both the natural east-coast route across the Tweed and down the coast of Northumberland and the line of the Roman road towards Scotch Corner were furnished, from an early date, with powerful castles which made it difficult for the Scots to acquire territory there. Admittedly David I in his 1138 campaign, opposed only by the hopelessly embarrassed Stephen, carried his frontier forward to the Tees and the Ribble and would have carried it to the Humber, if he had not been heavily defeated at the Battle of the Standard; but in 1174 his son William the Lion was brought up by the defences of the border, and eventually defeated.[18]

There were other borderlands which needed securing at a later date: in 1200 we find King John giving orders to the proprietors in the 'March of Ireland'.

> The King, etc, to all those having lands in the March of Ireland, greeting. We command and require you to fortify the castles in your lands of the March before the next feast of St. John the Baptist, so that through no failure on your part shall happen any harm to our land, as you have hitherto done ['*sic hactenus fec*'][19] otherwise we have ordered that your lands of the March be taken into our hand, and we will give them to other people who will fortify them.

On pain of forfeiture these tenants had to fortify castles, or possibly put them in repair[21] within a fairly short time, 'so that no harm befall our land'. Plainly, they were to take precautions to prevent the incursions of the 'Wild Irish' from gaining territory.

Returning to the few years after the Norman Conquest, we find one or two strange castles concerned with the pacification of England. It is noticeable that many early castles were extremely large in area, and have been reduced in size: Norwich, where the baileys were progressively abandoned to the town, leaving only the very large motte, is a case in point. This is likely to be due to the extra accommodation in the keep and other stone-built structures on the motte, which will have rendered the baileys unnecessary. But a more military story seems to be told in respect of the next two examples. Deddington stands close to the little Oxfordshire town of the same name. It was an enormous enclosure, very strongly banked and ditched; on one corner there was a motte (unusually, not ditched on the side of the enclosure). The great area seems never to have been utilised for permanent building; the motte was levelled and a small castle of twelfth-century character was built on its site. The whole has the appearance of a very large earthwork, replaced by a very small stone castle. The position is connected with Bishop Odo of Bayeux, who was left in part charge of England in 1067. Here he could well have stabled the horses and quartered the soldiers of a considerable field force such as he needed. As the soldiery were drawn off to fiefs of their own in the course of the settlement, there was less need for accommodation at headquarters, and eventually only need for a fairly small castle.

The story of Castle Neroche, in the Blackdown Hills to the south of Taunton, is more complicated. It consists of an exceedingly large motte at the point of a very strongly marked foreland, with a complicated system of embanked works on the level beside it. The outermost, hard to date, encloses the formidable area of 7.5 acres; the other works represent a progressive reduction of this excessive size. The Domesday tenant, Robert Count of Mortain, seems to have occupied the position — quite possibly already embanked — during the disturbances immediately after the Conquest. The communications of the site were good, and it would have made a good strategic position. Subsequently (as shown by an admirable excavation report by Mr Brian Davison)[22] two attempts were made to establish a fortified cantonment in the interior of the enclosure: the first was abortive; the second, involving a more radical reduction in area, was completed. The erection of a very large motte and a small inner bailey and the doubling of the ditch round what had been the cantonment, but was now the main bailey of an orthodox, if very large, castle, followed; it may have had some connection with the alienation to Montacute Priory of the powerful Mortain castle of Montacute, 13 miles away, about this time. But when Count William, son of Robert, forfeited his English lands in 1104, the castle was evidently abandoned. (The last stage of construction, which involved building a sort of miniature 'shell-keep' and bailey of clay-laid masonry *on top of the very big motte*, has evidently nothing to do with the rest of the narrative of construction; it was probably the work of obscure, and most likely nefarious, individuals in the Anarchy of Stephen.)

It seems likely that the final stage in the history of Lydford No. 2 — the earlier of the two castles at what, in Anglo-Saxon days, had been a considerable place — was concerned with this same disturbance in the newly conquered south-west: its interior structures consisted of a set of sheds, some at least containing grain — evidently a supply-depot for a field force.

The normal castle, at once martial and residential, could hold territory, and was intended to do so, but could not normally 'block' or 'command' a line of movement, in the manner of a latter-day fortress (which would have been much larger — normally a town — and would have mounted guns). This could only be done in cases where the castle occupied, or overlooked, a defile. Dover, overlooking what was a rather small harbour, but splendidly placed for movement between the French coast and the interior of England, is our foremost example of the sort; actual rocky gorges are few in England, and not many of these are commanded by castles. In the north-west, the mountain trench called Mallerstang is occupied by Pendragon Castle, and a north–south route (now followed by a motorway) through the fells passes close to the motte-and-bailey of Tebay, while the Roman road to Scotch Corner passes under the walls of a whole series of castles, mostly of early date; elsewhere it is unusual to find castles used in this barrier-fort fashion. Perhaps the most dramatic site is the deep rocky gorge of the Western Cleddau in northern Pembrokeshire (Dyfed); the place still goes by the name of

Wolf's Castle. 'In view, however, of the small size of the castle, it seems unlikely that the Wolf, whoever he was, was sufficiently powerful to take advantage of this significant position.'[23]

In any case, outside the very limited range of its missile-weapons, the castle could only interfere with enemy movements by means of sorties on the part of the garrison. At once it is clear that this can never have halted a field army. The garrison of the great Crusader castle of Saphet (Safad) in the early 1260s is enumerated as: 50 knights (Templars), 30 serving-brothers (presumably equivalent to serjeants-at-arms, two of whom were equal in value to one knight), 50 Turcoples (light horse), all the above with horse and arms; 300 crossbowmen, 820 workmen, 400 slaves. The last two classes were evidently non-combatants, and the crossbow, wickedly effective in siege or defence, was notoriously a mediocre weapon in the field. The castle, which evidently was still being built, could have put into the field about 200 effectives, of whom 80 would have been the all-important heavy cavalry.[24] Thus, when we hear that Le Krak des Chevaliers — which certainly was added to throughout and beyond its tenure by the Hospitaller knights — had a garrison of 2,000 in about 1212,[25] and if we assume the same proportions, it would appear that the Krak — surely the most formidable castle in Christendom — probably held 60 knights, 35 serjeants, 60 Turcoples, and a mass of non-combatants; perhaps not surprisingly, we find 60 knights in garrison in 1255.[26] When Château-Gaillard fell in 1204, the prisoners included 40 knights, 120 *satellites* (presumably serjeants) and many others.[27]

On the other hand, the Fair of Lincoln — the second battle of Lincoln in 1217 — was a notably small encounter to determine the succession to the throne of England: the Confederate (Capetian) faction numbered 600 knights, the Royalists (Plantagenets, who were victorious) only 400. The English army which won the great victory of Agincourt was notoriously almost pathetically small, with no more than 900 men-at-arms (knights and serjeants) and 5,000 archers.

It will be seen that even small medieval armies were far too strong for the garrisons of the most formidable castles. Any kind of field army could safely bypass a castle (where this was physically possible) both coming and going — provided, of course, that it moved in good order; in case of a hurried and disorderly retreat, the existence of a hostile castle on the road for home raised a number of sinister possibilities. A vigilant garrison could interfere effectively with communications — though these were comparatively unimportant for the relatively small, frugal and mobile armies of the Middle Ages. Even a little castle could serve to cut off messengers and scattered foraging-parties, and where castles were numerous, whether they were big or small, foraging could be dangerous or impossible.

But it would be a mistake to imagine that castles were founded according to the rules of fortification of a much later age; admittedly there were border fortresses: towards Scotland, Wark on Tweed, Norham and Liddel Strength stood on the very border, and a number of minor fortifications close behind, as they did on the Welsh border; in both cases everything was exposed to invasion, and everything needed to be fortified. Inside the borders, a number of castles are found at what would be accepted as strategic positions in the later period; but this merely means that they were built, for the most part, at towns, or at least places which, like the towns, had good communications. Some of these were lines of communication by sea: the first Norman landings in 1066, the Anglo-Norman penetrations into South Wales in the twelfth and thirteenth centuries, and the Edwardian castles around the coast of conquered North Wales, all depended in part on sea communications. Dunstanburgh was meant to have some maritime links in pursuit of its very dubious purposes. Pevensey — where, it is to be remembered, the Conqueror made his first landing — was evidently very hard to come at by land; hence its prolonged and successful defence against the Montfortians in 1264–5.

But what might be considered strategic routes, and strategic points, were frequently left unfortified, contrary to what one may think of as the rule of the science of war.[28] W. Mackay Mackenzie demonstrated this in the case of Scotland,[29] and Dr R.C. Smail in that of the land of the Crusades,[30] where medieval warfare was at its most serious and its most scientific. In England, the important road-junction of Coventry had a castle only in Stephen's reign; the strategic importance of the crossing of the Ure on the Great North Road at Boroughbridge was acknowledged by the building of a castle (Aldborough), but nearly a mile away; and this did not flourish, for the site seems to have been abandoned for about a century when battle was joined on Boroughbridge in 1322. The Thames crossing at Reading was surely important, but its only castle was a short-lived and illegal one built by King Stephen, which did not outlast his reign. Pembrokeshire (Dyfed) is a well-castled area, but its most evident strategic point, Canaston Bridge on the Eastern Cleddau, never boasted a castle.

Castles, in fact, were built to hold territory; if they could interfere with the movements of a hostile army, that would be something of an uncovenanted mercy.

For the mere holding of territory, a good many of the lordships of the Welsh March needed two castles (big lordships, like Pembroke and Glamorgan, required more); but the compact lordship of Grosmont contained three. The Three Castles formed a triangle of 5 miles/8 kilometres the side; Grosmont was the *caput*; Skenfrith was at least habitable, but the advanced and exposed White Castle was purely a military strong point. Even the constable's quarters, which had fireplaces, but also an earth floor, were none too luxurious, but the miserable little hall and the great central cesspit (next to the constable's rooms) suggest something far more unpleasant than usual, while the burnt-out Well Tower suggests an accident with a brazier (the towers had no fireplaces originally, and there is no record of any attack on

11

White Castle to explain the fire). This was plainly a purely military stronghold; whether it needed to be quite as squalid as it was remains uncertain. The rest of the hilltop on which the castle was built was embanked at some period; a large portion of this was given walls and towers, but no interior buildings whatever. It seems likely that the purpose of this addition (coming at the time when a Welsh advance had come close to the castle, and when its proprietors were members of the royal family) was to reverse the process which we have seen at Castle Neroche, and establish, alongside the very military castle, a strong cantonment for a field force.

Similar dependent enclosures in a great number of castles may have been intended as refuges for the local population; this, indeed, was a necessary business in war. These refuges are commonly called 'base-courts' in English; (the French *basse-cour* has more the sense of 'farmyard').[31] There are, however, castles whose principal purpose was simply the protection of the populace. Naturally, these are mainly to be found in threatened territory; they do not seem to occur on the Welsh March, but they are frequent on the northern border and in the Channel Isles. Facing Scotland, a number of the protective towers belonged to religious bodies or to magnates, none of whom had any use for them personally; it was to protect the tenantry that they were built. In the Channel Isles, close to the coast of France, there was need for a number of such refuge-castles. Of these, Grosnez (Jersey) has been excavated; inside its respectable military perimeter, of early fourteenth-century character, there are only the foundations of some half-dozen poor little huts.

Harbour-defence generally belongs to the period of artillery, but narrow entrances, like those of Fowey, Dartmouth, Plymouth (the Cattewater)[32] and Portsmouth, were defended with chains — their ends, and the windlasses with which they were raised, being protected by towers.

It is a truism that only a few castles were of major strategic importance; but, since castles and towers were built by a vast variety of individuals from kings to North-Country parsons and petty gentry, it would be amazing if this were not the case. If the strongholds of minor lords, or of officials on some remote corner of a great man's estates (such as Shilbottle), however well built and well sited they were, could stand up against an army — particularly a royal army — then Chaos would have come again, and the appropriate music would have been 'The World Turned Upside-Down'.

But collectively they could be important; such a mandate as that of King John to the castellans of the Irish March, mentioned above, makes no distinction between big castles and small. All were to be fortified, lest harm befall. John's son, engaged in building his new castle of Montgomery in 1225, gave orders to Godescal de Maghelins, to be passed on to 'all those who have mottes in the Vale of Montgomery, that without delay they have their mottes defended with good bretasches, for their own safety and defence and that of those parts'.[33]

This was a category of a very humble sort; that the King sent no mandate to any of them, but relied on Godescal to pass on his orders, suggests as much. In fact, the lords of these little earthworks (the 'good bretasches' commanded were timber towers) were of trifling importance, holding fractions of a knight's fee, from a half down to an eighth,[34] but yet a king's government valued them 'for the safety and defence of themselves and of those parts'.

Of the (Scottish) Border Surveys, that of Bowes and Ellerker, in 1541,[35] is the most important, and not merely from a military point of view. This is a document of social history, dealing with a rural culture lapsing back into barbarism.[36] The border towers plainly played an important part in holding back the darkness;

> the commissioners remark on the evil consequences of the lack of towers in exposed townships; in an alert, the inhabitants would abandon their holdings and retreat into England, taking along with them the able-bodied men who would otherwise have been of service in defending the border. It would be long before the husbandry of such an abandoned locality recovered, and in many places the refugees plainly never returned at all. The whole has the appearance of a process of progressive deterioration, which the provision of even a very modest tower could arrest.[37]

In all of these cases, the minor castles in question were of national significance in the opinion of the rulers of the country or their responsible officials.

Notes

1. J.G. Coad, 'Excavation at Castle Acre, Norfolk, 1972-6', *Château-Gaillard* viii (1976), pp. 79-85.

2. Brian Davison, 'Excavations at Sulgrave, Northamptonshire', *Archaeological Journal* cxxxiv, (1977), pp. 105-14.

3. Guy Beresford, 'The Excavation of the deserted medieval village of Goltho, Lincolnshire', *Château-Gaillard* viii, (1976), pp. 47-67.

4. 2nd edition (London, 1976).

5. '*Nomina Castrorum et Fortaliciorum infra Comitatum Northumbrie*' (1415), in Bates, *Border Holds of Northumberland* (Newcastle 1891), pp. 13-18.

6. Professor Leslie Alcock, 'Ringworks of England and Wales', *Château-Gaillard* iii, (1969), p. 109.

7. To take an extreme case — the Casa dei Pagani at Malvaglia (Ticino, Switzerland) is an example of a castle on an overhung ledge halfway up a vertiginous cliff. Its structures are altogether ramshackle; nevertheless the excavators found pieces of luxury material and expensive parchment: see Lukas Högl in *Château-Gaillard* ix (1978), pp. 175-86.

8. They held of the de Carews, who were honorial barons of the Earls of Pembroke, tenants in chief of the king.

9. In fact, it does not.

10. Rikke Agnete Olsen, 'Danish Medieval Castles at War', *Château-Gaillard* ix, (1978), p. 223.

11. D.J. Cathcart King, *Castellarium Anglicanum* (New York, 1983), vol. 1, xviii.

12. Close Rolls (1227-31) 359; Patent Rolls (1225-32) 346; the castle was seized by the sheriff and returned to its owner, who was ordered to guard it properly in future.

13. The story is more complicated; see *Archaeologia Cambrensis* cxix (1970), pp. 86-8. It is noteworthy that the Crown intervened here, even in the feeble person of Edward II.

14. This word is employed deliberately: Wales was not only racked by an unsuccessful war, but had fallen apart into its component princedoms, in most cases the subject of armed dispute.

15. As early as 1111, when he was murdered, we find Cadwgan ap Bleddyn looking out the site for a castle at Welshpool, and in 1116 Uchdryd ap Edwin built Cymmer castle.

16. Sir Goronwy Edwards, 'The Normans and the Welsh March', *Proceedings of the British Academy* vol. 42 (1956), pp. 155-77; D.J. Cathcart King, 'Castles and the administrative divisions of Wales: a study of names', *Welsh History Review* x (1980), pp. 93-6.

17. In 1092; *Anglo-Saxon Chronicle* ed. Whitelock (London, 1961), p. 169.

18. King, *Castellarium Anglicanum* vol. 1, xlv-xlvii.

19. These three words must probably be read *sicut hactenus fecistis* — 'as you have always done in the past.' The clerk who made this entry in the rolls seems not to have been very capable; *sic* is not a usual abbreviation for *sicut.*

20. *Rotuli Chartarum*, 98b-99a.

21. The verb *firmare,* 'to strengthen', is commonly used in medieval Latin as meaning 'to fortify' in the first place.

22. *Somerset Archaeological Society* cxvi (1972), pp. 16-58, and plates 1-3.

23. Quoted from an unpublished work of my own on the castles of Pembrokeshire for the County History.

24. '*De constructione castri Saphet*' ed. Huygens in *Studi Medievale*, 3rd series vi, part 2 (1965), pp. 378-87.

25. Wilbrand of Oldenburg; see Deschamps, *Le Crac des Chevaliers* (Paris, 1934) III n. 1.

26. Bull of Pope Alexander IV in Deschamps, ibid., p. 130.

27. William le Breton, *Gesta Philippi Augusti* ed. Delaborde (Paris, 1882), i, p. 219.

28. King, *Castellarium Anglicanum* vol. 1, xx-xxii.

29. W. Mackay Mackenzie, *The Mediaeval Castle in Scotland* (Rhind Lectures in Archaeology, 1925-6 (London, 1927), pp. 79-80.

30. Dr R.C. Smail, *Crusading Warfare, 1097-1193* (Cambridge, 1956), pp. 204-44.

31. The German word *Vorburg* has rather the same sense; the formal division of a castle into *Hauptburg* and *Vorburg* has little relevance to English practice.

32. Not the Hamoaze (the more modern harbour of Plymouth, from which a sailing-ship could get out — as it could not from the Cattewater — against the prevailing wind).

33. *Rotuli Litterarum Clausarum*, ii, 42a.

34. R.W. Eyton, *The Antiquities of Shropshire* (London, 1860) xi, pp. 71-8, 80-4, 93-4, 157-61, 166-74.

35. See Bates, *Border Holds*, pp. 29-49 (slightly abridged; an addendum at pp. xvi-xvii.)

36. The dismal word 'decay' is repeated throughout.

37. King, *Castellarium Anglicanum*, vol. 1, lxv, referring to p. xxiii.

2

Castle-Guard

The problem of garrisoning a castle could be solved in two main ways: in the later period, with a money economy well established, it was the natural thing to hire fighting-men for wages; earlier, one would expect to find a feudal solution, a specialised form of military tenure. And that is what in fact we find — tenure by castle-guard.[1] Sometimes we even find a castle's defences divided up, towers or portions of the perimeter being assigned to individual tenants, as we see at Dover in particular, where these names — Crevecoeur's Tower, Godsfoe's Tower, etc. — have endured to the present day.

This was a variation of Knight Service, and, like Knight Service, could be commuted for money. The term 'wardsilver' occurs as the equivalent of scutage, if only locally, for the castle-guard tenant. This close correspondence is indicated in Magna Carta (version of 1217, article xxiv):

> No Constable shall distrain any Knight to give him money for Castle-guard, if he be willing to perform it in his own person, or by another able man (if he cannot perform it himself, for a reasonable cause) and if we do lead or send him into the army, he shall be excused from Castle-guard, according to the time that he shall be with us in the army, on account of the fee for which he hath done service in the post.[2]

On the Continent, before castles burst on the English scene, we hear of *Châtellanies* (*Castellariae*), which appear to have been compact groups of fees appendant to particular castles and charged with providing their garrisons.[3] English conditions were unfavourable to such compact groupings, and the practice seems to have been to charge each of a group of honours or lordships, scattered over the country, and often themselves quite widely dispersed, with fixed services. Thus, we find the most important of the honours providing guard at Dover was that of Haganet, whose *caput* was the big castle of Haughley, in Suffolk. Stenton was able to enumerate only nine English holdings actually described as castleries: Clifford, Ewyas Harold and Montgomery, which are elsewhere credited with castle-guard services, and

15

Berkhamstead, Caerleon, Dudley, Nottingham, Pontefract and Richard's Castle, about whose services I have found nothing else. All these castles date from the eleventh century.

The services performed were wildly varied and inconsistent; in the first place, the normal service was performed by knights, with of course the use of serjeants to perform half a knight's duties; but at Huntington in 1299 the service required was by archers.[4] Periods of guard-duty varied; they were commonly of 30 or 40 days, but we hear of service for a whole year (presumably, not necessarily by the same man), and there are other variations. Honours burdened with numbers of castle-guard duties grouped the fees which had to perform them to permit a roster of duties covering the year so as to satisfy the overlord, who in the case of the mightier castles was likely to be the King.

Working on the existing documentation, Painter considered that the castle-guard element in the garrison of Richmond was a permanent 31 knights, at Hastings 15, at the huge fortress of Dover no more than 22 or 23, and at Norwich an improbable 50. These figures are likely to be misleading; Dover may well have had a considerable paid, permanent garrison, and something has plainly gone wrong with the figures for Norwich, which was hardly ever more than a second-rate fortress.

Other duties in respect of castles are bound up with those of castle-guard; in some cases the subordinate tenement was also bound to supply quarters for the tenants on duty; in others to contribute to the upkeep of the castle. This seems to have been more common in France than in England; but on this side of the Channel the duties of keeping the outer fences of the castle in repair (as to the main works, this sort of upkeep was plainly unsuitable), were sufficiently important to obtain the name, when commuted for money, of *heckage*.

We can hardly look forward to anything approaching a complete list of the castles which were owed castle-guard services, and my own compilation makes no pretence of being one. It represents a collection of the instances of castle guard cited by Round, Ballard, Stenton and Painter — a formidable body of authority, it will be admitted, though none of the learned authors was aiming at a catalogue — conflated with such examples as I have met with in a search of the *Calendars* of *Inquisitiones post mortem*, together with some less systematic research. My list is as follows:

Aldford, Alnwick, Anstey, Arundel.
Bamburgh, Banbury, Barnstaple, Baynard's Castle, Belvoir, Benington, Bishop's Stortford, Bramber, Brecon, Buckenham.
Callow Hill, Canterbury, Cardiff, Castle Frome, Chester, Clare, Clifford, Clun, Codnor, Colwyn, Corfham.
Devizes, Dodleston, Donington, Dover, Dunster.
Ewyas Harold, Eye.

Farnham, Folkingham, Forden, Framlingham.

Halton, Hastings, Hedingham, Helmsley, Higham Ferrers, Holgate, Holt, Huntington.

Kington, Knockin.

Lancaster, Launceston, Lewes, Lincoln (Ledbury, mentioned in 1223, is probably Bishop's Castle; see *Castellarium Anglicanum*, vol. 1, p. xvii).

Mitford, Montgomery, Mulgrave.

Newark, Newcastle-upon-Tyne, Newhall, Northampton, Norwich.

Oakham, Okehampton, Ongar, Oswestry.

The Peak, Pevensey, Plympton, Prudhoe.

Radnor, Reigate, Richmond, Castle Rising, Rochester, Rockingham, Ruyton of the Eleven Towns.

Salisbury (Old Sarum), Scilly, Sheffield, Shrawardine, Skipsea, Skipton, Stapleton, Stogursey.

Tickhill, Tonbridge, Tonge, Torrington, Totnes, Trematon, Trowbridge, Tutbury.

Wallingford, Warwick, Welshpool, Wem, Whitchurch, White Castle, Wigmore, Windsor.

In addition the Castleries mentioned by Painter add another six to the total.

It will be seen that most of these castles are important, but at the same time a not inconsiderable number of major castles are omitted. No doubt some of these have been left out simply because of the limited scope of the enquiry, but it would appear that there were too many of these missing castles for this to be a completely satisfactory explanation.

While the castles listed were generally large and powerful, this was not the case at Castle Frome, Newhall, Oakham, Ruyton of the Eleven Towns, Stapleton or Tonge; and two half-fees were owed at the totally unimportant and fugitive Callow Hill (Shropshire).[5]

Similarly, in view of the general movement towards money wages, it is not surprising to find such a purely feudal feature as castle-guard generally associated with the older castles; but here again there are exceptions. Holt (Denbigh, now part of Clwyd) is first heard of in 1311, being then a new castle; Folkingham was licensed in 1312, and its square moated earthworks are those of a late castle. Both of these were owed castle-guard services.

In a few cases, incidents of Welsh tenure were altered to form services of this kind, generally not very advantageous to the lord, as at White Castle and Radnor.[6]

It seems possible that even from the Conquest the tendency was against castle-guard as a personal service. The variety of castleries in England, the numerous gaps in the list of important castles guarded by feudal service, suggest as much.

Commutation of actual guard-duty for money could be convenient for both vassal and lord, and from Henry II's reign (1154–89) it appears to have become frequent. The actual terms of the composition evidently varied; Round suggested that the vassal normally bought out his services by the wages of a knight who could take his place, at a time when a knight's pay was 8d. a day;[7] but Painter, on this basis, proves that the actual rates of commutation 'vary from insufficient to ridiculous'. Like all medieval commutations, these were the outcome of individual negotiations. The tendency was towards a very modest settlement; the vassal's duty was not a very heavy burden, particularly compared to service with the host, and it was not worth very much to him to be released from it. As for the lord, the service was not worth a great deal to him; castle-guard, in peacetime at any rate, was very much of an anachronism under the Plantagenets.

We find differential rates of commutation for peacetime and war — the latter inevitably far dearer — and in some cases only peacetime duties were permitted to be bought off; in wartime the guard-service had to be performed. Nevertheless the cash-nexus was gaining ground. Eventually we find castle-guard assessed, not in terms of fees, but of cost; and when we hear of sixpennyworth of guard-service owed at Mitford, by Kirkley (Northumberland)[8] we have plainly come a long way from alternative Knight Service. Tenure by castle-guard thus lapsed into a curious sort of rentcharge, which in fact had no necessary connection with any actual garrison. There are some castles which disappear as anything but foci for charging rents of this sort. Eye (Suffolk), as a defended place, does not seem to have existed beyond the early thirteenth century, but its castle-guard rents appear in the Rolls for long years after. Higham Ferrers is another case of the same kind.[9] Even an opposite example is treated as in some degree inadequate because it had no appendent services of this kind; in 1283 the fairly new Red-Castle (Shropshire) was entered: *militum indiget ad sustentacionem* (short of knights).[10]

These curious rents appear to have continued beyond the Middle Ages and even to have survived Charles II's abolition of military tenures in 1660. So far were their martial origins left behind.

Notes

1. A good deal of work has been done on this subject, mainly concerned with the money commutation for the service: J.H. Round, 'Castle Guard', *Archaeological Journal* lix (1902), pp. 144-59; A. Ballard, 'Castle-Guard and Barons' Houses,' *English Historical Review xxv* (1910), pp. 712-15; F.M. Stenton, *The First Century of English Feudalism* (Oxford, 1932), pp. 190-215; Sidney Painter, *American History Review xl* (1935), pp. 450-9.

2. This is ch. xxix of the 1215 Charter, and ch. xx of the final Magna Carta of 1225.

3. Gabriel Fournier, *Le château dans la France médiévale* (Paris, 1978), pp. 114, 132.

4. *Archaeologia Cambrensis*, 3rd Series, xv (1869), pp. 229-30.

5. *Victoria County History of Shropshire*, viii p. 325.

6. William Rees, *South Wales and the March* (Oxford, 1924), pp. 64, 147n2.

7. It rose considerably; by Edward I's Welsh wars (from 1277) a knight's wage was 2s. a day.

8. Calendar of Charter Rolls (1257-1300), pp. 75-6.

9. *Victoria County History of Northamptonshire*, iii, pp. 266 and n48.

10. R.W. Eyton, *The antiquities of Shropshire* (London, 1854-60) ix, pp. 345-6. Red-Castle was licensed in 1227.

3

Control over Castles, at Home and Abroad

A castle, as a not entirely defensive weapon, of considerable potency, could be a threat both to the populace and to its ruler. The king, as warlord and avenger of the law, was inevitably what I have called 'inspector-general of fortifications' or he was nothing. Throughout our Middle Ages, the king reserved the right to grant or refuse a 'licence to crenellate' to intending castellans. Those who fortified in defiance of this built an *adulterine* or unlawful stronghold, which would be demolished at once, or at least as soon as the abnormal situation which enabled them to break the law was over.

That is the statement, simple and straightforward, of the situation in England; but, as often happens, the situation was neither simple nor straightforward in fact; it was subject to many limits and variations in respect of time and place.

To take first its geographical limitations: in the Palatine Counties — Chester, Durham and, much later, Lancashire — licences were granted by the earl (in Durham, the bishop was earl) and not the king. This did not mean any flood of licences; indeed, the king seems to have been considerably more tolerant than the palatine lords.

This did not exhaust the limits to the normal rule of law; the March of Wales — the area of that country into which the Anglo-Norman and Flemish conquerors and settlers had intruded themselves — was excluded in general from royal jurisdiction, in particular as regarded the building of castles; even when Edward I, the Conqueror of Wales, enforced his authority on the Earls of Gloucester and Hereford in 1290–1,[1] he did not pretend to be able to control the building of castles in the now pacified March. Nor was this all; the eastern parts of the counties of Shropshire and Hereford were part of normal, geldable England, outside the liberties of the March; and yet only a very few licences were granted there. When the northern border took fire as a result of English attempts at conquest, at first the new small castles and towers were subjected to the normal rule of licensing, but, from the middle of the fourteenth century, defences here also apparently needed no licence. A few cautious builders, alone, sued out licences for their strongholds, but it was certainly not the normal procedure.

As regards the historical process, it is clear that the Conqueror arrived in England as the principal partner in the exploitation-firm for the conquest of England. Though as Duke of Normandy he had considerable powers for curbing fortification, and plainly intended them to apply to England as well, the manner of application will have been completely different, in response to the wide divergence between conditions in the two countries. In Normandy there were too many castles; in England not enough. As Duke of Normandy he had been engaged in imposing order, since the battle of Val-ès-Dunes in 1047, on a duchy which had fallen into grave disorders during his minority. His position, while less favourable, was rather like that of his great-grandson Henry II after the anarchy of Stephen's reign; he needed to curb the power, and the castles, of his baronage. His sons made enquiry after his death into the laws of the land, and obtained the *Consuetudines et Justicie* of their father.[2] In regard to defences, this listed a series of unconditional bans; the phrase *nulli licuit* (it was unlawful for anyone) occurs over and over again; severe limits were placed on the depth of ditches and the arrangements of palisades; nobody was to erect a strong place (*fortitudinem*) on a rock or an island; nobody was to build a castle in Normandy.

It will be seen that this is a purely negative set of pronouncements; there is no suggestion that the duke might possibly relent and permit a deeper ditch or a stronger palisade; whereas in England the legal position was given (long after the age of castles) by the great lawyer, Coke: 'no subject can build a castle or house of strength imbattelled, etc., or other fortress defensible ... without the licences of the King ...'[3]

Here the licence to crenellate is in the foreground. We may suspect that at the time of the Conquest the necessity of the royal licence was not stressed very highly; the conquerors needed their castles, and they would strengthen the position of the Conqueror, their master. We find him founding castles — not all of which ended as royal fortresses — and bidding his vicegerents to do the same when he was out of the country. The word 'licence' to modern ears implies a document, but it need not do so in law, and these early licences, if indeed they were actually necessary in all cases, may well have been verbal. They could not, of course, be enrolled before about 1200.

The earliest written licences date from the reign of Stephen (1135–54). This may at first seem surprising, as this reign is so notorious for its adulterine castles. On the other hand, many of these places may not strictly have been adulterine at all; either Stephen or Matilda (or both, for there were many turncoats) may have authorised or condoned their building; but there seems to have been a sense that they were all temporary affairs, to be swept away when peace returned; as indeed they were. Accordingly the retrospective licence granted to William de Roumare, Earl of Lincoln, for his castle of Gainsborough, and those to the infamous Geoffrey de Mandeville, Earl of Essex, in respect of his castles, extant or prospective, are all contained in

21

regular charters, and in each case stress the permanent character of the grant.[4]

Not that it did any good; King Stephen, left in peace for the last year of his life, improved his time in destroying many of the castles of the anarchy, and his death released upon the remainder the formidable energies of Henry II, father of law and order, who made short work of them. It is unlikely that a great many licences were granted in Henry's reign; the odd case of Berkeley, which the king promised to fortify, presumably made one unnecessary.[5] Henry was more famous for demolishing the castles of rebels or suspects. One of these, at Framlingham, was rebuilt early enough to have a completely Norman character; it seems certain that it had a licence; and possibly a written licence, from Richard I or his regents.

With John's reign, the long series of enrolled licences begins; at present a considerable work is being conducted on these,[6] and only a few conclusions need to be put forward here:

(1) The licences are by no means only in respect of castles or fortifications of any kind; they were licences to *crenellate*, and all manner of medieval buildings were topped with a crenellated parapet — often merely ornamental. For reasons of caution or some other notion, the owners of these unfortified buildings sued out licences.

(2) There are some examples which suggest that not all effective licences were enrolled.

(3) A castle or other building could be licensed several times over. The owners were presumably acting *ex abundanti cautela*, taking precautions against changes in governmental policy, etc.

(4) Conversely, some licences were made out for a multiplicity of sites, or even in the style of a blank cheque, for anywhere on the grantee's property. These, naturally, are hard to assign to any particular place, but, like the multiple licences, may not have had full advantage taken of them.

(5) In most licences which could apply to castles, one obtains little help from the wording in reconstructing what was intended to be done. In some cases we certainly have restrictions on the permitted work. In 1261 — a rather troubled and dangerous date — Basing was licensed for a palisade on its existing earthwork;[7] in 1293 Moccas was licensed for a low wall — 10 feet (3 m) below the crenellations — and unflanked (*absque turri seu turrella*).[8] But in many cases we find a licence granted in respect of a manor-house, or merely a house (not a town-house, whose crenellation would be a much less serious matter). We cannot tell what the licensee had in mind; though in a few cases the concluding phrase *et inde castellum facere* reveals a complete licence to fortify. In a few other cases we find the house or manor replaced by a 'chamber' (*camera*). These are likely to be towers.

Soon after the establishment of the Rolls, we meet with a number of genuine adulterine castles and the fate that befell them. In the war of 1215–17 between the Confederates (the Magna Carta barons and their French allies under the future Louis VIII) and the Royalists, a number of natural anarchs seem to have seized on this period of strife to re-establish the happy times of good King Stephen. The victor of the war — the great William Marshall, regent for King Henry III — had studied under Henry II, and he and his associates knew exactly what to do with them. Whether in the earl's lifetime or after his death, the Council pursued them mercilessly to their destruction.

We do not get another set of condemned castles before the time of the Barons' War. Basing's restricted licence has been mentioned; castellation at Leybourne in 1260[9] and Dudley in 1262[10] and of Portland as late as 1270,[11] was forbidden, though the would-be builders were not steady opponents of the king.

Those who were opponents seem to have been looking forward to a new regime, in which the Montfortian faction should have everything their own way, and some of them embarked on programmes of fortification which they lived to regret.

Walter de Cantilupe, the Montfortian Bishop of Worcester, had begun a stone castle at Hartlebury, and his position must have been extremely uncomfortable after the defeat of his party. His death in 1266 released him from this and his other embarrassments in this world, which were considerable. Godfrey Giffard, a later bishop, was permitted to complete the castle.[12] A similar case of blighted hopes seems to have befallen Berengar le Moygne. In 1275, when he alienated Barnwell St Andrews to Ramsey Abbey, the Hundred jury presented that he had built a castle at Bernewell some ten years before.[13] There is no licence enrolled. The materials used were excellent, and the castle stands to this day. A grim sight it is: unfinished and slighted, a warning to future offenders. The towers have never received their upper storeys, and a great breach has been deliberately made in one curtain.

Though matters had not got anything like so far at Dunstanburgh, it is an extremely sinister fact that Simon de Montfort had possessed himself of this powerful natural site as early as 1256; for what purpose one may well guess.[14] It never came to fruition, and it was not until the time of Edward II and Earl Thomas of Lancaster — unworthy successors of Henry III and de Montfort — that Dunstanburgh was built. It was licensed in 1315[15] — a period when Lancaster was the effective master of England — and was probably defensible by the time of his fall and execution in 1322.

For the rest of the Middle Ages and beyond, licences to crenellate are found, first in the Patent, later in the Charter Rolls. They continue right into the Tudor period; an alternative form of licence was the 'pardon for crenellating without licence' which was not even subject to a heavier fee. The fact is, few of the new castles of the fourteenth century could have constituted any sort of threat to authority, and, where an earlier castle was being brought up to date, as at Warwick or Pontefract, no licence was legally needed.

Nevertheless, the royal licence was not without its importance. In 1371 the Commons petitioned that it should be abolished; their petition was refused.[16] Both facts show that it was still significant. It became less important in the fifteenth century, but only because government was less efficient, and the new castles feebler and fewer. Only the splendid Raglan — which was in the Welsh March anyway, and needed no licence — was a powerful castle of this time, surviving to the present.

Even as long before this as the golden age of Edward I, minor castles were treated surprisingly gently by the authorities; thus Marham, a castle in Norfolk, now vanished, was licensed in 1271,[17] but in 1277 was presented as to the prejudice and nuisance of the country.[18] This should be the end of the story, but the castle seems to have survived well into the fourteenth century.[19]

In other countries, rules were naturally different, and differently applied. Ireland, a region of incessant strife, was essentially an English March area, in which, as we have seen,[20] the king would be concerned to have the castles of his more dependable subjects kept up and guarded, rather than to control their numbers. Scotland used a licence to crenellate, but Mackay Mackenzie appears to have shown that it was neither usual nor obligatory in that kingdom.[21]

In the Holy Land, the king's authority was weak — fatally weak, if he was not a suitable military commander-in-chief — but once again, in the face of a powerful and dangerous enemy, was hardly concerned to apply limits to the number of castles in his realm; they were all too few, and the more powerful the better. As time went on (particularly after 1187, the year of the shattering Battle of Hattin) one lord after another transferred the burden of his fortress to the military orders, financed from Christian Europe: the Hospitallers, principally concerned with the fortification of the Homs Gap, where their main fortress was Le Krak des Chevaliers, and the Templars, manning their little police posts along the pilgrimage routes, which they had come into being to patrol. Both orders were happy to pick up other strongholds, small or great, and they supported the kingdom until its end. Even later, when the city of Acre fell in 1291, the Templars held on in the island of Aradus (Ruad) for another eleven years.

In the surviving kingdom of Cyprus the only castles permitted were those of the king.[22] Somewhat similarly, in the minor kingdom of Man there were no lay barons;[23] in Japan, where a feudal polity sprang up without any Western origins, the Tokugawa Shoguns forbade their *daimyos* (barons) from having more than one castle each.[24]

In those countries which had formed part of the Carolingian Empire, its disintegration left a situation in which a number of local rulers, to English ears mere subjects — dukes, counts, bishops — were in the habit of making war on one another. It is no surprise to find these local potentates granting licences, like our less boisterous palatine earls. These licences were frequently hard bargains leaving the grantee burdened with duties to his superior; in particular, the latter was commonly permitted to take over his vassal's castle in emergency. This duty of *rendability*[25] was enforced in England as a general rule of law, for the benefit of the king (and evidently of the king alone), being established by Henry II at the Council of Windsor, 1176.[26]

The position in the two Dutch provinces of Friesland and Zealand, where the palatine princes exerted no authority, or very little, was consequently abnormal. Friesland, it appears, was never feudalised; such authority as there was, was in the hands of the free peasantry. Inevitably a class of wealthier freemen appeared and not surprisingly built themselves earthwork strongholds; but the slight resources of these *hoofdelingen* restricted the size of what it is rather bold to call their castles: generally a tower on top of a miniature motte. The *ambachtsheren* of Zealand were petty feudal lords who held a similarly independent position; naturally, they built castles, but their holdings were so limited that these strongholds, too, were small; again mottes seem to have been the typical form, and only the wealthiest could afford brickwork, when this became available.[27]

The density of castles in Switzerland is very high indeed; this country has experienced little enough of an effective central authority, and the approximately 4,000 castles testify that castellation was generally unchecked. But where there were so many strongholds, most of them were bound to be small, and — unless the sample with which I am acquainted is highly unrepresentative — the inhabitant was likely to be a steward or bailiff: *Amt* or *Beamt*, *Vogt* or *Landvogt*. Latterly the cantonal authorities bought out or squeezed out the lords, and from that time their bailiffs were ubiquitous.

The case of Denmark is very interesting. This is not a country generally remarkable for castles; certainly it has hardly any quarries, almost all the stone available being in the form of intractable granite erratics. (Flint, certainly, is common, but there is no flintwork.) Earthwork and later brick castles account for the great bulk of fortified sites.

An extremely useful short history of Danish castellation, by Mrs Olsen,[28] reveals a very curious story: castles were hardly more natural to early Denmark than to pre-Conquest England, but the kings and their immediate circle began to build castles in the twelfth century, generally for coastal defence. The reaction of English readers to hearing of Danes as victims of piracy may be somewhat ironical; nevertheless, Denmark suffered severely from the depredations of Wendish pirates from across the Baltic, and royal strongholds to defeat them were wisely built. Other important people took similar action. Denmark reached its medieval apogee in the age of the Valdemars (1170–1241) under Valdemar I, the Great, and his sons, Canute VI and Valdemar II, the Conqueror.

This splendid period was followed by a most frightful decadence of the nation and its monarchy; wretched kings, so far from being able to control their subjects' castles, had to demolish their own. 'But not until the very end of the 13th century and especially from the beginning of the 14th century do private castles become widespread. Now the different motte-types appear.'[29] (Motte-castles in England, it should be noted, do not seem to have been built after 1154, apart from a few on the Welsh border; some Welsh examples may well be much later.)

The resurgence of the monarchy and the recovery of the nation were brought about by Valdemar IV Atterdag (1340–75), whose daughter, the great Margaret I, in 1396, banned all future building of castles, 'because so extremely little right has been done from within these castles'. (One can imagine one of Henry of Anjou's negotiators using very much the same words in the peace-talks in 1153.) Father and daughter had already got rid of many of the new private strongholds; and it seems (our authoress refuses to be dogmatic on the question) that Margaret's ban was effective, and the nobility built themselves simple moated gentry-houses; even when the ban was repealed in 1483, no outburst of castle-building occurred; the same style of gentry-house continued to be built, with a few vaguely military features (Danish peasants seem often to have been discontented and violent) deployed with less and less conviction. About 1520 the Bishop of Viborg built two powerful castles at Hald and Spøttrup; he was an opponent of the Reformation, and scented trouble ahead. This would seem to be the end of private castles in Denmark. The royal castles continued, taking on progressively the character of coastal forts, with their form following rather than leading European fashion in fortification.

Notes

1. Calendar of Chancery Rolls, 337.
2. See C.H. Haskins, *Norman Institutions* (Harvard, 1918), p. 282.
3. Coke upon Littleton, vol. 1, Ch. 1, sec. i (f)
4. J.H. Round, *Geoffrey de Mandeville; a study of the anarchy* (London, 1892), pp. 91, 142, 159 (Gainsborough), 168.
5. Thomas Dudley Fosbrooke, Berkeley MSS (London, 1821), p. 12.
6. By Dr C.H. Coulson, FSA.
7. Patent Rolls (1258-66) 197.
8. Calendar of Patent Rolls (1291-1301) 23.
9. Close Rolls (1259-61) 283-4.
10. Close Rolls (1261-4) 129-30.
11. Close Rolls (1268-72) 292.
12. Bishop Pearce, *Hartlebury Castle* (SPCK, 1926), pp. 20-1, quoting from the *Liber Albus Episcoporum Wigornensium*, fo 456.
13. *Rotuli Hundredorum*, ii, 7.
14. Cadwallader John Bates, *Border Holds of Northumberland* (Newcastle, 1891), p. 169.
15. Calendar of Patent Rolls (1313-17) 344.

16. *Rotuli Parliamentorum*, ii, 307.

17. Calendar of Patent Rolls (1266-72) 540.

18. Calendar of Inquisitions, Miscellaneous, i, 329 (no. 1089).

19. Francis Blomefield, *An essay towards a topographical history of the County of Norfolk* (Fersfield and Lynn, 1739-75) vii, pp. 378-9.

20. *Supra*, p. 8.

21. R. Mackay Mackenzie, *The mediaeval castle in Scotland* (London, 1927), pp. 215-29.

22. Baron Rey, *L'architecture militaire des Croisés* (Paris, 1871), p. 229.

23. The only lay notables, the Keys, were representatives of the ordinary freemen.

24. Professors N. Orui and M. Toba, *Castles in Japan* (Tokyo, 1935), pp. 33-4.

25. Dr C.H. Coulson, 'Rendability and castellation in medieval France', *Château-Gaillard vi* (1972), pp. 59-67.

26. King, *Castellarium Anglicanum*, vol. 1, xxiv.

27. J.C. Besteman, in *Liber Castellorum* ed. Hoekstra, Janssen, and Moerman (Zutphen, 1981), pp. 40-59.

28. Rikke Agnete Olsen, 'Danish Medieval Castles at War', *Château-Gaillard, ix* (1978), pp. 223-35.

29. p.232.

4

On the Development of Castles

There are certain general considerations to be taken in connection with the study of the development of castles. The modern observer is only too eager to take what may be called a Darwinian view of history, in which each period, if not actually better than its predecessor (we have learned by bitter experience that it need not be) is at least more highly developed in some branches of technology. Technological discoveries, indeed, are seldom forgotten, though the necessities of their age may not call for them, and its disasters may interfere with their use.

There is an earlier view; the Middle Ages looked back to a classical antiquity from which their age was decadent. Politically this was in some degree correct; technologically it made little sense. Even the glorious burgeoning of the twelfth century, with its advances in human knowledge and civilisation, was mounted against the opinion of the best minds of the age, that the world was perilously decadent and ripe for judgment: '*Hora novissima, tempora pessima sunt, vigilemus*' (It is the very last hour, the times are at their worst; let us keep watch).

In our own times, the technology of weapons has made such alarming strides that we find it natural to attribute any military success in the past to superior, and particularly more modern armaments. Such rapid progress is, indeed, typical of the twentieth century as a whole. In the 1914–18 war, mastery of the air over the Western Front changed hands no fewer than four times, and a fifth generation of fighters was appearing at the end. In a field where construction was inevitably much slower, an encounter between the battleships *Schleswig-Holstein* (1908) and *Warspite* (1913) would have been extremely one-sided, to say the least of it. A similar, but slower process went on in the nineteenth century; but in earlier ages we find types of armament, like the Tower musket (Brown Bess), surviving for long periods without change, or need of change. Worse still, we find victory going against the more modern weapon; as late as the Franco–Prussian War the French small-arms — the *chassepot* rifle and the *mitrailleuse* — were far in advance of the weapons of their enemies; but they did not bring victory. Worse again, at

Flodden (1513) a splendid Scottish army was slaughtered by an English force of no very high quality *because* the Scots used up-to-date weapons (pikes).

The above paragraphs have been provoked by encountering, in the work of a serious scholar, the extraordinary phrase: 'the ancient but militarily obsolete castle of the de Lacy earls' (Lincoln, in 1329).[1] Lincoln castle, in fact, had beaten off an important siege in 1216–17 and, though it was by no means a fine example of scientific fortification, was solid and powerful, and even in the Civil War — when it surely was obsolete — needed to be assaulted.

It was impossible to bring static armaments like castles to bear against one another, and even success and failure in a single campaign could not be a fair standard for comparison; there were so many factors to be considered: the numerical strength of the contestants, their morale, equipment and supplies, and their health; for then, as now, dysentery loved the soldier.

A well-sited castle, strongly ditched and strongly built, did not have any special need for scientific defences. Dr Smail, in his important *Crusading warfare,*[2] argues at length that the twelfth-century crusaders had learned little or nothing from Byzantine and Saracen fortifications. A particularly striking instance given is that of Kerak-in-Moab (Karak).[3] Here a fine natural site was chosen and improved with strong rock-cut ditches. The solid castle built inside has virtually no elements of scientific flanking; and yet the very idea of assaulting Kerak with the resources available in the Middle Ages is enough to make one's blood run cold. After their great victory of Hattin (1187) Saladin's followers had to starve the place out at great length.

It is not the policy of the present enquiry, or of much contemporary work on the subject, to present the development of medieval fortification as due to a series of definite lessons, learned in the hideously uncertain school of experience. Nor are the dates of these supposed lessons agreeable to the changes they are supposed to have brought about; the recognition of the problem of the 'dead angles' of the primitive rectangular keep is commonly related to King John's mining of a corner-turret of Rochester in 1215; yet round keeps had been built many years before in England, and a century earlier in France. The alleged disappearance of the central keep is generally connected with the great siege of Château-Gaillard in 1204, but there are a great many keepless castles, even in England, earlier than this. (In rather the same way, one author wishing to ascribe the building of Herstmonceux (Sussex) merely to the nostalgia and romantic yearnings of Sir Roger Fiennes, its builder, opined that Roger had been 'reading too much Malory'; as the castle was licensed in 1441 and Malory completed *Morte d'Arthur* in 9 Edward IV (1469–70), this explanation is somewhat unconvincing.)

It may be asked, in view of the increasing skill and professionalism of besieging armies, was there no possibility of such a thing as an obsolete castle — for instance, a timber fortification in the period of flanked stone defences, or a conventional castle in the age of fire-artillery? This was

29

certainly so, always provided that one does not understand 'obsolete' to mean 'useless'. On the Scottish border, a number of enclosure fortifications are called 'peels', i.e. wooden castles; though some of them, like the Peel of Staward, latterly received solid stone defences, they were plainly built in haste originally, and so in timber. A more august example is the Peel of Linlithgow. Edward I in 1302 determined to fortify Linlithgow with a castle built, at least largely, in stone. Shortage of finance or of time, or of both, constrained him to order instead a massively built timber structure.[4]

Even this example from the great master of English fortification does not end the story. The motte-and-bailey castle of Liddel Strength (Cumberland, now Cumbria) stands so immediately on the border that its best plan[5] includes a couple of acres on the far side of Liddel Water. This is a very powerful earthwork, but seems never to have been fortified in stone, which is not surprising on such a site. As late as 1346 it was held against a Scottish army under David II sufficiently effectively to attract a cruel vengeance on the part of the half-mad King of Scots.[6]

As to the progress of fire-artillery, most of our English defences, at least, were designed to permit full play to the artillery of the defence rather than to resist a battering from that of the enemy. This is not a feature confined to England; indeed we have nothing comparable to the towering brick structure called the *Magasinbygningen*, overlooking the approach to the Danish castle of Hammershus, on the Baltic island of Bornholm; the wall is little over six feet thick, but there were five storeys, of which the upper four were pierced with gunports. Nor are the defences of Noltland (or Notland) castle, in the Orkneys, particularly massive; but on all sides they bristle with elliptical ports on three or four levels — an amazing sight.

But in the course of the fifteenth century a practical siege-artillery was evolved; the iron cannonball and the cast gun supplied a threat that the normal castle was hardly adequate to meet. Before the appearance of the pentagonal bastion and the triumph of drawing-board fortification — which itself, it must be remembered, generally did no more than lengthen the siege, which must end in any case in the victory of the besiegers — various steps were taken to strengthen the defence, of which some at least persisted into the age of the bastion: a great strengthening of the batteries of the defence, especially with substantial guns; a great thickening of walls; ramping the curtains in earthwork; building outworks to keep the enemy at a distance from the place.

To sum up: the development of the fabric of the castle was important, but not uniquely important.

Notes

1. Dr C.H. Coulson, *Mediaeval Archaeology, xxvi* (1982), p. 77.
2. Cambridge University Press, 1956.

3. Pp. 218-21, 245.

4. *History of the King's Works*, i (HMSO, London, 1963-82), p. 413.

5. John F. Curwen, *Castles and towers of Cumberland and Westmorland* (Kendal, 1913), p. 26.

6. Calendar of Documents relating to Scotland, iii, 308 (no. 1670); *Chronicon de Lanercost*, ed. Stevenson (Edinburgh, 1839) p. 345.

5

The Origins of the Castle

The origin of the English castle was a question vigorously discussed at the turn of the century, when Clark's surprising theory that a motte could be equated with one of the *burhs* built by Alfred the Great and his family was contested and refuted by a remarkable body of scholarship, led by no less an authority than J. H. Round. The most important work in the campaign was Mrs Armitage's justly celebrated *Early Norman castles of the British Isles* (London, 1912). Though it was not strictly necessary for her purpose, Mrs Armitage took up the position that there was never such a thing as an Anglo-Saxon castle, and that the few castles built in England before 1066 were the work of Edward the Confessor's Norman 'favourites'. Her attitude was perhaps unnecessarily rigid, though she defended it with great erudition and skill — even going to the length of devoting a long and able argument against Dover Castle having been built by Harold Godwinsson,[1] the admission of which would have constituted no genuine objection to her chosen position — namely that Anglo-Saxon castles are an illusion — still less to her essential refutation of Clark's equation between motte and *burh*; for Harold was familiar with the castles of northern France, and at least one source states that he built Dover Castle to Duke William's orders.[2]

Though a number of corrections in matters of detail can be made to *The early Norman castles*,[3] its reputation remains high, and until recently its main thesis was never called in question: not only is a motte nothing to do with a *burh*, but 'history furnishes no instance of the existence of private castles among the Anglo-Saxons and the Danes (previous to the arrival of Edward the Confessor's Norman friends), and ... this negative evidence is of great significance';[4] mottes and all forms of castle, in fact, came in with the Normans. Recently, however, there has been a tendency to question the conclusion of Round and his school — uphill work though this has mostly turned out to be — and Mrs Armitage's treatise has passed unscathed, perhaps, but not unassailed; though we need hardly expect to hear anything more of Clark's *burhs*. Even if we should come across one or two Saxon castles of the eleventh century, would that mean any more than that one or two well-informed thegns disliked the look of the times, and were prepared to admit 'they order these things (I said) better in France'? Even on this admission, the castle would still have come to England as an imitation of continental practice.

It is certainly true that, in the last quarter of a century, the excavation of mottes has produced some extraordinary results, unforeseen by Ella Armitage or anybody else; but these mainly belong to periods well after 1066. Similarly, a good deal of research has been done on the ringwork — a type of inner earthwork constituting an alternative to the motte.[5] Mrs Armitage hardly recognised its separate existence,[6] but it would have made little difference had she done so, for she treated all the eleventh-century examples of this class as mottes[7] (to the considerable confusion of their study) and would obviously have accepted the two species as closely related, as in fact they are.

A recent enquiry on the part of the Royal Archaeological Institute into 'The origins of the castle in England' led to the publication of so praiseworthy and bulky a set of excavation reports[8] that it seems unkind to point out that none of them substantially advanced our knowledge of these origins, which remains as Round and Mrs Armitage left it. The moving spirit in this project was Mr Brian Davison, who had conducted a number of remarkably successful excavations, and also, by a tour of the recorded castles of pre-Conquest Normandy, has shown that, where these survive, they generally have no mottes.[9] This demonstration came as a surprise to most of his contemporaries, though it would evidently not have surprised the redoubtable Mrs Armitage.[10]

A further fact which appears to undermine the thesis of *Early Norman castles* has also been cited by Mr Davison: the allusion, in the eleventh-century document *Of people's ranks and law*, to a *burhgeat* as part of the necessary property of the thegn: 'and if a ceorl prospered, so that he possessed fully five hides of land of his own,[11] church and kitchen, a bell and a *burhgeat*, a seat and special office in the king's hall, then was he thenceforth of thegn-right worthy.'[12] This looks convincing enough at first; *burhgeat* should mean a fortress-gate, and there is no point in having a strongly defended gate if the perimeter of the place is not comparably strong; 'for the moment it is enough to note that a thegn was expected to boast some form of private defended enclosure or *burh*'.[13]

Professor Allen Brown, in a vigorous defence of Mrs Armitage's position,[14] points out that *burh* has a secondary meaning in such a connection as *burh-bryce*, the offence of breaking a gentleman's close,[15] and that this makes its appearance in the laws of Ine (688–94) at a time 'long before castles were invented on the Continent, let alone in England'. He goes on to adduce considerable evidence to show that a *burhgeat* is more likely to have 'fulfilled some symbolic and lordly function'.

But there is a more fatal objection to Mr Davison's argument: according to it a thegn (a king's thegn — the class of thegns was in fact more extensive) 'was expected to boast some form of private defended enclosure'. King's thegns formed a very numerous class of men,[16] and if they all had 'private defended enclosures' there must have been literally hundreds of these. Since these enclosures will have been strong enough to be defended, a very large proportion of them might be expected to have survived in some recognisable form down to the present day. In which case, what can they look like, and why has none of them been identified by excavation? We know sufficient about the archaeological dating of mottes, ringworks of the castle type, and even homestead moats, to be reasonably sure that no great mass of serious defences of the Saxon period is to be found among any of them. Thus not only does history furnish no instance of a private castle among the Anglo-Saxons, but a great body of excavations, of a pretty miscellaneous description, has also failed to discover one.

In fact, the earliest castles recorded in England — and recorded with the name, never hitherto used, of 'castel' — were those of the Norman followers of Edward the Confessor, which briefly appear in 1051–2. Three appear by name, either in the Anglo-Saxon Chronicle or in Florence of Worcester,[17] but their names are those of their owners. Pentecost's Castle has been fairly convincingly identified as Ewyas Harold (Herefordshire); Robert's Castle, though identified as Clavering (Essex), is quite unlike the remains of an eleventh-century castle; and Hugh's Castle is unidentifiable. In addition, two more castles in Herefordshire — where the Normans were mainly settled — are fairly convincingly attributed to these foreigners: Richard's Castle is supposed to take its name from Richard fitz Scrob, a Norman of the period, and it is also reasonably presumed that the Norman Ralph 'the Timid', created Earl of Hereford, must have built a castle there.There is a formidable motte at Richard's Castle, and Hereford had an even bigger example, now destroyed. As regards the dating of mottes, both of these castles could perhaps have had their mottes added at a later date, in the manner of Castle Neroche; but this would not have been possible at Ewyas Harold, which occupies a dropping-ridge site, where the bailey was completely indefensible without a lofty motte on the uphill side. This is the more important because Ewyas Harold, whether or not it can be identified as Pentecost's Castle, is the one certain pre-Conquest castle in England; it is described as having been refortified[18] by 'earl William' (fitz Osbern, who reached the border in 1067, quitted England for ever in 1070, and was slain next year).[19]

We must thus look for the origins of both the motte and the castle outside England. The castle, being typically the stronghold of an individual, commonly belongs to feudal times and feudal practice. In the dangers of the end of the first Christian millennium — the inroads of the Magyars and the Northmen — Alfred the Great's *burhs* and Henry the Fowler's *Burgen*, the work of great and centralising kings, were communal, large-scale fortresses; but where the question of defence had to be answered by the individual — the powerful individual, it should hardly be necessary to add — his natural reaction was to fortify himself inside his own house. This could be done in more than one way: he could either strengthen the house itself to resist assault, or fortify the curtilage, the enclosure in which it stood; or he could do both. In the first case — which would only be appropriate for small proprietors — we should have an isolated tower, or motte, or ringwork; in the second, the result would be an early example of the keepless castle, a fairly large fortified enclosure with no interior stronghold; in the third, the castle would be a tower-and-bailey, a motte-and-bailey, or a ring-and-bailey, depending on the manner in which the house itself was fortified. This last was generally the best system for lords of the early Middle Ages — it was certainly the most usual. Surviving Roman fortifications and more recent communal defences supplied examples for the castle-builder, and it seems likely that stone and earthwork defences occurred from the first as alternatives. As regards the enclosure, the natural course was to deepen its ditches and raise its banks, so that its formal boundaries became lines of defence, with battlemented walls of timber or stone. The sort of defence that we must visualise is perhaps best expressed by the prohibitions of the *Consuetudines et Justicie* of Normandy, attributed to William the Conqueror.[20]

No ditch was allowed beyond a stringently shallow limit — the ditcher must be able to throw out the upcast without climbing on a plank or staging (*scabellum*) to do so; the fence had to be plain, without battlements (*propugnacula*) and similar features. Strongholds on rocks and islands were not to be built, and nobody was to make a castle in Normandy. This last provision may either have been intended as a summary of the whole paragraph of the *Consuetudines*, or as a prohibition against stone castles; though the word 'castellum' is not elsewhere confined to masonry structures.

Even including the limitations on ditching, banking and palisading in general, these prohibitions seem likely to be directed mainly against the practice of fortifying *houses*. The main danger to the dweller in a house, large or small, was — then as now — fire. Most houses were wooden, most roofs were thatched; the practice of setting fire to the building and besetting the door or doors, so as to cut down the household as they broke cover, is likely to have been of some antiquity when it achieved its best-known example in the 'Saga of Burnt Njal'; a more cowardly variation, suitable for villeins to use, in which the door was barricaded from the outside, is not long forgotten among the rural population of many parts of the world; one thinks particularly of Ireland.

With this menacing possibility to be reckoned with, the intending castellan could have recourse to any of a number of expedients. He might rely on the defences of his outer enclosure; he might construct a powerful bank and ditch round the actual house (a ringwork); he might build on a rock or an island — as foreseen in the *Consuetudines*; he might put his house on the top of an artificial hillock (a motte); finally, he might build in stone. This by itself would not be enough; a low stone building could be attacked by throwing torches in, or shooting through its windows, or setting fire to the door or the roof. But a stone first-floor hall had inherent defensive possibilities: its windows — which at that period would not in any case have been large — were well up from the ground, and so was the door. If no doorway was built at basement level, and if the roof was covered in a reasonably fire-resistant substance, such a building would give considerable protection against casual violence; indeed, little more was needed to turn it into a fortress: extra protection needed to be given to the door, either by using a ladder for access, or by constructing the type of fortified porch and stair known as a 'forebuilding'; the walls needed to be battlemented; here convenience dictated a level wall-walk, which could not be built below the level of the gable-ends. Thus the roof was protected by the upper extension of the walls, and became invisible from outside; the whole building took on the characteristic cuboidal shape of the 'Norman' keep as we know it in England. It is significant that Langeais (Indre-et-Loire), the oldest known keep of this type, dated to 994, is a comparatively lightly built structure of very simple first-floor hall character. By 1066 — let alone by the late twelfth century, when such towers as Dover and Newcastle were built — Norman keeps had become far more complicated structures; but even as late as the 1060s a powerful keep like that of Chepstow could be designed basically as a first-floor hall. Indeed, this inherently defensible type of building appears again and again throughout the medieval period and beyond, in buildings of decreasing defensibility, as the style worked down to lower and lower social levels without ever becoming contemptible in point of strength. It first appeared in defensible twelfth-century hall-blocks like Grosmont in Monmouthshire (Gwent), Monmouth itself, and Manorbier in Pembrokeshire (now part of Dyfed), continued by way of a set of solidly built oblong two-storey buildings in Wales — Mold (the Tower) and Northop Hall Farm in Flint (now part of Clwyd), Newton (Newhouse) and Rhoscrowther (Eastington) in Pembroke, all apparently of the fifteenth century — and developed into the large number of peasant fortifications in sixteenth-century Northumberland and Cumberland (Cumbria) known as bastle-houses, with a cottage 'hall' over the cowshed.

It is clearly to the inherent advantages of the first-floor hall that we owe the origins of the standard rectangular keep, which we in England call 'Norman', though its Continental distribution extends far outside Normandy.[21] The other common types of inner defence in post-Conquest England were both earthworks: the ringwork and the motte. As to the ringwork, little need be said of its origins; it is merely an example of the normal bank-and-ditch fortification of north-western Europe, of powerful dimensions, carried round an unusually compact enclosure — typically, round a dwelling-house. It shows no difference in character from other earthworks of its general type; larger and less compact examples of ring should probably not be counted as ringworks proper. Rather than alternatives to the motte, they should appear as baileys without any motte;[22] in fact the upper limit of size for the class is of necessity very vague.

The origin of a class of defence so little specialised is obviously a simple enough affair. The late M. Héliot has drawn attention to the contraction in area of private strongholds in France, beginning perhaps in the ninth century, certainly by the tenth, and accompanied by a strengthening of the defences:

> La nouvelle formule, appelée à triompher au XIe, différa de la précédente par la resserrement du périmètre, le renforcement du rempart, et l'addition d'une motte artificielle. Imposée par le souci d'améliorer les conditions de la défense, la contraction semble avoir été progressive . . .[23]

Such a process would automatically produce something in the nature of a ringwork if the defences were carried out in earthwork and if no motte was constructed.

This brings us to the far more difficult question of the origins of the motte itself. It is clear that one possible explanation, and perhaps the most probable, is that it was produced by the progressive contraction of defensive perimeters described by M. Héliot.[24] The singular feature of the motte is that the defended area is a table-top level with the head of the scarp, the whole having the shape of a vast mud-pie. Now it is not difficult to imagine such a work coming into being as the final result of a progressive *resserrement* and strengthening of inner earthworks. There was a limit to the closing-in of perimeter possible with ordinary earthworks; the powerful line of defence of a ringwork occupied a great deal of room itself, and yet had to leave space for the inhabited area inside. The motte represents a higher degree of *resserrement*; here there is no inner face to the bank; the scarp falls directly from the circumference of the inhabited area. In particular, we know from a number of excavations that existing earthworks were often raised and strengthened; what would be the result of doing this to an already fairly strong and compact ringwork? In England we have recorded cases of transition, and transitional forms between the motte and the ringwork: mottes which were produced by filling in a ringwork;[25] ringworks on foreland sites which were embanked only on the exposed side, so that they were ringworks there, but mottes to the rear; ringworks — generally large and powerful examples — where the central cup has been partly filled in so as to afford more room for the buildings inside the banks.[26] All these English examples are only of value in tracing the beginnings of the motte in so far as they preserve some older tradition, for the motte itself had been evolved well before the Conquest. English evidence by itself cannot relate to an earlier period.

The principal work concerning the antiquity of the motte in France and Normandy is that of Professor de Boüard, published in *Château-Gaillard*.[27] M.

de Boüard shows that the word 'motte' is used first for a turf or sod, then for a turf bank — in every case apparently that of a mill-stream — and does not come into use for a castle mound before the middle of the eleventh century; the chroniclers indeed never use it before the twelfth, when *mota* or *motta* appears in the works of Ordericus Vitalis and Suger. The word applied to a motte in early times is more usually *dungio*, and it is under this name that the first plain mention of one, built by a Count of Blois in 1026,[28] is found. With a further mention of a *mota* near Vendôme which was clearly a castle, M. de Boüard concludes: 'Ainsi, dans la région de la Loire moyenne, l'existence de mottes est-elle solidement attestée dès les années 1020–1040? Sans doute, à la même époque, la Normandie en possedait-elle aussi.' He goes on to cite a number of persuasive examples, in Normandy and outside, including the pre-Conquest Norman castles in England and the Italian motte of San Marco Argentano, built, or built upon, by Robert Guiscard — *Guiscardus terror mundi* — between 1045 and 1050.

It will be seen that he gives no evidence for the existence of any motte much earlier than 40 years before the Conquest, and that the unfamiliarity of the word 'motte' might seem to suggest that the thing itself did not appear in large numbers till a fairly late date — perhaps later than 1066; but it would be incautious to develop this argument for more than it is worth; we may recall how the biographer of the Blessed John, Bishop of Thérouanne, writing in 1130 or soon after, gives a most vivid description of the motte at Merchem, and assures his readers that such defences were common in those parts — but without once mentioning the word *mota* or even *dungio*.[29]

It would not be surprising, moreover, if research should find earlier examples of mottes, and M. Michel Rouche has put forward a very convincing one: Vinchy (Nord) on the banks of the Scheldt. Built in 979 as a threat to Cambrai, it was finished or almost finished when the bishop, calling up his allies, fell upon it and demolished it; an air-photograph shows the typical outlines of a ploughed-down motte-and-bailey. The author mentions other possible early mottes in the region.[30]

In closing, M. de Boüard draws attention to examples of artificial mounds, on the North Sea shore of Germany and the Low Countries, and also in the flood plain of the Rhine, which were raised rather to place their owners' households above the high spring tides and the flood-waters. This afforded scope for confusion between the two classes of antiquity, which until recently was apparently unresolved. I can recall my first visit to a Dutch castle — Limbricht (Limburg) in September 1972. Here we were warned by our excellent Dutch hosts that, though it looked as if it was a motte — as all out instincts bade us to accept — this was something different: a mound raised to escape from disastrous floods. Now Limbricht, as well as having steep, defensible scarps and a defensive wet ditch, stands some 24 feet (7.25 m) above the level. What sort of flood was envisaged for this to be necessary? And Millem is 17 feet (5.18 m) high, and Montfort 18 feet (5.50 m), and

Kessel 26 feet (8 m), by my measurements, while the Leidse Burcht at Leyden is 9 metres, that is, 30 feet high. These are by no means the highest figures in the most recent catalogue of mottes in the Netherlands, made by Mr Jan C. Besteman, in a paper to which I am already in debt.[31] Here he shows that in the early Middle Ages the difference between the refuge-mounds (*terpen*) and the military mottes (*werven*) was recognised, but the term *werf* (motte) fell out of use in the later thirteenth century, and so the confusion between the *terpen* and the real mottes, latterly called *bergen*, arose, and was not resolved until very recently (a symposium of great significance in 1969 is referred to in this connection). Here we have something like a Batav ian version of Clark's *burhs*, rectified only at a much later date.

Here we must also note an English suggestion as to the origin of mottes. This is that of Dr Brian Hope-Taylor, who sees the motte as accessory to a class of stilted watch-tower, known to the Romans (though not necessarily invented by them), and used on their frontiers in Germany, frequently on a circular platform with a surprising resemblance to a motte, though not artificially raised. As to the origins of the motte, he suggests:

> It is highly probable that the earlier towers stood inside a protective earthwork enclosure, which survived as the bailey. The stilts of a tall tower standing on normal ground level must necessarily be set into very deep holes dug into the subsoil for their reception. Sockets of narrow diameter and great depth are extremely difficult to dig, and this may have been the main factor which gave rise to the mound. If the holes were dug too shallow or too wide, the tower would soon begin to lean, and the obvious method of reinforcement would be to dig a gully or ditch about it and to pile the excavated earth against the lower portions of the stilts. This would suggest the natural defensive advantages of a mound, which would so sheath the vital cornerposts as to baffle enemy sappers. Once it was adopted, the stilts need no longer be set in into holes dug in the ground. Placed on a firm basis, at or very slightly below ground level, and held in position by some temporary framing, they would be suitably embedded as the large mound was heaped around them ... the tower was of the essence of and integral with the motte.[32]

This theory is put forward in so brilliant a paper, and is itself so ingenious, that it is with regret that one points out its weaknesses. The watch-tower element, to begin with, is of doubtful application; admittedly the central building on the motte at Abinger was small in plan, and could well be interpreted as a structure of this sort; but many mottes, both short and tall, have table-tops far too wide to be needed for anything as small as a watch tower; we hear of buildings on mottes, even in early times, which are certainly more substantial; thus Arnold of Ardres's castle was a remarkably highly developed timber structure for the early twelfth century; but it stood upon a dungio;[33] the bishop of Thérouanne, in the passage mentioned above, is described as crossing the bridge of the motte with the intention of changing his vestments in his *hospitium*; he would hardly have chosen a watch-tower to stay or change in.

As to the question of Roman origins: between a type of monument which is not heard of before the tenth century and another which is not known after the fourth, a great gulf of time is fixed; such resemblance as there is may well be fortuitous, or the product of some species of convergent development. Finally, the suggested narrative whereby the mound was added to consolidate the post-holes of an unstable tower is not really compelling; 'the obvious method of reinforcement' would either be by way of adding struts and shores to the tower itself, or by wedging its supports tightly in their post-holes with stones or timber wedges.

Notes

1. Mrs Ella Armitage, *The early Norman castles of the British Isles* (London, 1912), pp. 138-44.

2. Eadmer, *Historia Novorum* ed. Rule (Rolls Series 81), pp. 7-8. See also William of Poitiers, 104, where the expression *Traditurum ... Castrum Doveram, studio atque sumptu suo communitum* can very well be understood to mean that Harold was promising to build the castle (he is certainly described as promising to fortify others, wherever William wanted them). The language of Guy of Amiens, *Carmen de Hastingae proelio* ed. Morton and Muntz (Oxford, 1972), pp. 38-9, strongly suggests the existence of a castle in 1066; see editorial comment, xlv-xlvii.

3. She should not have included Norham, and probably not Clitheroe in her catalogue; and the following should have been included: Goodrich, Clare, Kirkby Malzeard, Burton-in-Lonsdale, Brinklow, Eardisley and the unidentified 'Walelege' of Domesday, also Folkestone and probably Lewes No. 2. Bourne (Lincolnshire) should be Bourn (Cambridge).

4. *Early Norman castles*, p. 63.

5. An introductory study of this class of earthwork has been written by Professor Leslie Alcock and myself, 'Ringworks of England and Wales', *Château-Gaillard iii* (London, 1966), pp. 90-127.

6. She mentions at Corfe 'an earthwork which might be called a 'Ring and Bailey'; *Early Norman castles*, p. 138. This is 'The Rings', Corfe No. 2.

7. *Ibid.*, p. 152 n2. She includes Castle Acre, Exeter, Preston Capes and Old Sarum (Salisbury) as mottes.

8. *Archaeological Journal cxxxiv* (1977), pp. 1-156. Introduction (A.D. Saunders), pp. 1-10; Bramber (K.J. Barton, E.W. Holden and C.R. Sladden), pp. 11-79; Hastings (Philip Barker and K.J. Barton), pp. 80-100; Montgomery no. 2 (Barker), pp. 101-4; Sulgrave (Brian Davison), pp. 105-14; York no. 2 (P.V. Addyman and J. Priestley), pp. 115-56.

9. *Château-Gaillard ii* (Cologne, 1967), pp. 39-48; also *Château-Gaillard iii*, pp. 37-47. In so far as this second paper suggested that the motte might have been invented by the Norman Flemish-French invaders under William the Conqueror in the actual conquest of England, it had a very hostile reception from the continental participants

at Battle in 1966 — perhaps not surprisingly.

10. *Early Norman castles*, p. 78 n1.

11. Five hides of land was the quantity which was, in some parts of England at least, expected to produce one fully equipped fighting-man.

12. Bishop Stubbs, *Select Charters* (9th edn, Oxford, 1946), p. 88.

13. Brian Davison, 'Origins of the castle in England', *Archaeological Journal, cxxiv* (1967), p. 204.

14. 'An historian's approach to the origins of the castle in England', *Archaeological Journal cxxvi* (1969), pp. 131-48.

15. Latterly, at any rate, it was equally an offence, if a cheaper one in point of penalty, to break a ceorl's close; this was *edorbryce*.

16. Stenton, *Anglo-Saxon England* (2nd edn., Oxford, 1947), p. 482.

17 *Anglo-Saxon Chronicle*, ed. Whitelock *et al.*, (London, 1961), p. 125, version L, Florence of Worcester (*Chronicon ex Chronicis*), ed. Thorpe (London, 1848-9) i, 270. Only Florence mentions Hugh's castle.

18. *Domesday Book*, i, 186a, 1.

19. Mr Davison seems inclined to suggest that fitz Osbern added the motte; *Château-Gaillard iii*, p. 38: 'However, no-one seems to have asked of what such a refortification, on a scale worthy of record in the Survey, might consist: the motte has always been taken to a primary part of the castle of the 1050's.' This would appear to be rather a desperate argument; it could not be advanced on the site.

20. C. H. Haskins, *Norman institutions* (Harvard, 1918), p. 282.

21. M. Pierre Héliot, in *Bulletin Archéologique, NS, v* (1969), pp. 144-5, gives its area of distribution: 'en Angleterre ... en France jusqu 'aux abords du Massif Central et aux rives de la basse Garonne; enfin dans la zone des terres d'Empire ou l'on parlait français ... Son aire de diffusion ne s'étendit guère au Midi ...

22. D.J. Cathcart King and Leslie Alcock, 'Ringworks of England and Wales', *Château-Gaillard iii* (Chichester, 1966), pp. 95-6.

23. *Journal des Savants* (1965), p. 492.

24. This explanation was suggested as long ago as 1936; Braun, *The English castle* (London, 1936), pp. 15-16.

25. King and Alcock, *loc. cit.*, pp. 100-1. Since the date of publication, two further examples of ringworks filled in to form mottes have been discovered: Aldingham (Lancashire North-of-the-Sands) and Loughor (Glamorgan).

26. King and Alcock, *loc. cit.*, pp. 93-4.

27. 'Quelques données françaises et normandes concernant le problème de l'origine des mottes', *Château-Gaillard ii* (Cologne, 1967), pp. 19-26.

28. *Ibid.*, p. 23, citing the *Annales Vindocinenses* ed. Halphen in *Recueil d'Annales angevines et vendômoises* (1903), p. 60.

29. *Acta Sanctorum* (Bolland, Antwerp, 1643) January, vol. II, p. 799 (27 January). See also Clark, *Medieval military architecture in England* (London, 1884) i, pp. 33-4; and *Early Norman castles*, pp. 88-9. (The bridge of the motte had collapsed under the weight of the bishop and his flock; miraculously without loss of life.)

30. In *Mélanges d'archéologie et d'histoire médiévales* (Geneva, 1982), pp. 365-9.

31. 'Mottes in the Netherlands', in *Liber Castellorum*, ed. Hoekstra, Janssen and Moerman (Zutphen, 1981), pp. 40-59.

32. In Bruce-Mitford (ed.) *Recent archaeological excavations in Britain* (London, 1956), pp. 247-8.

33. *Lamberti Ardensis Historia Comitum Ghisnensium* ed. Heller, *Monumenta Germaniae Historica xxiv* (Hanover, 1979), p. 624.

6

The Primitive English Castle — Earthwork

The approximate century after the Conquest can be treated as a single more or less homogeneous period. Not that there was no development in design — one would certainly expect something of the kind from the period in which occurred the First and Second Crusades, the early stirrings of the Gothic, and the coming of the House of Anjou to England — but there was little strictly military development in this country, and probably not very much elsewhere in Christendom. In Outremer the Crusaders found Byzantine models and Syrian masons; military technique in fact was far in advance of anything they were accustomed to use in their own countries. They did not interfere with this, but wisely followed the advice and methods of local masters; only they seem to have lived in keeps — as they had done in the lands from which they came — rather more than had previously been usual in the East. What is more interesting is that the many who returned from the Crusades did not attempt to build Crusader castles in Europe (see Chapter 8, *infra*).

As far as England was concerned, builders of castles followed a variety of courses. At first, since the newly arrived Normans were entrenching themselves in haste, they used earthworks mainly of the motte-and-bailey type. The principal early alternative was the ringwork; at present the ratio between the two classes is 1 ringwork to 3.6 or 3.7 mottes, but the proportion of rings was probably originally higher: in several cases rings have been turned into mottes, merely by filling in the central hollow.

Considerable examination of the problem of the ringwork has suggested — subject to possible correction as a result of excavation — that the ring is contemporary with the motte, and is a straightforward alternative to it. The reason why one castle should be built with a motte and another with a ringwork seems to have been a matter of mere personal preference on the part of the castellan, and the local groups in which many rings are found cannot easily be explained by any historical, geographical, or ethnographic factor; the local castle-builders are likely to have been influenced in their choice either by emulation or by the expert advice available in their own district.[1]

There are also strongly ditched works like Framlingham (Suffolk) which are not raised significantly above the general level; also there were shapes of castles which were dictated by the ground: much of England may lack spectacular rocky ridges and summits, but strong sites exist, and strong sites were occupied. These can give us shapeless castles, difficult to put into any predetermined category, but rocky sites are advantageous for stone construction rather than timber. Where the castle-builders were at all free to lay out earthworks, they remained singularly true to the normal compact curvilinear types of defence — a circumstance which was not to be to the advantage of some of their successors, who found themselves trying to erect, on these unpromising earthworks, defensive systems of straight curtains and enfilading towers.

Sometimes, however, we find baileys laid out with straight sides, as at Windsor and Warkworth — though where, as in these cases, the defences are in massive stonework, we may wonder whether the whole plan may not have been remodelled. But straight lines are rare in ringworks, though there are two straight sides at Old Buckenham (Norfolk) and at Llanfaethlu (Anglesey), while Sheriff Hutton No. 2 (North Yorkshire) appears to have been a complete rectangle. Mottes are even more rarely angular; in England there seems to be only one plain square motte — Cabal Tump at Pembridge (Herefordshire) — though there is a handful of others complicated by stone revetments or by an appendage to the motte, which seem likely to be of very late date.[2] Indeed, such a date seems likely for the Pembridge motte as well; we are informed that in Denmark, where the mottes are in general far later in date than those of England, they are predominantly square.[3]

The motte itself provides the greatest variety and calls for the most discussion. Even on surface indications the variations between individual mottes are enormous; excluding the few square or squarish examples, they can be perfectly round in plan or distinctly elongated ovals. In dimensions they vary enormously: in height they may be over 40 feet (12 m) from the level, some perhaps as much as 50 feet (15 m); or again as little as 5 or 6 feet (1 m.50 or 2 m). Some low-lying mottes with wet defences, especially on the Welsh border, are lower still — an intermediate form between the military motte and the homestead moat — but these are not numerous.

The diameter of the summit ranges from about 380 feet (116 m) at Norwich (Norfolk) — the largest motte in England, though it is partly natural — to as little as 20 feet (6 m). These very small tops, however, probably do not represent the original state of their mottes, nor their own original size; erosion has played its part in reducing their diameter over the centuries. Indeed, there are some mottes which have no table-top left, and not all of these have been reduced to their present miserable condition, it would appear, by human agency.

6.1: *Primitive castles: England*

Ringworks

Mottes

Other early castles

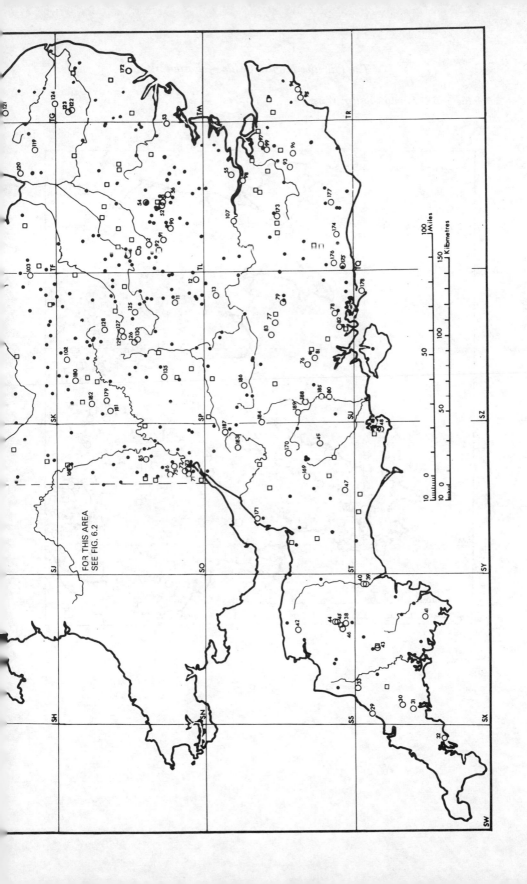

FOR THIS AREA
SEE FIG. 6.2

Figure 6.2: Primitive castles: Wales

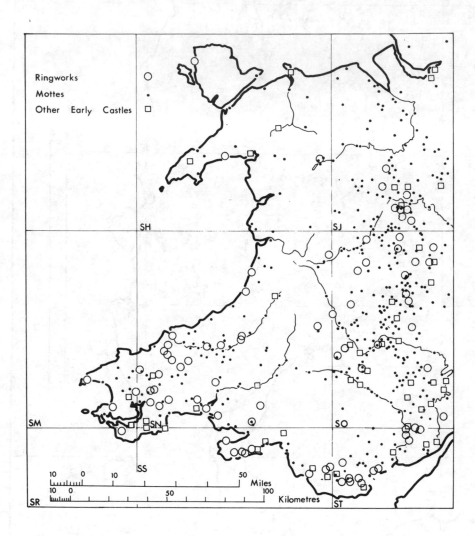

An example of a very small motte might be Legsby (Lincolnshire) which is 30 feet by 40 (9 m by 12 m) across its summit, and a mere 4 feet (1 m 20) above the general level (7 feet/2 m 15 from a boggy ditch 3 feet/90 cms deep). Norwich can serve as our largest example, with an average diameter of 380 feet (116 m), a height of 27 feet (8 m 20) on the crest of the ridge uphill, but 40 feet (12 m) on the other three sides. For a low flat example, we take Haresfield (Gloucestershire) with an average diameter of 180 feet (55 m) and a height of 5–6 feet (1 m 50 to 2 m) — the ditch is wet and fairly wide. An example of a very tall, but relatively narrow motte is Arundel (West Sussex). My own measurements (of limited accuracy) make its height, on an average side, 54 feet (16 m 40); its top is 105 feet by 90 feet across (32 m by 27 m 50). Between these remote extremes lie the mottes of England and Wales, numbering 741 at a recent count.

It is a characteristic of castles that they typically consist of a set of enclosures with a strong inner work — earth or stone — and one or more outer wards or baileys. Mottes and ringworks are generally, but not necessarily, associated with baileys, sometimes as many as four or five of diminishing strength, as if what they were intended to shelter was less and less important to the lord of the castle. An extreme case is Kilpeck (Herefordshire), a castle of no great importance, with no fewer than five baileys, and a village enclosure into the bargain. A stone fortress with a number of enclosures is Barnard Castle (Durham). In any castle, there is nothing unusual about two or three subordinate enclosures; certainly in England and Wales there is no rigid division into *Hauptburg* and *Vorburg* such as we find in parts of the Continent. It seems clear, however, that small castles could be built as mottes with comparatively roomy tops housing all the very modest establishments of their owners, and in such cases there would be no need of a bailey. Ordinarily, however, the main bailey was an important part of the defences.

The position of the motte relative to its bailey, unless dictated by strong movements of ground, is regularly on the perimeter of the bailey defences. The area of the motte and its ditch being considerable, we find very few instances where it stands actually inside the bailey, though such exist. The cross-ditch between motte and bailey was commonly filled in, particularly in stone-built castles.

Where the castle stands close to a strong natural defence, the motte normally stands on this line; in particular, on a ridge-point site, so that the bailey protected it on the exposed sides. The opposite arrangement is found in a few cases, where the approachable side is level, but relatively narrow, so that the motte blocks it, apart from the entrance; we often find a stone keep posted to overawe the entry in this way, but more rarely a ringwork; it is very uncommon in the case of an inner and an outer ward.[4]

As to the motte itself, its character is a more complicated affair than had been realized down to the last 20 years. A motte, I have written elsewhere, 'is an inert mass of earth, sand, marl or stones. It cannot itself be inhabited or defended, and is always an adjunct to its associated constructions of timber, brick or stone.' It is of course the relation of these structures to the motte itself that is so complicated. It had already been realised that the motte typically started by carrying a wooden structure of some sort, surrounded by a palisade. As to the central structure, we knew little, and are hardly better informed now.

The first important excavation of a motte, at Abinger (Surrey) in 1949, thus produced a plan which was very much what could have been expected; the only matters which seemed to call for notice were the small area of the central building — interpreted by the excavator, Dr Hope-Taylor, as a watch-tower — and the double line of posts for the palisade.[5] The latter was a feature which had been observed elsewhere, and turned out to have numerous parallels in many countries. It should be noted in passing that the successful excavation of a motte — in the sense that any of the original arrangements of the top are recovered — is an extremely rare event: either the motte or its superstructure may prove never to have been completed; or the summit has been eroded or dug away; or else whatever original structures were built on top of the motte have been cleared away to make room for later construction.

The many stone structures associated with mottes had always been considered to represent replacements in more permanent material for the timber tower and its palisade, installed when the artificial earthwork had gained sufficient solidity to bear their weight. These 'replacements' were of remarkable variety: first, the motte could be topped with a tower, and these towers are of all shapes and descriptions; alternatively the palisade could be replaced in masonry, either by a plain ring of walling — a 'shell-keep' — or by some more developed ring of walls and towers. At Launceston we have both the central tower and the 'shell-keep', with an outer revetment in addition; at Guildford and the very much later Clun a rectangular keep has been built down the slope of the motte so that part at least of its foundations could be laid on the natural ground level. In the same way, a number of the stone 'shell-keeps' and more complex perimeter defences are carried down the face of their mottes to form revetments, often resting on the natural ground. It had also been observed that some at least of the centrally-situated towers had foundations carried right down to ground level through the body of the motte, and it was suspected that this might be true of others. On the hypothesis that all masonry adjuncts to mottes are later in date than the mottes themselves, this seemed to involve some very ambitious foundation-trenches; but that hypothesis had already begun to wear thin. The well-known castle of Caldicot in Monmouthshire (Gwent) has a massive round tower with its foundations carried down to ground level through a motte so small and unimposing that practically all of it must have been removed to make way for the tower — always supposing that it was in existence at the time the tower was built, as seems unlikely.

Since 1945 there has come to hand a good deal of more positive evidence. In 1946–7 Messrs Jope and Threlfall excavated the castle of Ascot Doilly (Oxfordshire) where they uncovered the base of a small, roughly square, tower in the middle of the rather insignificant motte. Their conclusion was: 'The evidence shows that the mound was piled in stages against the tower as its masonry was raised. If there had been an earlier motte on the site ... it must have been virtually removed before the tower was started.'[6]

As the tower was built in rather poor materials, the base might have needed the support of a low mound. There was nothing particularly surprising about this, nor about the revelation by Dr Ralegh Radford that the motte of Tretower (Brecknock, now part of Powys), composed of very friable alluvial soil, had been revetted in crude masonry from the first.[7]

There were some real surprises to come. Farnham (Surrey) was well known as an example of a large motte revetted in stone with small rectangular towers. The masonry suggested the later twelfth century, and it was naturally, and correctly, supposed that it had been added to the motte; Farnham, indeed, is heard of in 1138.[8] But the motte itself had a more complicated history than anyone had supposed, as the excavations in 1958–60, under Dr M. W. Thompson, were to reveal.[9] It was shown that the original motte was built around, and contemporaneously with, a massive pier of masonry enclosing the well-chamber and rising to the top of the motte, where it was enlarged horizontally to form a wide rectangular foundation, with the projecting portions supported on the well-rammed marl of the motte. Whatever may be said of this dubious expedient in terms of engineering, it is clear that the substructure was meant to carry a substantial square tower, and that the construction of the latter was intended from the outset. (Its disappearance probably dates from the slighting of the castles of its owner, Henry of Blois, Bishop of Winchester, in 1155).[10]

Still more surprising were the results of Dr J. P. C. Kent's excavations at South Mimms, from 1960 onwards. This appeared to be a very ordinary motte when I visited it in February 1942, but it proved to have been a most remarkable structure in its original form. In the first place, its slopes were revetted in vertical wooden shuttering, so that, instead of the usual truncated-cone shape, it formed a flat cylinder. In the middle of this — rising from stone sleeper-wall foundations laid on the natural soil — was a square wooden tower in the form of the frustum of a very steep-sided pyramid. The basement was not filled in; its walls revetted the earth filling of the motte which was piled all round it. The entry was at ground level, by a tunnel through the body of the motte into the basement of the tower. The motte and its wooden structures were coeval; the only stonework was formed by the sleeper-walls under the tower.[11]

Lydford Castle (Devon) was the scene of another disconcerting discovery. It had long been realized that the square keep of this castle, standing apparently on a low motte, had its foundations at natural ground level, for one section of its basement had been kept clear, to be used as cellar or prison. The excavation of the remainder of the basement by Mr A. D. Saunders for the Ministry of Works in 1958 revealed three lighting-slits which had been blocked by the erection of the 'motte'.[12] A similar sequence was also reported from Aldingbourne (Sussex), where the low mound was shown to contain the stump of a tower faced down to ground level in excellent ashlar — thus, a tower which was intended originally to be seen for its whole height.[13]

The relation between the motte and its superstructure was clearly more complex than had been supposed, and as the natural human tendency, faced with such a complexity, is to attempt to enforce simplicity on it, there were attempts to suggest that every motte could be expected to contain substructures of wood or stone, destined to support its central tower. In support of this view, further examples could be cited: the square foundation in piled stone in the middle of the great motte of Totnes (Devon), presumably intended to carry a timber tower; the posts passing through the earth of the motte at Kaersgaard in Denmark without excavated post-holes, so that they must have been in position when the motte was raised.[14] Nevertheless, it was difficult to accept this position without reserve: not only was Abinger itself an exception, with its tower built on the summit of the motte, but there had been a great many earlier excavations of English mottes which had found no substructures. Some of these excavations admittedly were fairly butcherly affairs, and several of the mottes in question were treated as barrows; but even the worst excavator would have reported a stone substructure, and many of those who undertook work of this sort were fully capable of detecting the remains of timber constructions. More recently also the masonry structure discovered in the course of a minor excavation at Langstone (Monmouth) had had its foundations carried down to natural level through an existing motte, while the important work at Winchester has shown that the early twelfth-century keep was driven into the motte in the same way.[15] Conservation work done at Longtown (Herefordshire) and Whittington (Shropshire) has revealed that the stone keeps of both these castles were built on top of their mottes with very shallow foundations indeed.

There is indeed nothing simple about the relation between the motte and its superstructure; perhaps the best analysis of all possible situations is that composed by Dr Thompson, the excavator of Farnham; and this may serve as the basis of any discussion on the matter:[16]

(1) No substructure, the superstructure erected on top of the mound (Abinger and Hoverberg, near Cologne.)

(2) Substructure erected on old ground surface and entirely buried, within the mound:

    (a) In wood (Kaersgaard; possibly Burgh Castle, where post-holes were found on the site of the destroyed motte)

    (b) In stone (Totnes)

(3) Substructure erected on old ground surface, its exterior only being buried, the interior retained as a cellar:

(a) In wood (South Mimms)

(b) In stone (Ascott Doilly, possibly Wareham. 'Farnham ... is peculiar but evidently belongs to this category.')

(4) Free-standing tower to which a mound was later added (Aldingbourne, Lydford).

In classes 2 and 3 there is the further possibility that the substructures may have been inserted into an existing motte rather than built at the same time as the earthwork; this, we have seen, is what happened at Langstone and Winchester. It will be noticed that class 4 — where the motte did not form part of the original plan — stands apart from the rest. As Dr Thompson states, the purpose of this sort of added motte (or false motte, as we might call it) is military; it gave the tower some protection against mining, and probably a great deal against the use of ladders. He is inclined to look to this class — but with a tower probably of wood — as coming earliest, with class 1 representing the final stage of evolution; but he very reasonably suspects that 'by the time mottes appeared in this country in *c.* 1050 this earlier evolution had already been completed'. In fact, the earthing-up of the bases of towers is sometimes found to have occurred at a fairly late date; that of Lydford is ascribed to the late thirteenth century, while at Néaufle (Seine-et-Oise) the round tower is built up in a later motte, which partly blocks a pointed window.[17] Other examples of class 4 are Christchurch (Hampshire)[18] and Doué-la-Fontaine (Maine-et-Loire); at the latter the motte was raised around the foot of a tower built by raising and consolidating a strongly-built unfortified house of the tenth century.[19] The German example of Hardtburg has its motte heaped round a square *bergfried* of the early twelfth century. The motte and tower are of the same date, and the tower had cellars; we have thus an example of class 3b.[20] An interesting group of Dutch fortifications in the Rotterdam area, all very small and all now destroyed, contained examples of class 2b, in the form of structural arches buried in contemporary mottes. At Holy, Vlaardingen, built in about 1250, four arches carried a small tower, nearly square. Also at Vlaardingen, at Juffer Aechtenwoning, a tower built down the slope of the motte was flanked by a single arch of what seems to have been a continuous buried arcade intended to carry a ring of wall around the summit of the motte — a 'shell-keep' in fact. This, too, was dated to about 1250; a complete set of arches to carry a shell at Overschie apparently was a little earlier.[21] Such sophisticated substructures, of fairly late date, may well represent a development from buildings of class 3b. The latter represents the obvious way to build a stone tower and its motte starting from scratch; but in this class, as well as in class 4 where the motte was an afterthought, the basement was utterly dark and of questionable usefulness. At Lydford most of it was eventually filled in; at Doué the whole. If the substructure was going to be useless for occupation, the best thing would clearly be to build it from the first as a structural element only — a mere support to the upper stages of the tower. The sole English example of this class is at the eleventh-century castle of Totnes (Devon) where there is a crude drystone foundation for carrying a tower; this method is little removed from class 1.

Dr Thompson's class 2a — where the substructure was made of wood, entirely buried in the motte — represents what should be the basic form of a motte and its tower according to Dr Hope-Taylor's theory of the origin of mottes. This form is represented, singly and most awkwardly, by Kaersgaard, which is apparently very late in date, even by Danish standards; for it was destroyed in 1340, and there seems to be no evidence that it was at that time at all old.[22] So far from being an indication of the original method of supporting the central tower on a motte, it seems more likely to be a timber version of such a tower as Holy.

To return to England, recent excavations have revealed a number of examples of mottes containing no substructures at all. Of these the most important is Hastings,[23] whose erection is shown in the Bayeux Tapestry; other examples are Hen Blas (Flint No. 4), Therfield (Hertfordshire) and Sycharth (Llansilin, Denbigh, now part of Clwyd).[24] The present writer is strongly of the opinion that class 1 of Dr Thompson's scheme accounts for most English mottes; that wooden houses and towers, and in many cases stone ones, were simply built on top of the motte. It is at least clear that this arrangement is not likely to be exceptional or anomalous. Where, however, it was intended from the beginning to have a stone tower emerging from the motte, the obvious method was to build tower and motte together, as at Ascott d'Oilly. Where the basement structure was made to be buried in the first place, this could be a crude expedient like that at Totnes, or a sophisticated structure like that of the Rotterdam mottes. The frequency or rarity of any class of substructure, among so small and erratic a number of completed excavations, cannot be taken as significant. Also the absence of any early example of Dr Thompson's class 2a (buried wooden substructures) is not necessarily as important as it appears, while the surprisingly numerous instances of class 4 may also be misleading. We may not expect future excavation to reveal many more examples like Farnham or South Mimms. The latter, however, at least shows us what curiosities an apparently simple motte can conceal; the vertical timber revetment, in particular, may well prove to be a common feature — in any case it is a possibility to be taken into account by future excavators. Certainly Mr Addyman has found similar wooden revetting in the outworks of Ludgershall (Wiltshire),[25] and Mr Davison has noted a trench across the slope of the motte at Aldingham (Lancashire) which could hardly be intended for any other purpose.[26] Few though these examples are, one has only to consider the consequences of the collapse of wooden shuttering of this sort to see that it could completely mislead all but skilled and tenacious excavators; in particular, it could destroy any sign of the defences of the perimeter, and greatly affect the apparent area of the summit.

Generally the material of the motte has been dug out of the surrounding ditch, but any convenient source of earth and stones could be brought in to help. Where excavators have been able to note the stratification of the material, this is commonly found to have been tipped inwards from the outer edge — a fact which would seem to suggest the origin of the motte as a development from the ringwork, though such a method of working is very much what one might expect in any case. Some large examples were built in layers, each carefully rammed, and it is perhaps this fact that accounts for the intimidating gradient of the slopes of many of these bigger mottes. In other cases steep-faced mottes are due to a high angle of repose in the local soil; the red sandstone clay of Herefordshire is particularly notable in this respect. Sometimes the soil, being deficient in its angle of repose, was reinforced by a clay casing on the outside. Where it was possible to use existing features, a natural hillock or even a round barrow, as at Rûg (Corwen No. 1, Merionethshire, now part of Gwynedd), made a good base for a motte,[27] or the builders might collect stones and make a central pile to start with, as at Kaersgaard and Sycharth. In some cases the bulk of the motte is made of 'imported' material; Modrydd (Brecknock, now in Powys) seems to be a mass of river-boulders laid in clay dug out of the ditch. At Cwm Prysor (Gwynedd) a site where scree was abundantly available, the Welsh produced the ultimate in this category — a solid mass of stone laid mainly in earth, with the faces battering only slightly from the vertical, and small offsets, the whole almost cylindrical in form. In some places the motte was of basically natural formation, a steep hill artificially flattened and scarped down. Such are the powerful Somerset mottes of Dunster and Montacute. The natural rock summit of Clitheroe, crowned with a masonry 'shell-keep', was treated as if it were a motte, but the only examples of rock bosses with artificially scarped vertical sides seem to be those at Halton (Flint, now part of Clwyd) and Mouse Castle (Cusop No. 2, Hereford). Halton is badly damaged; and Mouse Castle has every appearance of being an unfinished earthwork; it is therefore possible that their present appearance is misleading.

The contemporary name for the central tower of the motte's timber defences was evidently *bretasche* (*breteche, bretagium*, etc.). This identification is clear from such a case as Henry III's order to the owners of the mottes in the vale of Montgomery to have their mottes fortified with good bretasches,[28] but there is more in the word than this. We find bretasches in castles that had neither motte nor ringwork: for instance, a bretasche was removed from the castle of Nafferton,[29] a large squarish earthwork whose completion had been forbidden in 1218. As this was to be set up 'at the gate of the drawbridge' at Newcastle it must have been a gate-tower. Some castles had more than one bretasche: in 1241 two were being built at Rhuddlan and two more at Ellesmere;[30] in 1244 the castle of Coleshill (Flintshire, now part of Powys), which is at present unidentified, was to be fortified with the best garillum and at least three bretasches.[31] On his lines of circumvallation and contravallation around Château-Gaillard in 1203–4 Philip Augustus of France set up double bretasches in seven places, that is to say, very strong wooden castles.[32] Presumably these double bretasches extended from one line to the other; and though only Philip's panegyrist could have described them as 'very strong wooden castles' they were wooden towers, and so were all the other bretasches which we have noticed. Some were at the gates of castles, like that at Wolvesey 'on the new bridge' in 1240;[33] we even note that a bretaschia could be nothing more than a bell-cote.[34] At Worcester[35] in 1204 the gateway was rebuilt in stone with a bretasche above it. This is an example of particular interest in view of the later history of the word. Bretasche, or its later form brattice, is used to describe a form of defence of the nature of hoarding or machicolation, which enabled the defenders to drop missiles on an enemy at the very foot of the walls. Antiquaries tend to use the word of a roofed gallery below the actual parapet, sometimes very short, and generally of stone, not wood — a type of defence common in Palestine and not unusual in France in late-medieval defence; it is very rare in England, but curiously common in Ireland. Whether the word should rightly be confined to this type of structure is uncertain. Mrs Armitage knew of no use of 'bretasche' in this connection before the fourteenth century.[36] At Worcester the timber superstructure of the gate was something less than a complete tower and much more than a mere gallery.

It is remarkable that the same word could mean at different times a timber tower and a mere overhanging defence; but the inescapable conclusion seems to be that the towers themselves were built so as to overhang their bases. Such a style of building in timber is perfectly sound, even advantageous, since it balances the projecting walls against the weight of the joists. It would also offer a considerable measure of safety against the grave danger of fire; openings in the floor of the overhanging portions would enable the defenders to extinguish a fire laid at the foot of their tower or kill the incendiaries themselves. Wooden blockhouses, such as those of the American West,[37] almost inevitably take on this form.

In fact, the bretasche on the motte was not normally directly exposed to attack — so far as we know; some mottes have such small tops that there seems little room for an outer line of defence. At Abinger the traces of the central tower were found to be surrounded by a very clearly marked double row of post-holes. Literary sources of the Norman period suggest the likelihood of some sort of outer defence of this kind, but no other example has yet been excavated around the summit of a motte, although similar sets of double palisading have been found in other positions: at Bishopton in Gower (West Glamorgan) on the defences of a small ringwork;[38] at Therfield on the line of a bailey,[39] and at the Hüsterknupp in the Rhineland in a similar position.[40] A very weak example, with the post-holes widely spaced, is found at the medieval level of the defences of Mount Caburn (Sussex); this was interpreted as the perimeter of a Stephanic castle, but probably was only a village-defence.[41] Other examples are reported from the bailey of Launceston (Cornwall)[42] and the inner work at Søby on the island of Aerø, Denmark.[43] The outer line of post-holes is generally the more regular and continuous. The normal interpretation put upon these remains by archaeologists is that the outer line of posts carried the face of a timber wall, planked or wattled, probably daubed in clay as some protection against fire, and topped by a parapet, much like that of a stone curtain and most likely designed to imitate one. Meanwhile the inner posts were shorter, and helped to carry a wall-walk along the rear of the parapet. At Abinger — where the uppermost levels had been dug away before the start of the excavations — Dr Hope-Taylor reconstructed the defences as built entirely of timber, with cross-bracing between the two lines of posts; but at Bishopston, at the Hüsterknupp, and at Therfield and Launceston there was abundant evidence that the space between the two lines of posts had been filled with earth and stones, and that the wall-walk was carried on this filling.

The only modern name for a defence of this kind is the German *Holzerdemauer*, but it seems that the contemporary name was *garillum*.[44] The order to fortify Coleshill castle *optimo garillo* in 1244 has already been mentioned; this should refer to timber walls, just as the bretasches were timber towers. Plainer examples come from Dover Castle: in 1247 the building of a double wall and half a turret 'where the garoll' is' was ordered, and in 1256 instructions were given to pull down the 'jarollum' round the church in Dover castle and replace it by an embattled stone wall of the same height.[45] This is plainly the light wall whose base is still visible, running along the crest of the massive bank behind the church and the Roman *pharos*. (The bank could easily be taken for part of a great ringwork; it proves to be of several periods, the last as late as the thirteenth century, which will explain why it received its stone defences only in 1256.) A palisade along the crest of a bank, as high as the embattled stone wall that was to take its place, was plainly a defensive structure, not a mere obstacle, and this jarollum at least was plainly a *Holzerdemauer* of the familiar type.

Palisading of this kind was not invariably used; at Hen Blâs there was only a single line of post-holes, rather widely spaced. The case of Clough Castle (Co Down, Northern Ireland) is less satisfactory, and it may be doubted whether it had in fact only a single row of palisading.[46]

Access to the summit of the motte was commonly supplied by the sort of timber flying bridge which figures in the Bayeux Tapestry at Dinan and Bayeux, and which is described in considerable detail in the narrative of the Bishop of Thérouanne's adventure:

a bridge, which first springing from the counterscarp of the ditch (*ab exteriori labro fossae*) was gradually raised as it advanced, supported by

Figure 6.3: The garillum

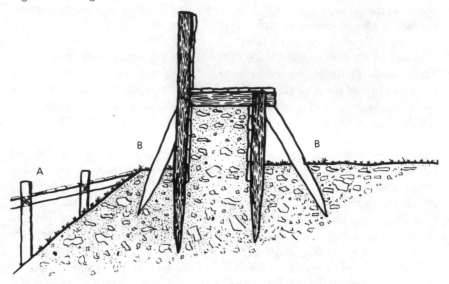

Typical section A: bridge of motte (in background). B, B: timber shores (only found at the Hüsterknupp).

sets of piers (*columnisque*), two, or even three, trussed on each side over convenient spans, crossing the ditch with a managed ascent (*eo ascendendi moderamine per transversum fossae consurgit*) so as to reach the upper level of the mound, landing at its edge (*limen prima fronte contingat*).[47]

From the pictures and the description we can get a good notion of a type of bridge leading up to the head of the motte, which was certainly in use around the time of the Conquest. But even the Tapestry appears to show us, at Rennes, a different means of access to the summit; here, a straight stair apparently runs up the slope of the motte, presumably from a horizontal bridge across the ditch.

Excavation reveals both sorts of approach; at Hen Domen (Montgomery No. 2) a long succession of flying bridges has been revealed, while the classic excavation of Abinger motte has uncovered 'a massive block of rock-sand ... left intact across the ditch by its makers, to serve as foundations for a bridge giving access to the motte-side. It was about 12 feet wide ...'[48]

More recently, a causeway across the ditch of a motte at Newton Longville (Buckinghamshire) by the name of Hangman's Hill was excavated ahead of the inevitable farm bulldozer, and proved to be original. These solid causeways were presumably less satisfactory from a military point of view than a timber bridge, parts of which could presumably be removed in defence.

It is not without relevance to consider the access to the top of the motte in stone castles. These are similar, but the parallel is not complete. There seem to be no surviving causeways, and flying bridges have certainly disappeared. In a number of cases there are signs of an approach across a level bridge and up the slope of the motte; for instance, at Crickhowell (Brecknock, now in Powys) and at Caerleon (Monmouthshire, now Gwent) there are the bases of pairs of small round towers, originally forming gatehouses at the foot of the slope and at the abutment of the bridge. A different means of access is afforded in a number of cases by a staircase built along the top of the wing-wall linking the defences of the motte and those of the bailey, as at Berkham-stead (Hertfordshire) and Launceston (Cornwall). It does not seem likely that the timber garillum was ever strong enough to support stairs in this position.

Ringworks call for less discussion in general than mottes, though they show a much greater degree of variety. Thus, though on level ground or on a summit the typical ringwork forms a fairly complete and symmetrical loop of bank and ditch, there are many cases where its perimeter is backed against powerful natural obstacles, and only requires artificial defences on part of its front, so that a powerful bank on this side will afford all the earthwork defence required for an effective castle: this type of work we have called a *partial ringwork*. Certain variations are to be observed; there is a type commonly found on sloping ground, where the surrounding bank, conspicuously tallest where it faces the high ground, slopes away to nothing, or to very little, on the downhill side. These *crescentic* rings are graceful and attractive earthworks. Less agreeable, but evidently effective, was an example like Cefnllys No. 2 (Radnor, now part of Powys) where the ground is level on all sides except one; the bank drops sharply to nothing on the edge of the obstacle. At St Mellon's (Monmouthshire, now Gwent), which stands on a projection overlooking the low ground beside the Severn estuary, the bank is exceptionally short.

These economical little earthworks are naturally common on broken ground, and useful for small castles. Very few larger castles are built on partial ringworks: Castle Acre (Norfolk) is the only one that comes to mind; its bank has been raised (and walled) twice. On the other hand, some more important promontory sites are occupied by complete rings: the large Castle Leavington (Yorkshire, North Riding; now North Yorkshire), on its formidable foreland, is a complete ring, and so, it appears, is the powerful earthwork at Devizes (Wiltshire). The really massive ringworks are few in number: as well as Castle Acre and the Devizes there are the central earthwork round the great tower of Castle Rising (Norfolk), the badly-damaged Downton (Wiltshire), New Buckenham (Norfolk), also the powerful ring-bank that supports the masonry of Exeter (Devon); above all, the huge inner perimeter of Old Sarum (Wiltshire), our biggest example of the kind — a mighty ellipse 360 to 310 feet (110–95 m) across from rim to rim, with a scarp 55 feet (17 m) high facing a counterscarp of 20 feet (6 m). Of approximately 200 rings in England and Wales the bulk are considerably smaller than these, even some with banks only 6 feet or 2 m high. One particularly singular small ring is considerably stranger than this: Llanlleonfel (Brecknock) on a fine hilltop site has a scarp of 11 feet (4.25 m); the ditch is only 4 feet deep, but is cut in hard rock. The actual ring is only 54 feet by 48 feet (16.50 by 14.50 m) across the top of the banks, and the floor of the enclosure is only about 25 feet by 12 (7.50 m by 3.65). The little stronghold looks, paradoxically, as if it was designed to be defended, but not inhabited.

Conversely, the *petites enceintes circulaires* in Normandy, described by Professor de Boüard in a paper that did much to set on foot the modern enquiry into castle ringworks,[49] are seldom of a real military character, nor do they stand close to a village and its church, as castles generally do. They seem to have been meant as some sort of protection for those who were assarting woodlands, or otherwise exploiting the fertility of the district. Nevertheless — as one would certainly have supposed — we find a Norman example of a ringwork, le Plessis-Grimoult (Calvados).[50] This is a *grande enceinte en fer de-cheval* — a fine crescentic ringwork on a sloping site, with a flat meadow on the downhill side, which is likely to have been marshy. It received stone defences, some of which survive. Its last de Plessis lord chose the wrong side at the battle of Val-ès-Dunes in 1047 — a mistake for which he paid with his lands and his life — and nothing more seems to have occurred at the castle; if this is so, le Plessis-Grimoult was a ringwork, crowned in masonry, before any castles existed in England.

The conversion of one sort of earthwork castle into the other is fairly frequent. Most commonly this involves the filling-in of the central depression of a ringwork so as to form a motte. This would be a likely consequence of raising the bank, or it might be due to a desire to increase the available area inside the palisade. Two examples of different technique may be cited, but it must be stressed that the story in each case has been composed on the strength of surface appearances, and that excavation might have a different tale to tell.[51] At Kemeys Inferior (Monmouthshire), backed against a head-long slope to the river Usk, is what appears to be a crescentic partial ringwork of some strength, whose bank has been cut through at two points close together, so as to form a very small motte; Middleham No. 2 (Yorkshire) is a complete ring and bailey, with a main bank which is not only very strong, but on the uphill side quite extraordinarily wide on top — no less than 45 feet (13.50 m). It is difficult to suggest any reason for this appearance more convincing than the earthing-up of a small motte and bailey to the level of the top of its motte.

A subordinate feature of medieval earthwork is the outer bank found at many castles. In its simplest form it is a plain bank outside the castle ditch — the counterscarp-bank of normal archaeological reference. This formed an obstacle, but its existence might not be due to original planning; Professor Leslie Alcock found that the counterscarp-bank at the long-inhabited motte of Langstone (Monmouthshire) was formed of upcast from the periodical scourings of the ditch.[52] In more complex examples there are double and treble ditches with banks between them. Of the numerous cases of this sort a few that come to mind are Thetford (Norfolk), Caus (Shropshire), Ludgershall (Wiltshire) where Mr Peter Addyman has shown that the intermediate banks were heavily revetted in timber, front and rear,[53] Whittington (Shropshire) which has perhaps the most complicated set of banks and ditches of all, and Helmsley (North Yorkshire) where the powerful bank between the great rock-cut ditches is the noblest thing of its kind in England. In dealing with this sort of outer defences, the principal question to be asked is which were simply obstacles and which outer lines of defence, to be occupied and held by the garrison. There are certain superficial indications which can offer a possible answer to this question, for instance whether or not one of these outer banks is attached directly to some substantial work of the main defences. Nevertheless, only excavation can give us a satisfactory answer, and even that may be uncertain.

Notes

1. King and Alcock, 'Ringworks of England and Wales', pp. 103-6. However, C.J. Spurgeon argues with considerable force that 'a geological determinant is apparent in Glamorgan, the crucial factor being the presence or absence of glacial drift' (which is seen as favouring the construction of mottes), *Château-Gaillard* xiii (Caen, 1987), pp. 206-7. See also, by the same author, *Castles in Wales and the Marches; essays in honour of D.J. Cathcart King* (ed. Kenyon and Avent; University of Wales Press, Cardiff, 1987), pp. 32-6.

2. Aughton (Yorkshire, now in Humberside); Kirkby Fleetham, licensed in 1314 (North Yorkshire); Llangattock (Brecknock, now part of Powys).

3. Hans Stiesdal, 'Die Motten in Dänemark; eine kurze Übersicht', in *Château-Gaillard* ii (Cologne, 1967), p. 95; 'ist der grösste Teil quadratisch'. Cf. the same author's 'Late earthworks of the motte and bailey type' in *Château-Gaillard* iv (Ghent 1968), pp. 219-20.

4. The only examples of this kind seem to be Powerstock (Dorset) and Scarborough (North Yorkshire).

5. Brian Hope-Taylor,'The excavation of a motte at Abinger in Surrey', *Archaeological Journal*, cvii (1952), pp. 15-43; also in Bruce-Mitford, *Recent archaeological excavations in Britain* (London, 1956), pp. 223-49.

6. E.M. Jope and R.I. Threlfall, 'The twelfth-century castle at Ascot Doilly, Oxfordshire, *Antiquaries Journal*, xxxix (1959), p. 233.

7. Guide Book to *Tretower Castle* (HMSO, 1950), p. 1.

8. *Annales Wintonienses* (ed. Luard, Rolls Series, 36.2), p. 51.

9. M.W. Thompson, 'Recent excavations in the keep of Farnham castle, Surrey', *Medieval Archaeology*, iv (1960), pp. 81-94.

10. Pipe Roll, 2 Hen. II, p. 54; *Robert of Torigni* (ed. Howlett, Rolls Series, 82.4), p. 186.

11. Reports in *Medieval Archaeology*, v (1961), p. 318; vi-vii (1962-3), p. 322; viii (1964), p. 255; see also Brian Davison, *Current Archaeology*, i (1967), p. 130. No adequate report seems to have been published.

12. See reports in *Medieval Archaeology*, ii (1958), p. 195, and iii (1959), p. 307. Its history seems to have been even more complicated: A.D. Saunders, 'Lydford Castle,

Devon', *Medieval Archaeology*, xxiv (1980), pp. 123-87.

13. Report in *Medieval Archaeology*, vi-vii (1962-3), p. 323.

14. Stiesdal, 'Die Motten in Dänemark', *Château-Gaillard*, ii (Cologne, 1967), p. 97 It should be noted that the posts rested on a foundation-layer of stones under the motte, and the post-holes were only about half a metre (20 inches) deep.

15. Excavation reports: Leslie Alcock, *Medieval Archaeology*, ix (1965), p. 193; Martin Biddle, *Antiquaries Journal*, 1 (1970), p. 291.

16. M. W. Thompson, 'Motte substructures', *Medieval Archaeology*, v (1961), pp. 305-6.

17. M.A. De Caumont, *Abécédaire d'archéologie* (Caen, 1869), iii, pp. 470-2, verified and photographed by Mr Davison.

18. Thompson, 'Recent excavations in the keep of Farnham Castle, Surrey', *Medieval Archaeology*, iv (1960), p. 88.

19. Lecture of Prof. de Boüard to the *Château-Gaillard* meeting at Ghent in August, 1968.

20. Adolf Herrnbrodt, *Château-Gaillard* iv (Ghent, 1968), p. 142. Cf. the cases of Moers in the Rhineland and Huissen in the Netherlands, cited by Dr J. G. N. Renaud in *Château-Gaillard*, i, p. 111. At Moers the motte is later than the tower. A tower of about 1400 at Icht (Düsseldorf-Lohausen) has a motte (contemporary?) heaped round it (*Ex. inf.* Herr G. Binding).

21. C. Hoek, in *Rotterdam Papers* (ed. J. G. N. Renaud, Rotterdam, 1968), pp. 81-8.

22. Stiesdal (as n[14], *supra*).

23. Philip Barker and K. J. Barton, 'Excavations at Hastings castle, 1968', *Archaeological Journal*, cxxv (1968), pp. 303-5.

24. G. B. Leach, 'Excavations at Hen Blas, Coleshill Fawr, near Flint', *Flintshire Historical Society*, xvii (1957), pp. 1-15; Martin Biddle, 'The excavation of a motte and bailey castle at Therfield', *Journal of the British Archaeological Association*, 3rd series, xxvii (1964), pp. 53-91; Douglas Hague and A. Warhurst, 'Excavations at Sycharth Castle, Denbighshire,' *Archaeologia Cambrensis*, cxv (1966), pp. 108-27.

25. P. V. Addyman, 'Excavation at Ludgershall castle', *Château-Gaillard*, vi (Caen, 1973), p. 9.

26. Brian Davison, Report in *Medieval Archaeology*, xiii (1969), pp. 258-9.

27. Other examples are St Weonard's (Hereford), the destroyed motte of Tre-Oda (Whitchurch No. 2, Glamorgan) and the great chambered tomb of Knowth, Co. Meath, Southern Ireland).

28. *Rotuli Litterarum Clausarum*, ii, 42a (30 May 1225).

29. *Ibid.*, 459b.

30. Calendar of Liberate Rolls (1240-5), pp. 69-70, 92-3.

31. Close Rolls, (1242-7), p. 175.

32. William le Breton, *Gesta Philippi Augusti*, cap. 125 (ed. Delaborde, Paris, 1882), p. 216.

33. Calendar of Liberate Rolls, (1240-5), p. 26.

34. *Ibid.*, p. 32.

35. *Rotuli de Liberate*, p. 93; Pipe Roll 5 John, p. 52.

36. Armitage, *Early Norman castles*, p. 387.

37. I was delighted to find that this comparison had also occurred to the late Professor U. T. Holmes of the University of North Carolina.

38. Llywelyn Morgan, *Antiquarian survey of East Gower* (London, 1899), pp. 180-3; also *Archaeologia Cambrensis*, 5th series, xvi (1899), pp. 249-58.

39. Biddle, as at n[24].

40. Herrnbrodt, *Der Hüsterknupp* (Cologne, 1958), pp. 65-9. This German example seems to have been more skilfully built and more generally sophisticated than the rest.

41. A.E. Wilson, 'Excavations in the ramparts and gateway of the Caburn', *Sussex Archaeological Collections*, lxxix (1938), p. 183, 186; lxxx (1939), pp. 195-6.

42. A.D. Saunders, 'Launceston Castle; an interim report', *Cornish Archaeology*, iii (1964), pp. 63-9.

43. *Ex. inf.*. Hr. Stiesdal.

44. The word is capable of great variations in spelling, also in gender: *geroillum, jarruylium, jarullus.*

45. Calendar of Liberate Rolls, iii (1245-51), p. 120; iv (1251-60), p. 323.

46. Waterman, 'Excavations at Clough Castle', *Ulster Journal of Archaeology*, 3rd series, xvii (1954), pp. 104-63. This otherwise thorough excavation stopped short at what appears to have been an inner row of post-holes; it does not seem as if any attempt had been made to search for anything in front of them. In addition, a number of pits inside the palisade were apparently positions for archers; the stone-on-edge lining of the loophole of one of these lay *outside* the line of posts, and clearly was designed to revet the sides of an opening passing through the earthen filling of a garillum. Additionally, there seems no point in the archers standing in pits unless it was to give them headroom under a low rampart-walk, such as this sort of defence would be likely to have.

47. See Chapter 5, n[34]. (Translation by Clark).

48. Brian Hope-Taylor, in Bruce-Mitford, *Recent archaeological excavations in Britain* (London, 1956), p. 233.

49. Professor de Boüard, 'Les petites enceintes circulaires d'origine médiévale en Normandie', *Château-Gaillard*, i (1964), pp. 21-36.

50. E. Zadora-Rio, *Château-Gaillard*, v (1972), pp. 227-39.

51. King and Alcock, *Château-Gaillard*, iii (1969), p. 101.

52. *Medieval Archaeology* ix (1965), p. 193.

53. *Château-Gaillard* iv (Ghent, 1968), pp. 9-12.

7

The Primitive English Castle — Stone

Masonry construction, being a much slower business than timberwork, was less suited to the immediate needs of the Norman conquerors. Undoubtedly the great bulk of the earliest castles in this country were of earthwork and timber, and one very important result of this would be to delay still further the installation of stone defences. Until the passage of time had compacted the large masses of earth in the banks and mottes of these timber castles, the garillum could not be replaced in masonry; and it was in the largest strong-holds, where the earthwork was massive, that the process of replacement would have begun. Mrs Armitage apparently believed that only three pieces of masonry in English castles could be dated to the eleventh century: William I's great keeps at Colchester and the Tower of London, and the gate of Exeter, with its Saxon features; later she added the keep of Pevensey, and tentatively the tower of Bramber.[1]

However healthy such scepticism may have been in its day, later writers have been able to bring forward other examples of eleventh-century work: the enclosure of Richmond (North Yorkshire),[2] the inner ward of Ludlow (Shropshire),[3] the inner enclosure of Corfe (Dorset),[4] and the main defensive line of the Castle of the Peak (Derbyshire),[5] all of which stand on strong rocky sites (Corfe on a summit of chalk). Chepstow keep (Monmouthshire, now Gwent) is another important addition to the canon.[6] None the less, it is clear that the great bulk of castles of earlier type received their stone defences in the twelfth century; it must be remembered that by the end of that century castles of scientific flanked design were already being built.

The stone castle of primitive type could exhibit considerable variations in layout and detail, but typically it consisted of a keep — either a Norman tower or a 'shell-keep' — and a single ward. Outer wards are normally addi-tions. Where the two main parts are not contemporary, the keep is usually later than the ward. A shell-keep needed a motte compacted by time; a Norman keep required considerably more skill to build and more time in building than an enclosure of the relatively low and simple walling used in this early period.

The defence of the ward is generally simple; the curtains — often low by later standards — follow either strong natural features or the line of existing earthworks. As a result the trace is irregular or curvilinear, in spite of the builders' general preference for straight walling when this was possible. In fact, very commonly the line of a curvilinear bank is fortified with a wall of polygonal trace, made up of a number of short faces, meeting at very obtuse angles; in the more carefully built castles these are capped with quoins — a very characteristic twelfth-century feature — or even with buttresses. The main front of the Castle of the Peak is straight; Wolvesey (Hampshire), built on level ground, is a quadrilateral, arranged round a courtyard.[7] The reason for any use of straight lines is plainly convenience (not, as in the fortification of a later period, military advantage). There were indeed not enough towers for the use of any scientific defence based on enfilade; without capping towers, any markedly salient angles were only a source of weakness, and straight faces presented no advantage to the defence. Even in a case like Ludlow, where there is an unusally generous set of flanking towers — four besides the very large gatehouse, and not ill arranged — there is no real scientific employment of flanking. A single exception must be mentioned: the eastern side of Richmond, where Robin Hood's Tower, the Gold Hole Tower, and the fallen tower between them cover the front by flanking in the manner of a far later period. But even here it is not quite clear whether this is a real or only an apparent example of scientific flanking; Robin Hood's Tower contains a chapel, the Gold Hole Tower is a latrine turret;[8] while several other small turrets of the castle, existing or vanished, were not disposed in any very military fashion.

Mural towers indeed, when they occur in this period, are generally not very imposing: rather small, square, projecting from the curtain, often closed at the rear so as to form proper rooms, if not very useful ones, on each floor; rising (as is normal in towers) a stage above the curtain. They do not usually cap angles, and have no arrangements for archery, except perhaps from the battlements.

Gates are often more imposing; the common type is a square tower, with the entry forming the basement stage, and arches in the front and rear walls, the former closed by the doors. Examples of this sort are to be found at Richmond — where the gatehouse was raised to form the imposing Great Tower — at Tickhill (Yorkshire, West Riding; now in South Yorkshire) Egremont (Cumberland, now Cumbria), and Castle Rising (Norfolk), but from the very beginning a more highly-developed type appears. Here there are three arches spanning the way, and the gates were set in the central arch. The presumed advantage of this arrangement is that the defenders were able to interfere, through an opening in the floor over the outer part of the passage, with enemies attacking the gate. Exeter is an example of evident eleventh-century date; Newark (Nottinghamshire) and Sherborne (Dorset) are others, dating from about 1130. The great early Norman gate of Ludlow is an example of a rather more complicated type, and has been greatly altered; it was elongated, with its outer end widened so as to form a T-shape in plan; nevertheless, it is clear that its great doors hung in an archway well inside the entry, though nearer the front than the rear. There is an ingenious and unique mural passage to bypass this middle archway and serve as a substitute for a wicket; unless the doors hung at this point this arrangement was pointless.

This more complicated type of gatehouse had probably some relation to certain wooden gate-towers of a variety of dates.[9] Itself it had little future; the more ambitious sort of gate in the period of scientific defence which was to follow was usually designed on quite different principles; Trematon (Cornwall) has a rare example of a three-arch gatehouse of the later thirteenth century. But the simple rectangular tower with the entry driven through its basement and the defences of the gate concentrated at its outer arch is a feature which appears throughout the Middle Ages; we can cite such cases as the inner gate at Llanstephan (Carmarthenshire, now part of Dyfed) which dates from the early thirteenth century, the rear gate of Bodiam (East Sussex) built about 1386, and the smaller gate of Raglan (Monmouthshire, now Gwent) of about 1440. So elementary and satisfactory a type of entrance was likely to endure for a long time.

Only one of these early gatehouses — that at Castle Rising — has grooves for a portcullis.

The 'shell-keep' is a familiar feature of our early castles. The name is well established, and was popularized if not invented by Clark; but it is not altogether a happy one. A keep should be a tower; it should also be a defence of last resort, and the shell was a 'last resort' to which a later resort in the form of a tower was sometimes added.

In essence a shell was simply a replacement in stone of the timber garillum round the top of a motte. These rings of wall are generally not very lofty, in such position they did not need to be, while the depth of made earth under their foundations made it unsafe to build them too high. The caution of their builders may not have been excessive; a number are represented by fragments only. By itself, a 'shell-keep' is a simple structure; a well-preserved example, with the broken skyline of its weathered battlements, looks altogether like a colossal pork-pie, set upon the gigantic sandcastle of its motte. A mere ring of crenellated walling — a sort of small ward on top of the motte — is all that we understand by the name of 'shell-keep'. Unlike every other sort of keep, it did not house — though it may have protected — its lord's living quarters, and the arrangements for life inside one of these ring-walls remain one of the principal mysteries in the study of medieval fortification. Most inner structures have perished; generally they are likely to have been of wood. It seems likely that in some cases the timber tower continued in use after its protective garillum was rebuilt in stone; but there seems little doubt that the typical arrangement consisted of a ring of buildings around the inside of the shell-wall, enclosing a courtyard. Such buildings perforce were generally one-storey affairs, for their protective wall was low. Surviving examples (often rebuilt as these must have been) show a pattern of this kind: the buildings enclosing a square courtyard inside the Round Tower (so-called) at Windsor and an irregular polygon at Tamworth (Staffordshire). A very fine example of such a row of buildings, with its inner wall concentric with the shell, is to be seen at Restormel (Cornwall), but this is not associated with a motte; Restormel is a ringwork and both the shell and the later inner walls stand on the natural level. A ring of buildings may in many cases have formed part of the original plan, as it certainly did at Trematon. Here, around the inner face of one of our finest shell-keeps, there is a continuous row of stout corbels, intended to carry the roofs of a ring of buildings, perhaps of two storeys, for the shell is a lofty one. Surprisingly it contains neither latrine-chamber nor outfall, and as a matter of fact these features are far from numerous in shell-keeps — a weakness in sanitary arrangements which greatly contrasts with the generally good sanitation of the contemporary Norman towers. A row of single-storey penthouses round the inside of a blank wall hardly suggests comfortable quarters from other points of view, and it is possible that some shell-keeps were designed for occupation only in emergency. This conclusion may not be correct; it has to be considered against the background of other facts and probabilities — the likelihood that the original timber building on the motte was a dwelling-house; the obvious habitability of the numerous stone towers which stand on mottes; the general equation between the innermost stronghold of a castle and the dwelling of its lord.

A shell-keep is thus a simple affair, appropriate to the primitive period of the English castle; but it neither follows that any example will belong to this early age nor that it will itself be particularly simple in its final form. The two fine and lofty shells of Arundel and Trematon are dated to the early twelfth century by their early Norman gateways, but Pickering (North Yorkshire), which appears to have been a simple polygonal shell of no great height, was pierced by long arrowslits which forcibly suggest a thirteenth-century date; the features of the big shell-keep of Cardiff also indicate a date well into the thirteenth century; the very simple shell of Totnes (Devon) was rebuilt in the fourteenth century without undergoing any serious alteration in design.[10] Some of the later defences of mottes, especially those which are carried down to revet the earthwork, hardly deserve the name of 'shell-keep'. So well are many of them equipped with flanking towers that they can more profitably be considered as small inner wards built on or round the motte.

More ordinary is a case like Tamworth: more or less completely inhabited down to a recent date, it has had its ring-wall raised twice (once in post-medieval times) to house the buildings within. In its original form it was a plain, rather low polygon, of apparently thirteenth-century date, with a contemporary square tower on the side of the approach, buttressed by the massive wing-wall that carries the way up on to the motte; whether the tower was actually a keep is not now very clear. (The great wing-wall[11] is older than any of the masonry on the motte.) An example of a shell-keep heavily reinforced to make a most formidable stronghold is Launceston, the ancient *caput* of Cornwall. Here a strong, rather crudely built ring-wall, crowning a lofty motte, dates from the twelfth century; in the thirteenth century a low battlemented terrace — a *chemise*[12] — was carried round its foot, and a short, massive round tower was built right inside; on its brief perimeter the motte of Launceston thus presented to an enemy something like the threefold terrors of the great land-wall of Byzantium. Finally, the approach was fortified; little or nothing remains of the actual gates in the shell-wall or the chemise, but they were reached by a fortified stair along the wing-wall on the east, running south to join the defences of the bailey with a towered gate at its foot.

The wing-walls of a stone-built motte-and-bailey castle, joining the structure of the motte — whether tower or ring-wall — to the defences of the bailey so as to close the gap between the two loops of defence show a considerable complexity and variety of design. Frequently one curtain is thickened so as to carry the stair to the top of the motte — both Tamworth and Launceston[13] are examples of this very common practice, which appears also at Windsor, Berkhamstead, Carisbrooke, Pickering, Cardiff, Arundel and Tickhill; there is something rather similar at Trematon and Tonbridge. Wing-walls not used for access were commonly kept low, so that the wall-walk did not constitute a threat to the keep; some are lowered as they approach the top of the motte; some run straight into it, leaving a gap — presumably closed with a palisade — between their ends and the wall of the keep; others end as a screen-wall — a mere obstacle without any wall-walk at all. All these expedients weakened the wing-wall against attack, but only close to the keep. An assault here, delivered first up the slope and then across it, on impossible ground for ladders, and within a literal stone's throw of the battlements of the keep, would have had little hope of success. We come across these wing-walls in connection with many other works besides the motte, where inner and outer lines have to be connected over the cross-ditch which separates their enclosures; similar expedients are found to those we have mentioned, at a number of places of this ticklish kind; the screen-wall, with dummy battlements or none at all, but protected by flanking fire from the inner ward, is the most usual of these.

Enlarged wing-walls provided the means of access to the top of the motte in many cases, but not in all; at Crickhowell and at the enormous motte of Caerleon there are the remains of pairs of small round towers low down on the slopes of the motte, well away from any possible position for a wing-wall, which were plainly the gatehouses of fortified stairs from the bailey. In other cases the means of access is obscure, but one thing is certain: there are no indications of any version in stone of the sort of timber flying bridge, connecting the counterscarp of the ditch directly to the lip of the motte, which is described in the story of the Bishop of Thérouanne and depicted in the Bayeux Tapestry.

The last and most typically Norman feature is the great rectangular keep. Greatly though this imposing class of structure varies — and no attempt can be made here to trace all the variations — there are certain features that occur in almost every example: the stepped plinth of the base, with the characteristic sloping 'treads' of the steps; the shallow pilaster buttresses, on the faces dying away below the battlements, but developed on the angles into clasping-buttresses, rising to form turrets, the latter of increasing size and importance as time went on. Internally the interior was divided — typically, into two unequal parts — by a stout cross-wall, which served to carry the floor joists. Vaulting was unusual above basement level — a normal feature of English castles of any period.

The Norman keep, it will be seen, was a strangely stylised structure; in particular, the flat pilaster-strips, only a few inches thick, were functionless, adding no appreciable strength to the invariably massive walls of the tower. Similar, though more functional buttresses are encountered elsewhere in Norman work; it is interesting to note that they are uncommon on mural towers: a large tower at Wolvesey (Hampshire) has them, and so has the flat solid buttress-turret added to the long front wall of the Castle of the Peak.

The original entrance to Norman keeps is generally on the first floor, though in two of the latest and most formidable examples (Dover and Newcastle-upon-Tyne) it has been carried up to the second. Exceptionally, Colchester's enormous keep has a ground-level entrance, protected by a portcullis. It is usual to find that a ground-floor entrance has been pierced for convenience at some later date; at Canterbury this was made when the defence of the keep was still important, and a small gatehouse was built to protect the new doorway.

The upper-floor doors in some early Continental keeps, and probably in some of our smaller and simpler examples, like Goodrich (Herefordshire), were reached by wooden stairs — perhaps ladders which could be drawn up into the tower. The round and polygonal towers of later date were generally entered in much the same way, but the bulk of Norman keeps in England were entered by a stone stair along the face of the wall, and in fully developed examples this is enclosed by a battlemented wall on the outside, and defended by doors at the foot. The whole structure is known as a 'forebuilding'; typically it is part of the same design as the tower itself, but always it is lower and much more lightly built. The stair is wide, but may be interrupted by bridge-pits or intermediate doorways, and an assailant could also be attacked from overhead. The upper and the lower ends, over the inner and outer entrances, were often formed into small towers, and chambers formed above and below the stair were turned to a variety of uses — chapels, latrines, prisons.

The entry of a Norman keep was thus strongly defended; its walls were of massive thickness, and its lofty top was battlemented. All this made it a formidable defensive structure, but beyond these elements any account of it must be concerned with domestic features; a Norman keep is essentially a house — a house which had been made into a military stronghold without any real interference with its domestic functions. At this stage it is necessary to differ very strongly from the great Clark, who had picked up the notion that keeps were intended for occupation only in emergency,[14] and typically did not allow his own vast knowledge of the subject to prevail against his *idée fixe.*. We are all too familiar with the prevailing modern argument that, because we, the comfortably circumstanced part of the population of the eighteenth, nineteenth or twentieth century, would have found life extremely disagreeable in the Middle Ages, therefore we must visualise the medieval population, high and low, as disinherited moderns, living a life of permanent suffering, grieving for the absence of all those comforts which we now consider necessary to the human condition, but which had unfortunately not then been invented. Clark made himself responsible for a singular variant of this notion: that the great Norman keep was impossibly uncomfortable or inaccessible for occupation in its own period. In fact, by even Victorian travellers' standards, it represented a degree of comfort not to be despised: Gertrude Bell or Edward Lear would often have been glad to have been entertained in such comfortable quarters as the average Norman keep afforded. There was no nineteenth-century drawing-room standard of comfort, it is true, anywhere in a Norman castle, but such comfort as there was was very conspicuously concentrated in the keep. The great thickness of the walls helped to preserve an even temperature; the cellarage was capacious and cool, and its lack of a doorway of its own, if inconvenient in some ways, served at least as a defence against pilfering; all the main quarters were housed in the building, for in almost every case the hall was included. This was in extreme contrast to other kinds of keep, which generally had no space for this very large room. The multiple doors of the forebuilding may have served to reduce draughts; the windows were admittedly small, but this was inevitable in a period when the art of glass-making was in a backward state. Moreover, these were perfectly normal domestic windows, very commonly of two lights, with window-seats, and they were numerous enough; in large examples the hall had windows at two levels — surely a luxury feature in buildings of this period. The thick walls gave space for numerous handy wall-chambers and latrines, and the height of the latter above their outfalls reduced the unpleasantness due to their primitive style of sanitation. The complete absence of any sort of arrowslit in almost every example serves to confirm the general picture of a dwelling-house given great passive strength with the minimum of interference with its domestic character. The final element is the line of the pitched roof or roofs visible in most cases on the inside faces of the tower. A flat roof would, of course, have been much more convenient for military purposes, and later owners of Norman towers frequently removed the pitched roof and added in its place an extra storey with a flat leaded roof level with the wall-walk.

For domesticity and habitability, any large Norman keep is a remarkable structure by the standards of its period; where any Norman domestic buildings, pure and simple, still exist, these do not show any advance in comfort on the rooms in the fortified towers. Comparison with late-medieval living quarters would be false; in the course of the Middle Ages standards of comfort rose fairly sharply. Nevertheless, from the relatively comfort-loving thirteenth century it is possible to glean a couple of examples of comparative discomfort such as White Castle and Penmaen already mentioned.[15]

The Norman keep, we can safely agree, was already highly developed at the time when it was introduced into England. Chepstow might pass for a primitive example, but the White Tower at the Tower of London and the enormous keep of Colchester are not only the largest things of their kind (Colchester being very much the larger of the two) but also highly complex in design, both containing large chapels with projecting apses. The angle-turrets are well developed for the period; one of those at the Tower is round.

It is well known that the normal distinction between our Norman keeps depends on the relative position of the hall and the lord's private chamber, commonly called the solar. In the former of the two main categories, hall and solar are at the same level — normally the first floor — side by side and separated by the familiar cross-wall.[16] The building is thus normally only two storeys high, presenting rather a squat appearance; a very fine example is to be found at Castle Rising (Norfolk). In the second type, which appears to be generally later in origin, the solar is placed above the hall, the resultant building being at least three storeys high — the normal number for a tower. So persistent is the cross-wall — and so structurally necessary in the larger towers — that we find the architect of Rochester (Kent) obliged to carry it across his hall, pierced by an arcade to throw the two parts into one. Rochester keep, built by Archbishop William of Corbeuil in about 1126, is an extremely fine example of this sort of tower; as it has an extra entrance-floor above the basement and below the hall, and as the latter has an upper gallery with a second row of windows, this is a very lofty and impressive tower. Hedingham (Essex) is another very handsome example, very closely resembling Rochester; the cross-wall, however, has been replaced by a series of great arches which carry the floors. As it stands today — roofed, floored and with glass in its windows — it conveys a good idea (perhaps even a flattering idea) of the quality of life in a Norman keep.

In some of the smaller and later Norman keeps, however, the movement was away from domestic convenience, or even comfort; for the first time there was no room for a hall in the tower, which now took the form familiar in most later great towers: a suite of private quarters for the lord of the castle or his constable, not a complete house. The 'suite' in some cases was extremely limited in size and lacking in amenity. The most ungracious of all

69

would seem to be the keep of the Lacy castle of Clitheroe (Lancashire), a very exposed little tower on a lofty rock.[17] Above a low, unvaulted basement there is a single room, with no fireplace, two wretched little prison-windows — probably three originally — and a latrine. There is no upper room,[18] access was by an outside stair with no forebuilding, and the basement can only have been reached by ladder. Little less Spartan were the comforts of the tower of the Castle of the Peak, which again had no forebuilding and nothing above the single room on the first floor. It is worth noticing that this very austere chamber was likely on occasion to be occupied by the king himself, and royalty was several times in residence. To these smaller, hall-less towers Mr Braun has given the name 'chamber-keeps'.

Several individual towers call for particular remark for one reason or other: the first of these curiosities is surely Chepstow, a very simple if very large[19] first-floor hall. Another very curious structure, commonly treated as a sort of Norman keep, is the great tower of Pevensey, now only represented by a lofty base without any internal detail. Its basement, about 55 feet by 30 feet (16.5 m by 9 m), is believed to have been filled in with clay to the first-floor level; from the plain ashlar of the external faces project four (apparently orginally six) great apsidal buttresses of very bold projection, one of them founded on a solid bastion of the Roman fort. Whatever this extraordinary structure may have been, or whenever it was built (Sir Charles Peers dated it to c.1100),[20] it is hardly what we are accustomed to consider as a Norman keep. Norwich certainly has a keep of a normal sort, very large, and with its outer faces splendidly carved in blind arcading — crudely restored in recent times; built on made ground, on the top of its huge motte (which was at this point only partly artificial) it has a fairly solid basement storey, but its whole superstructure is flimsy by the standards of the period, though at least well calculated in relation to the dangerous foundations, which have nowhere given way.[21] A more remarkable example still is that of Richmond (North Yorkshire) built over a plain square gatehouse, with inner and outer gate-arches; the outer of these is blocked, but the inner — a fine Norman arch — is open at the present date and has been open since the oldest antiquarian drawings of it were made. There is no possibility of its having been left unblocked in the twelfth century, when the tower was built. The latter is a Norman keep of typical exterior detail and commanding height. It is, however, defective in several respects; it lacks a forebuilding, and the entrance is from the wall-walk (orginally it was entered from the wall-walk on both sides) while its accommodation is poor and rough. There is a single large chamber on each side of three levels, the two lower rooms having each a central pillar. In spite of one or two mural chambers, the general aspect of the tower is uncomfortable; in particular, it does not contain the hall of the castle. This was in fact already in existence when the tower was built — Scolland's Hall, in the corner of the main ward. This is 100 yards (914 m) from the tower, and it is difficult to imagine the tower rooms being used in connection with it in a Swaledale winter; in fact the castle's private quarters were built close to the hall. As a strong point of the castle's defences the great tower of Richmond, standing close to the entrance and on the exposed angle of the perimeter, is most impressive, but considered on both the military and the domestic side of a keep's character, it is an ambiguous building.

Next, two great and complex towers call for notice less because of any curiosities of their structure than on account of their date; for the keeps of Newcastle-upon-Tyne and Dover are first mentioned as being built in 1172 and 1182 respectively[22] — built, that is to say, by Henry II during the period of scientific fortification which had begun in his reign, and after he himself had already begun to experiment with polygonal keeps at Orford and Chilham. This reversion to the square keep has been treated as a sad backsliding on his part, and these two powerful Norman keeps can be seen as a pair of dinosaurs outstaying their day on earth. Both are remarkable structures in any case: very massively built, with numerous mural passages and chambers; in each the entrance is on the second floor, the forebuilding being very large and highly developed; at Dover it is formed into a row of three square towers. Internally there is one main room on each floor at Newcastle, but Dover is divided by a massive cross-wall on all stages — a strangely archaic feature.

But there is one other large keep to be considered, whose extraordinary and in many ways anomalous character has prevented it from being mentioned earlier, for nothing else resembles it.[23] This is the great tower of Kenilworth, called in early times Caesar's Tower. It is remarkable for its huge passive strength, for the very advanced features of its defences — which suggest a date later than that of Dover — and finally for the fact that its recorded history appears to indicate a time for its building much earlier than this.

Repairs to the *turris* of Kenilworth are recorded in 1190,[24] which certainly suggests that the present keep was then in existence. At that time the castle had been in royal hands since 1179,[25] perhaps since 1173-4, when it had been garrisoned by Henry II in the Young King's War.[26] Neither in 1190 nor at any other time is there any recorded expenditure which could possibly refer to the building of a tower of this size; only in the reign of John is any substantial amount of money spent on the castle. Mainly between 1210 and the end of the reign (1216) a sum of £1,115 was expended at Kenilworth,[27] though the enormous works of this castle could easily have swallowed such a sum without any part of it going to build or complete a new keep.

As to the fabric of the tower, it is without parallel among English castles, and probably among castles anywhere; it is elongated in plan, its main body being about 80 feet by 60 feet (24 m by 18 m) and from its angles project not mere turrets, but regular square towers. There is no ground floor, properly so called; the lowest stage is 10 to 20 feet (3 to 6 m) above the irregular ground outside. Up to this level the basement of the tower is filled in solid

71

with earth (it has been suggested that this filling may be part of an original motte); while the outside of the tower is covered in an enormous stepped plinth, far larger and higher than the usual plinth of a Norman tower, and carried up to the level of the first floor. Even above this impressive base the tower is extremely strongly built, with walls as thick as 17 feet (5 m 18) on one side; at this stage too the angle-towers were completely solid, except that one of the four contains a latrine and another a newel-stair. The one surviving light in the walls is a very narrow slit.

This impressive strength might well be taken as an advanced feature; in particular the large and boldly projecting corner-towers suggest an intention to use enfilade shooting (in fact, they were fitted up for the purpose, as will be seen). Also, though alterations by Robert Dudley, the Elizabethan Earl of Leicester and lord of Kenilworth, have completely gutted the forebuilding, it would certainly appear that the entrance to the tower was on the second floor,[28] as at Newcastle and Dover. A final feature, far more advanced than anything found elsewhere among the Norman keeps of England, is the series of arrowslits around the upper part of the keep. These are all of a single pattern, the same as those on the round north-east tower of the outer ward (Lunn's Tower), a remarkable building which has been universally accepted as part of the work of King John. Two of them are placed on the flanks of one of the angle-towers so as to enfilade the adjacent faces of the keep. They may well have formed no part of the original design, but if so, they will have been introduced in the last stages of the building, not as an alteration to a finished tower; the work is too tidy, and the arrangements too complicated, for an insertion of this kind.

The mention of a *turris* at Kenilworth may possibly apply to an earlier keep; in any case it is difficult to imagine that a tower of so advanced a character could have been built before 1179 by a member of a baronial family, and not one of the foremost importance.

Even when the round tower had replaced the rectangular Norman keep in all new first-class fortifications, we must not exaggerate the extent to which Norman keeps had fallen out of favour. Existing examples were not abandoned; most of them continued long in occupation, though they were esteemed rather for their accommodation than for their military strength. Even so, as late as the Barons' War of 1264-5 the keeps of Rochester and Dover were successfully held against the Montfortians;[29] even King John's triumphant mining of Rochester in 1215 seems to have been regarded less as evidence of the vulnerability of a Norman keep than as an indication of how terrifyingly hard and competent John 'Softsword' could be when he set his heart on it.[30]

That rectangular keeps, and isolated towers of the same plan, should have been common throughout the Middle Ages is not in the least surprising; the shape, after all, is the most natural one for a tower. It is the more remarkable to find a certain number of keeps built in the style of Norman keeps into the thirteenth century and beyond, though admittedly none of these are of the first importance. This involves us with a semantic monstrosity: 'Norman' keeps which are actually Gothic buildings, but the fact is real enough. Thus at Moreton Corbet (Shropshire) there is what for most purposes would be accepted as a small Norman keep, but its interior features are Early English, and it is dated to about 1200.[31] Brandon (Warwickshire) shows the typical base of a small Norman keep, but the excavators found only Early English elements.[32] At Tamworth the square tower on the line of the 'shell-keep' has big corner-buttresses in the manner of Norman keep construction, but it forms part of a general campaign of building which seems to belong to the thirteenth century. At Oystermouth on the Gower peninsula of Glamorgan (now West Glamorgan), the keep is an oblong building with square corner-turrets, but its detail is entirely of the thirteenth and fourteenth centuries, with conspicuous pointed drop-arches of late thirteenth-century appearance in the oldest parts of it. Lastly, there are two Shropshire towers which so much resemble Norman keeps that they are commonly accepted as such: Clun and Hopton.[33] Of these Clun is built down the slope of a motte, like the Norman tower of Guildford; its lower end, standing on natural ground, has angle-buttresses like those of a typical Norman keep, though its battered base is not of strictly Norman type. Its internal detail includes a Caernarvon arch and a number of recesses with pointed heads, while the openings in the lower part of the tower were long and narrow — almost certainly arrow slits, though all have been broken out for their cut stone. This has every appearance of being a thirteenth-century tower, but Hopton, its near neighbour, shows no detail earlier than the fourteenth century. This is a medium-sized square tower, emerging from a low motte; it has a Norman general plan, with clasping-buttress turrets on three of the corners, dying into a battered plinth; but the plinth is nothing like the characteristic Norman form, being a plain batter, under a roll-moulding, while the internal plan is also anything but Norman, and the fourteenth-century detail nowhere appears to be secondary to the original structure.

In short, what we may call 'Norman' keeps survived beyond the primitive period of fortification in England, and well into the Gothic age.

Perhaps a little more discussion of stone fortification is needed. It includes both standing masonry and revetment, though revetment by itself is rare; normally the above-ground walling is carried down to revet the scarp.

The quality of the masonry, in respect of both elegance and performance, can vary enormously. Only the most opulent castle-builders could send long distances for considerable quantities of stone and lime; in any case, the ditch of the castle is, in most cases, the principal quarry. To the English antiquary, in particular from the western part of the country, it comes as a surprise to find that in much of northern and eastern Europe there is little or no stone, and timber defences were employed until the introduction of brick. Even in the mainly soft rocks of England's south-east, use was made of such materials as the hard chalk called *clunch* and Kentish ragstone, or recourse was had to flintwork.

Ordinary building-stone may be easily worked or intractable, soft or hard, and it may or may not be a source of lime. Old Red Sandstone makes the most beautiful ashlar, though some of it weathers badly, and it is often hard to get good lime for mortar near to sites where it is available. Castles built in this material are accordingly often very badly preserved; the damage is very often due to human agency, for a source of fine building material held together by feeble mortar is a standing temptation to the stone-robber. The position is very different on the limestone, and particularly on the long belt of the Mountain Limestone that runs across South Wales. Not a particularly tractable building-stone, it is hard and scarcely weathers at all, and it yields a most tenacious and enduring mortar; at Pembroke (built c.1200) one can safely say that the only damage to the masonry has been by the hand of man; at Manorbier (Pembrokeshire, now part of Dyfed) even the battlements of the twelfth-century hall are still in place, a monument more lasting than brass. But on the Middle Marches of Wales, great castles have vanished into the grass, like Caus (Shropshire), or into a muddy heap, like Blaen Llyfni (Brecknock, now part of Powys); or into a mass of broken rubble, like the great hilltop Dinas in the same county; in each case, the only standing masonry is a patch (at Blaen Llyfni, several patches) of repair-work carried out in properly-mortared masonry.

It is not uncommon to find an economical use of lime mortar; when there was not enough to go round for a proper use of it, the all-important faces of the wall were pointed in lime, while its hearting was laid in something inferior, clay, or even sand, which some Crown agents, undertaking repairs to the keep of Kenfig (Mid Glamorgan) seem to have been shameless enough to use. I personally have had the unpleasant experience of accidently knocking off the corner of a tower at Newport (Pembrokeshire — Dyfed — but well to the north of the Mountain Limestone belt) and finding its weak hearting falling out.

Elsewhere, limited supplies of lime have sometimes been applied to the more important elements of the defence; at Beeston (Cheshire) the faces and basements of the towers on the Outer Ward seem to be well-mortared in comparison with the rest of the defences. Very often we find the lime used on the keep, which in any case would be higher than the perimeter of the ward; this occurs in several Welsh castles, but the extreme case is Castle Combe (Wiltshire) where there is a small square keep built in mortared masonry, whereas the ringwork and bailey have walls laid in the traditional Cotswold materials — stone slabs with no mortaring whatever.

Notes

1. Armitage, *Early Norman castles,* p. 186 (Pevensey) and p. 110 (Bramber).
2. Sir Charles Peers, *Guide book* (HMSO, 1935 and 1953).
3. W.H. St John Hope,'The Castle of Ludlow', *Archaeologia,* 1xi (1968), pp. 257-328.
4. Sidney Toy, 'Corfe Castle: its history, construction and present condition', *Archaeologia,* lxxix (1929), pp. 85-102; Royal Commission on Historical Monuments (England), *Inventory for the County of Dorset,* ii, part 1, pp. 57-78 and plates.
5. B.H. St J. O'Neil, *Guide book* (HMSO, 1934 and 1950).
6. J.C. Perks, 'The architectural history of Chepstow castle during the middle ages', *Bristol and Gloucestershire Archaeological Society,* 1xvii (1946-8), pp. 307-46 and *Guide book* (HMSO, 1955 and 1967).
7. Martin Biddle, 'Excavations at Winchester: fourth interim report', *Antiquaries Journal,* xlvi (1966), p. 326-8.
8. 'Gold Hole' is apparently an euphemistic name for a cesspit.
9. Leslie Alcock,'Castle Tower, Penmaen: A Norman ring-work in Glamorgan', *Antiquaries Journal,* xlvi (1966), pp. 187-90.
10. Stuart Rigold, *Totnes Castle* (Guide book, HMSO, 1952) 3, pp. 7-8.
11. Owing to extensive use of herringbone masonry in its fabric, this wall has often been put forward as Anglo-Saxon work.
12. A feature also found at Barnstaple (Devon). No other example of a *chemise* round a shell-keep is known.
13. For Richard's Castle, see P.E. Curnow and M.W. Thompson, 'Excavations at Richard's Castle, Herefordshire', *Journal of the British Archaeological Association,* 3rd series, xxxii (1969), p. 110; for Launceston, A.D. Saunders, Excavations at Launceston Castle, 1965-1969, interim report', *Cornish Archaeology,* ix (1970), p. 84.
14. Probably from Harrod (see Henry Harrod, *Gleanings among the castles and convents of Norfolk* (Norwich 1857), pp. 44-7. For Clark's own views, see *Mediaeval military architecture,* i, p. 136.
15. See Chapter 1.
16. Hugh Braun, *The English castle,* (London, 1936) has a good diagram on p. 40. The names 'hall keep' and 'tower-keep' have not found general favour.
17. See Clark, *Mediaeval military architecture* i, pp. 397-402. Some of the features have been obscured by repairs, well-intended but rather too vigorous, undertaken by a former Duke of Buccleuch.
18. Clark shows one (p. 398) but with neither window nor access to the stair. This is probably merely an empty space inside the tower-head to accommodate the roof.
19. About 100 ft by 40 ft (30 m by 12 m) externally.
20. Sir Charles Peers, *Pevensey Castle* (Guide book, HMSO, 1933), pp. 5-6. For a contrary opinion, see D.F. Renn, 'The Turris de Penuesel, a reappraisal and a theory', *Sussex Archaeological Collections,* cix (1971), pp. 55-64.
21. Proper plans seem only to be found in Samuel Woodward, *The history and antiquities of Norwich Castle* (Norwich and London, 1847), *tab.* V, VI, VII.
22. Pipe Rolls, 18 Hen II, p. 66, and 28 Hen II, p. 150.
23. In correspondence, Judge Perks has written: 'when dealing with the great towers of 1154-89 ... every time I made a generalization I had to say *except Kenilworth*'.
24. Pipe Rolls, 2 Ric I, p. 37.
25. *Ibid.,* 27 Hen II, p. 79, where the sheriff accounts for the farm of three years (1179-81).
26. *Ibid.,* 19 Hen II, p. 178, 20 Hen II, p. 139-40; for the whole story of the king's acquisition of the castle, see Allen Brown, 'A note on Kenilworth castle: the change to

royal ownership', *Archaeological Journal,* cx (1953), pp. 120-4. There seems to be little evidence for the earlier dates given by Baillie Reynolds, *Kenilworth Castle* (Guide book, HMSO, 1948), p. 1.

27. Allen Brown, 'Royal castle building in England', *English Historical Review*, 1xx (1955), p. 394.

28. The present entrance to the keep is through a rather crude and narrow passage at the lower (first-floor) level. This seems to be original, but is likely to have been merely the access from the tower to the basement chambers of the forebuilding.

29. *Flores historiarum* (ed. Luard, Rolls Series, 95) ii, pp. 490-1, iii, p. 8; *Wykes,* in *Annales monastici* (ed. Luard, Rolls Series, 36.4), 146-7, p. 178; *Annales prioratus de Dunstaplia* (ed. Luard, Rolls Series, 36.3) pp. 230-1; Rishanger, *Chronica et annales* (ed. Riley, Rolls Series, 28.2), p. 22; Trivet, *Annales sex regum Angliae* (ed. Hog, London 1845) p. 268.

30. Wendover, *Chronica* (ed. Hewlett, Rolls Series 84.2), pp. 162-3; *Walter of Coventry* (ed. Stubbs, Rolls Series 58.2), p. 227.

31. Lord Harlech, *Ancient monuments* (HMSO, 1955), iii, p. 41.

32. Philip B. Chatwin, *Birmingham Archaeological Society* 1xxiii (1955), pp. 63-83.

33. For recent datings of this kind, see Pevsner, *Buildings of England 16,* 109, p. 153.

8

The Influence of the Crusades

An English castle built in masonry in, say, 1150 could be expected to have the following characteristics: an enclosure of irregular or curvilinear plan, following strong natural or artificial obstacles; few towers, and those square and of little defensive significance; probably a gatehouse, which might be an impressive structure; probably, but not certainly, a keep — either a shell on a motte or a Norman tower. There would be other features not yet mentioned: the curtains might be rather low by later standards; a portcullis would be unlikely, particularly in the main gate; nor would there be any arrowslits. This feature is perhaps the most important of all; the absence of shooting-slits in Norman keeps (except at Kenilworth) has frequently been commented on; their loops were for light alone. 'Shell-keeps' may have shooting-slits, but they themselves are often of a date long after our chosen 1150. The gatehouses and mural towers of this early period are equally without arrowslits, and the merlons of the comparatively few parapets of the date which survive are also unpierced.

But a typical stone-built castle of 1200 presents a very different picture;[1] its general plan may have been imposed by an irregular site or an existing curvilinear earthwork, but as far as possible it will have been resolved into a polygon — better still a quadrilateral — with straight sides enfiladed by towers on the intervening angles. These towers, after a series of early forms — rectangular, polygonal and round, solid and hollow, with open or closed backs — would probably be taking on the typical thirteenth-century 'drum-tower' form: round (much more rarely polygonal) on angles, half-round on straight faces or very obtuse corners, stoutly built and enclosing a chamber on each floor. The upper rooms were often capable of use as living quarters, thus enhancing the quality of life in the castle. The basement chambers were generally dark and uninhabitable, only for use for storerooms or prisons, though there are basements with arrangements for habitation in a few castles. But whether habitable or not, any level or all levels could be looped for archery, and a good proportion of these loops would be right round to the flank, enfilading the faces of the curtains and the ditch in front of them. The curtains themselves were perhaps generally higher than in the previous period, perhaps somewhat thicker, but the straight trace that they followed (as far as this could be arranged) is their principal difference from curtains of primitive type. Occasionally they are pierced at or near ground level by long shooting-slits for direct grazing fire, but this arrangement was never very common in England. The parapets on towers and curtains alike generally had arrowslits alternating with the embrasures; thus plunging fire from the wall-walks could have been very powerful, some of it direct, some (from the tower-heads) in enfilade. The gates of this new period vary enormously; some are mere openings in the curtain, some pass through the basement of rectangular towers like typical gatehouses of the earlier period, a very few are pierced in the flank of a half-round tower, but the general tendency is towards a type of gateway not unfamiliar to the Romans — an opening between two half-round towers which join above the passage to form a single block of building. Almost invariably the defences of the entry would include a portcullis,[2] sometimes more than one. We know too little of drawbridges — especially in their early history — to be sure about them; but they seem to have been in increased use. Finally the keep itself would have been polygonal or cylindrical rather than square, and in some cases, probably for economic reasons — for the new defensive arrangements were far more costly than the old — it was dispensed with altogether. These later keepless castles have been over-emphasised by modern antiquaries. They were hardly more numerous than those of the earlier period; but in one respect they demand more notice, for, whereas early keepless stone castles like Corfe, Richmond, Ludlow and Rochester had great towers added to their defences by later owners, the progressive contraction of defensive areas — M. Héliot's *resserrement* — had by now reached a point where there was likely to be little or no room for a keep of secondary date. As if in recognition of this fact, we find the word *donjon* misapplied to refer to some small thirteenth-century inner wards, particularly those of Montgomery, Degannwy, (Caernarvon, now part of Gwynedd) and Beeston (Cheshire).

It was quite natural for antiquaries to look for the reasons for this very substantial change in the methods of defence to the introduction of a more scientific approach from some region of greater martial enlightenment — which in this context could only be Outremer, the land of the Crusades, where war was certainly a far more scientific affair, and was commonly carried on on a far larger scale, than in Europe. It was a reasonable guess that the Crusaders would have learned a good deal from their opponents, the Saracens, whose civilisation was notoriously superior to that of Western Europe — not to mention from the Byzantine Empire, which had played schoolmaster to the Saracens, and had never known a Dark Age.

Thus, we hear the legend of Lalys, the Palestinian architect brought back from the Crusades, who was responsible for a great improvement in the castles of South Wales, and settled at Laleston in Glamorgan. Many of us later antiquaries were ready to accept Edward I's great master-mason, James of St George, as a native of St George of Lydda. There was also an instinctive acceptance of a famous castle, built by a famous Crusader, as a great step forward towards the new fortification. But now, when Lalys is totally discredited, and Dr Arnold Taylor has plainly demonstrated that the 'St George' in Master James's name is Saint-Georges-d'Espéranche,[3] so that he was a Savoyard — a Westerner — we must make short work of Richard I's Château-Gaillard. Admittedly it is a most enthralling castle, majestic even in ruin, most impressively sited, a sign and a wonder to the traveller. It is a Crusader's castle, but it is not a castle of the Crusades; it represents, no doubt, an advance on earlier fortification in England and France; but the direction of this advance was not to be maintained. The outer perimeter, with its straight curtains and round towers, is pretty typical work for 1196 — good work, *bien entendu* — but not particularly advanced in character compared with, say, the closely contemporary Pembroke; Château-Gaillard, indeed, seems to have been defended from the battlements alone, which would make Pembroke a more advanced (and indeed a more Levantine) castle, with its numerous arrowslits at lower levels.

The massive works over the Seine on the summit are unique, and, being unique, have no part to play in any history of development. The towering round keep, with its massive angular beak on the most approachable side, has only a very few analogues in France, and none at all in England; as for the land of the Crusades, there are no round keeps there of any sort except for a single half-round tower built by German Crusaders. The machicolations on the perimeter of the tower, carried on buttresses of inverted-pyramid shape, are not found elsewhere; nor are the extraordinary arrangements of the inner ward, where the curved face of its more approachable sides is made up of a series of round tower-fronts, abutting one against the other.

For the change to scientific fortification in the West to have come about by a direct invasion of advanced military science from the East, the timing is wrong; it should have come in about 1100, when Robert of Normandy and other victors of the First Crusade returned to Europe; if indeed it could not have come earlier. There was already traffic between east and west, and there seems no reason why some noble pilgrim, some time-expired Varangian Guard from the Emperor's service, could not have brought home with him the science of fortification as it was known to the Byzantines.

Indeed, as Dr Smail has pointed out,[4] there was no need; there were a good many examples of a developed military art in the Roman remains still surviving in the West; those of the late Empire were commonly based on a complete system of flanking by round towers, generally solid; in England medieval castles were established in four of the Saxon Shore forts, of which Pevensey and Portchester were important. In wealthier Gaul there were more Roman remains, while in 1091 the Spaniards of Avila surrounded their city with a good imitation of Roman work.[5]

It is difficult to say how much the Crusaders can have copied from the Saracens, for there is not a great deal of information about the work of the latter — though Saladin, as can be seen from his building at the Citadel of Cairo, used a developed style of fortification.[6] The Byzantines, however, clearly had an enormous amount to teach; a short stroll along the Land Wall of Constantinople would have shown to any Crusader who was not simply dumbfounded by what he saw a system of defence by multiple lines of regularly flanked walls, with towers square, round and polygonal — even one of the beaked pentagonal plan so strongly advocated by Greek theoretical writers.[7]

We must divide the survivors of the First Crusade into those who stayed in the East and helped to establish the Crusader states — the Kingdom of Jerusalem, the Principality of Antioch, and the Counties of Tripoli and Edessa — and those (the great majority) who returned home, having delivered the Holy Places as they had intended to do. The first class built a number of castles in Syria and the Holy Land between the conquest at the end of the eleventh century and the disastrous battle of Hattin in 1187; some of these, on powerful sites, were very strong. Kerak in Moab has already been mentioned; perhaps an even more important fortress was Saône (Sahyun) in Syria,[8] on a long rocky ridge between two frightful gorges, where a Byzantine fortress had long stood. With a greater degree of originality than was usual among their contemporaries, they abandoned the existing defences (which were arranged in some depth across the one short approachable side) in favour of a single line along a most formidable ditch cut in the rock. (Who cut it is uncertain.)

But in a greater number of cases we find that the founders of the earlier castles were quite unenterprising; generally they placed themselves very much in the hands of their Syrian master-masons, only commissioning towers to live in, such as they had had at home in the West; as carried out by the Syrians, these were square towers, vaulted and rather plain, with none of the ornamental features of the 'Norman' keep. The enclosures of castles on relatively level sites tended to take on a form derived from the *castra* of the Roman *limites,* by way of the little Byzantine forts known as *tetrapyrgia,* from their four corner towers. The latter were square, with little projection. There were variations; a *castrum* could be combined with a tower, either on an angle or in the interior. At Giblet (Jebail), where there is a powerful keep in the middle of the ward, an extra flanking-tower projects to defend the entrance.[9] Coliat (al-Quleiyat), a rather weak castle, had shallow projections on three sides, and a bold one only at the gate.[10] Nor was the handy castrum-plan confined to early Christian work; Saladin built a little castrum on the hilltop of Ajlun,[11] and the massive castle of Belvoir (Kawkab al-Hawa), built by the Hospitallers after 1168 and in a manner worthy of a later and more splendid period of castellation, is essentially a castrum, though considerably developed: with the double *enceinte* typical of a large Crusader castle, with extra towers on the curtains of the outer line, and a very complex entry, ending at a gate-tower projecting from one of the sides of the inner perimeter.[12]

Even at Belvoir, where the towers project boldly, they are square or rectangular; round flanking-towers in fact do appear in the twelfth century, but not on any large scale, and not very early. Deschamps — admittedly *obiter* — gives his opinion that there were none before 1164[13] (except a half-round tower at Tripoli, which I have seen, and would rather ascribe to the thirteenth century). He assigns to the period before 1187 only three round towers at Beaufort (Schekif Arnoun)[14] and five at the very advanced Saône. These are all small — a tower at Saône 21 feet (6.40 m) in diameter by my measurement; towers of Beaufort 25 feet (7.6 m) and 20.5 feet (6.25 m) according to the published plans — much the same size as Saladin built at the Citadel of Cairo.[15]

As to the returned Crusaders of the twelfth century, they brought no master-mason Lalys with them, and no serious memory of Eastern methods. Neither in France nor in England was there any multiplication of *tetrapyrgia;* instead, the process of primitive fortification was carried on without any visible halt until the 1160s, when Henry II of England, a king who had never been on Crusade, ushered in an age of scientific defence in the West.

But the 'primitive process' did produce, apparently in France, one novelty: the round donjon. Very common on the Continent, it is rare in England — there were or are only about 40 examples; much more remarkable, there are none at all of French origins in Syria or Palestine[16] — for the great tower of Margat (Qalaat al-Marqab) was not independently defensible, but simply an enormous angle-tower at a vulnerable point of the castle's defences.[17] The only round keep is at the headquarters of the Teutonic Knights, the castle of Starkenberg (Montfort des Teutoniques; Qalaat Quorein) where the most exposed angle is capped by a massive round tower.[18]

After the end of the Third Crusade (1192) neither side was in a position to feel victorious, or even secure from an enemy in force. Both Christians and Muslims, accordingly, fortified themselves to the best of their ability, and this is, in general, the age of the great castles for which the Crusading period is famous.

The death of Saladin, soon after the end of the war, left his Empire to fall to pieces, divided between his younger kinsmen, and it was not for ten years that it was reunited by his brother al-Adil (the 'Saphadin' of the Crusades). He was a notable builder, with a style of his own: very large towers, generally of rectangular or derived forms, covered at all stages with massive groined cross-vaults.[19] These very imposing structures are found at the citadels of Cairo and Damascus, at Bosra and (in a fragmentary state) at Mount Tabor;[20] they exerted great influence over later Muslim work, the plans of

Figure 8.1: Location of round keeps

individual towers being repeatedly copied; but they do not seem to have had any influence on Crusader building, except perhaps in favouring the use of large oblong towers, like those at Pilgrims' Castle ('Atlit).[21]

Among the Christians, this was predominantly the age of the Military Orders, to whose guardianship, financed from all over Christendom, many of the barons of Outremer conveyed their castles and lordships. They built or remodelled a series of the most magnificent castles: Le Krak des Chevaliers (Qalaat el-Hosn), the most splendid of all,[22] Margat and Belvoir,[23] built by the Knights Hospitallers of St John; Tortosa (Tartus),[24] Pilgrims' Castle,[25] and Saphet (Safad[26] by the Knights Templars; and Montfort des Teutoniques (Starkenberg)[27] by the Knights of the Teutonic Order. This last was a sort of Germanic rock-castle; the rest were all (except possibly the now very shattered Saphet) concentric castles, with two complete *enceintes* — a style of building which was widely copied over Europe in general, and in particular was associated in England with the work of the Crusader king, Edward I. Some attempt has been made elsewhere to differentiate between the building-styles of the two major Orders, but the variations in detail in the works of both make this an impossible task; neither used any single consistent style. Only their great strength and their use of concentric defences were common to the whole group, and certainly these had their influence on Europe.

Of the individual elements of the defence, thirteenth-century towers are much more commonly rectangular in the East than the West. Gates in Crusader and Saracen work are of a great diversity of forms, but one characteristic type is encountered frequently, which made very little impact on the West: here the gate opens in the flank of a tower, generally square.[28] This is obviously a promising site for a postern, but many of these oblique gates are main entrances; they imposed an abrupt, tight double-turn on an assailant, but also on anyone else using the gate. Perhaps the reason why this type of gate, so common in Outremer, is so rare in the West, is the difficulty it would cause to civilian traffic, for main entrances were meant for the delivery of supplies and munitions; in Europe the bulk of these would be conveyed in wains, in the East — particularly the Saracen East — by camel. Negotiating such a gate — particularly with horses in tandem — would have presented difficulties to any waggoner; to the master of a string of camels, no difficulty at all. I am not familiar with any examples of this type of gate in France; as far as England is concerned, there is only a tiny group of examples in South Wales. Apart from a singular, unexplained example at Caldicot (Monmouth-shire, now Gwent),[29] the only real case is the Horseshoe Gate of the inner ward at Pembroke; both are in the flanks of round towers. The remaining examples are formed in the sides of semicircular barbicans rather than actual towers; they are more roomy (as if the troubles of the carters had been considered), but the arrangement is very much the same: such are the outer gate of Pembroke Castle, and the gate of Tenby (Pembrokeshire, now part of Dyfed). The principal gates of the towns of Tenby and Pembroke were evidently of this form, as was the barbican added at the surviving gate of Tenby town, known, from its mutilated state, as the Five Arches. (Edward I employed a similar barbican, of very large size, at the Tower of London; and there is another, of fourteenth-century date, at Goodrich (Herefordshire). Both these are on the outside of the ditch. The link between the members of this very localised group is plainly the great William Marshal, Earl of Pembroke in 1189–1219, and latterly Regent of England.[30] He was a returned Crusader, and incorporated in his new Pembroke Castle another Eastern feature: a fighting-gallery in the thickness of the curtains on the exposed side of the outer ward.

Arrowslits in the West show a great diversity of shapes, which owe nothing to Outremer, but in that area there is a far greater use of loops on positions below the battlements. Even in the West, the round flanking-towers are pierced generously for archery; but in the East the curtains as well were loopholed at a number of levels; principally at ground level, but also from the floors of buildings along the curtain, or passages (fighting-galleries) pierced lengthwise in its thickness. Both of these appear in England about as early as any sort of shooting-slit is found: at Framlingham (Suffolk), rebuilt remarkably early after its demolition in 1174-5, there are a series of big ground-level loops; and Pembroke's fighting-gallery dates from about 1200, perhaps earlier. Nevertheless, neither expedient is particularly common in England before Edward I's aggressively designed castles, which make considerable use of both. Modern antiquaries are inclined to condemn these methods as dangerous — liable to weaken the curtains structurally — and a similar opinion seems to have occurred to contemporary builders. This was mistaken, as we can see from examples in the East; for example Ba'albek, where the great western curtain of the Saracen castle, honeycombed with no less than three levels of arrowslits, set under vaulted recesses, below the parapet proper, has survived for 700 years in a region notorious for its earthquakes.[31] A similar multiplication of loops is to be seen in the surviving fragment of the inner ward curtain at Tortosa.[32]

If the low loops and fighting-galleries of the East are relatively unusual in the West, the Eastern *double parapet* does not appear there at all. This very familiar feature in Outremer is found at Saône, and in general in thirteenth-century work, among both Crusaders and Saracens. Here the walls of a tower-head towards the field were carried up above the roof about another 8–10 feet (2.5-3 m), with the actual wall-walk and battlement above again. This high screen could shelter the slinging-engines of the defence, while arrowslits and passages to the brattices were pierced in the lower level. Double parapets could also be contrived on curtains. The few examples in Europe — Pierrefonds (Oise), Caesar's Tower at Warwick, and the Great Tower of Tattershall (Lincolnshire) — belong to periods far too late for any derivation from the Crusades.

Vertical defence in the West in the earlier Middle Ages was provided by the wooden galleries called hoards, carried on timber joists. From the late thirteenth century we find this system replaced by the stone defence called machicolation. Hamilton Thompson explains the change as follows: 'The general tradition is that [machicolations] were invented by the Crusaders in Syria, where wood for hoarding was not easily obtained.'[33] In other words, the

Figure 8.2: The development of machicolations in the West

Joist-holes for a timber hoard (Kidwelly)

Reinforced joist-holes (Caldicot)

Stone consoles for timber superstructure (Newcastle-upon-Tyne town walls, Durham Tower). The intervals are far too wide for stone lintels.

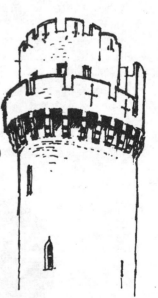

Perfect stone machicolations (Warwick Castle, Caesar's Tower)

Drawings by Derek Crowe; the rendering of Durham Tower, Newcastle-upon-Tyne, is after Barbara Harbottle

Crusaders evolved the common Eastern form of bratticing from their own timber hoards, and reimported the improved product into Europe. This, unfortunately, is a case where 'the attractiveness of the theory does not supply any guarantee that it is correct'; indeed, it can be shown to be entirely false. There is a stone brattice — a short corbelled-out projection for dropping missiles — at Qasr el-Hair, built in 728–9,[34] and Creswell has shown that the Eastern brattice was in use long before the Crusades, and was evolved from the corbelled-out latrines used on Eastern buildings since very early times.[34] They continued to present very much the same appearance: small, short projections built of flat slabs of stone, carried on corbels, with a sloping penthouse roof and a loophole (two on corner brattices) too short for archery. Very seldom, and virtually only in late Saracen work, do we find continuous bratticing covering the whole front of a tower or a curtain. Like the archetypal latrine, they project from a stage lower than the battlements — very often from the lower level of a double parapet.

Western machicolations, on the other hand, are typically found in complete series, defending a whole tower or curtain; they are at battlement level — indeed, it is the parapet itself that is carried on the stone consoles. Moreover, their derivation can be traced; the pedigree begins with the hoard supported on timber joists. Next, we find joist-holes reinforced by stout corbels, as at Caldicot (Monmouthshire, now Gwent) and the middle gate at Corfe (Dorset); then at Coucy (Aisne) and on the towers of the town wall of Newcastle-upon-Tyne the joists are replaced completely, by heavy stone corbelling. This was massive enough to carry the parapet itself, and accordingly we find this done; by 1285 the end-curtains of Conway, in which were the gates, were machicolated in masonry.

There was, in fact, little direct influence — in the sense of direct copying — between Outremer and the West. In particular, the actual appearance of flanked defences in England, which occurred in the 1160s, owed nothing to Crusading influence; and the two illustrious returned Crusaders who actually copied eastern features — with no great following outside their own constructions — belong to later periods.

This must not be taken to mean that the Crusades went for nothing, even in the limited sphere of military architecture. The immense scale of war and fortification in the East inevitably increased the appetite of the rulers of Christendom for powerful castles and for armies, which, if not perhaps as large as those in Outremer, could be equally competent. It also brought them into closer contact with a weapon, not really unfamiliar, which was to prove the catalyst in the change — the crossbow.

Notes

1. The following works, cited by the name of their authors, are mentioned in the footnotes of this chapter: Meron Benvenisti, *The Crusaders in the Holy Land* (Jerusalem,

1970); T.S.R. Boase, *Castles and churches of the crusading kingdom* (London, 1967); Paul Deschamps, *Les châteaux des croisés en Terre Sainte* (3 vols., Paris, 1934, 1939, 1973). This splendid project devotes the whole of vol. 1 to Le Krak des Chevaliers; vol. 3 has an unbound (and probably unbindable) collection of plans and photographs. It does not cover the County of Edessa, as was presumably originally intended; Wolfgang Müller-Wiener, *Castles of the crusaders* (in translation, London, 1966); G. (Baron) Rey, *Etude sur les monuments de l'architecture militaire des croisés en Syrie et dans l'Ile de Chypre* (Paris, 1871, a great founding treatise); R.C. Smail, *Crusading Warfare* (Cambridge, 1956), cited as Smail (1956); R.C. Smail, *The crusaders in Syria and the Holy Land* (London, 1973), cited as Smail (1973).

2. Significant exceptions are the gate of the middle bailey at Chepstow and the Horseshoe Gate at Pembroke; both of these are plainly the work of the great William Marshal, Earl of Pembroke and Striguil (Chepstow) 1189-1219. On his entry to the earldom he was a mature soldier (aged about 46) and for some reason seems to have distrusted a portcullis. The fact that his great Outer Gate at Pembroke was fitted for two portcullises does not mean that he trusted a single portcullis any more than before.

3. A.J. Taylor, 'Master James of St. George', *English Historical Review*, lxv (1950), pp. 433-47; and 'The Castle of St Georges-d'Espéranche', *Antiquaries' Journal*, xxxiii (1953), pp. 33-47.

4. Smail (1973), p. 94.

5. Bevan, *History of Spanish architecture* (London, 1938), pp. 116-17.

6. K. A. C. Creswell, in *Bulletin de l'Institut français d'archéologie orientale*, xxiii (1924), pp. 89-158.

7. The projecting part of such a tower would consist of four sides of a regular hexagon. In fact, they are not particularly common; and even at the citadel of Angora, where beaked towers are systematically used, they are not of the form recommended: Jerphanion, *Mélanges de l'Université Saint-Joseph, Beyrouth*, xiii, fasc. 1 (1928), pp. 144-219, esp. pp. 155-9.

8. This baronial castle, which is probably the best design of the Crusader 12th century, is widely written-up: Boase, pp. 48-51; Deschamps, iii, pp. 217-47; Müller-Wiener, pp. 44-5, 96-7, plates 12-21; Rey, pp. 105-113, pl. xii (plans not to be trusted); Smail (1956) pp. 236-43, 250; and (1973) pp. 104-8. Paul Deschamps also contributed papers on the castle to *Gazette des beaux-arts*, xxx (1930), pp. 329-64, and *Syria*, xvi (1935).

9. Boase, p. 45; Deschamps, iii, pp. 203-15; Müller-Wiener, pp. 64-5; G. (Baron) Rey, pp. 217-19; Smail (1956), pp. 227-8, plate v; and (1973), pp. 96, 98.

10. Deschamps, iii, pp. 203-15.

11. C.N. Johns, 'Excavations at Pilgrims' Castle, 'Atlit', *Quarterly of the Department of Antiquities in Palestine*, i (1931), pp. 21-33; Boase, pp. 71-3; Müller-Wiener, pp. 58-9.

12. Benvenisti, pp. 294-300; Boase, p. 43; Deschamps, ii, pp. 121-3, slight; Smail (1956), pp. 231, 249 (obsolete plan) and (1973), pp. 100-2.

13. Deschamps, ii, p. 168; he gives no reason for this conclusion.

14. For Beaufort, see Boase, pp. 66-7; Deschamps, ii, pp. 176-208, pl. liii-lxxv; Müller-Wiener, pp. 62-3, pl. 84; Rey, pl. xiii; Smail (1956), pp. 221-3, 226-7, 246, pl. iii.

15. K.A.C. Creswell, *Bulletin de l'Institut français d'archéologie orientale*, xxiii (1924), pp. 89-158, an outstanding study of a medieval fortress.

16. This is evidently fatal to the theory of T.E. Lawrence, that Crusader castles were copied from French originals; Lawrence, *Crusader castles* (London, 1936).

17. For Margat, see Boase, pp. 56-60; Deschamps, iii, pp. 259-84, Müller-Wiener, pp. 56-8, and pl. 52-61; Rey, pp. 19-38, pl. ii-iii; Smail (1973), pp. 113-15, pl. 26-9.

18. This is a powerful half-round structure; see R. Denys Pringle, 'A Thirteenth-

Century hall at Montfort Castle in Western Galilee', *Antiquaries' Journal,* lxvi (1986), pp. 52-81. Earlier plans appear to be misleading.

19. See Creswell, *loc. cit.,* esp. p. 118.

20. For Cairo, see Creswell; for Damascus, see D.J.C. King, *Archaeologia,* xciv (1951), pp. 57-94 and plates; for Bosra, Müller-Wiener, pp. 67-8, plates 92-4; for Mount Tabor, Kitchener and Conder, *Survey of Western Palestine* (London, 1881), i, pp. 367-8, 388-91.

21. C.N. Johns, 'Medieval Ajlun', *Quarterly of the Department of Antiquities in Palestine,* i (1931), pp. 111-129; ii (1933), pp. 41-104; iii (1934), pp. 145-64.

22. Principally dealt with by Deschamps, vol. 1. See also Boase, pp. 51-6; Müller-Wiener, pp. 59-62; plates 16-83, Rey, pp. 39-67, plates iv-vii; Smail (1956), pp. 243-4, 248; (1973), pp. 108-13, plat. 16-20.

23. For Margat, see n17, *supra;* for Belvoir, n12. (This castle is in fact a twelfth-century structure.)

24. Boase, pp. 60-1; Deschamps, iii, pp. 287-92; Müller-Wiener, pp. 50-1, plate 33; Rey, pp. 69-83, planche viii.

25. See n21, *supra.*

26. Benvenisti, pp. 199-204.

27. Benvenisti, pp. 331-7; Deschamps, ii, pp. 138-9; Müller-Wiener, pp. 74-5, pl. 104, 105; Rey, pp. 143-51, pl. xv; Dean, *Bulletin of the Metropolitan Museum of Art,* xxii (1927).

28. Deschamps, *Syria,* xiii (1932), pp. 378-9.

29. Morgan and Wakeman, *Monmouth and Caerleon Antiquarian Association* (1854). There may have been another, now demolished, at Caerleon; Coxe, *Tour in Monmouthshire* (London, 1801) i, p. 89 and plate facing.

30. D.J.C. King, 'Pembroke Castle', *Château-Gaillard,* viii (1967), pp. 164-5, figs. 2, 10, 11.

31. Wiegand, *Baalbek* (Berlin and Leipzig, 1921-5) iii (by H. Kohl); Müller-Wiener, p. 54 (the curtain seems to be that shown between the numbers 1213 and 1224).

32. Rey, pp. 74, 75; here there are defences at five levels, though one has been blocked, and another forms the actual battlements.

33. *Military architecture in England during the middle ages* (Oxford, 1913), p. 176; see also Enlart, *Manuel d'archéologie française* (Paris, 1904) ii, pp. 528, 650.

34. K.A.C. Creswell, *Early Muslim architecture* (Oxford, 1932) i, pp. 330-43, 345-7.

35. K.A.C. Creswell, *Bulletin de l'Institut français d'archéologie orientale,* xxiii (1924), pp. 159-64. For a similar opinion, see Deschamps, i, p. 262. It is interesting to note that a very similar process occurred in Ireland, where small corbelled-out latrines were introduced by the English, and similar structures were employed by Irish notables as machicolations, which finally took on not only the functions, but very much the form, of the oriental brattice. H.G. Leask, *Irish castles and castellated houses* (Dundalk, 1944), figs. 27, 29, 31, compare figs. 8, 48, 51 and 68.

9

The Introduction of Scientific Fortification

It would appear that the castle-builders of the eleventh and early twelfth centuries knew, or could very easily have found out, a lot more about military science than they cared for or needed to use.[1] Early medieval armies frequently lacked the sheer professional skill required for the successful pursuit of the siege of a strong castle, and there are a number of instances, especially from France, of powerful princes being held up for humiliatingly long periods by single sieges. Professionalism among fighting-men, under the comparison of the Byzantine army and the Military Orders, was bound to grow as a result of the Crusades; but there was another professionalism: the technical skill of miners who could undercut the angles of a fortress, the skill of expert carpenters to make siege-engines. The increase in professionalism and the added power it gave to the attacking force might be expected to put a greater call on the knowledge and energies of the builders of castles.

We normally expect to find the process beginning in France, the heartland of medieval architecture, the Western nation most deeply concerned in the Crusades. In medieval matters, we generally have to accept the relatively unimportant and peripheral position of England. It is the more interesting to notice that French archaeologists have for many years regarded English castles, particularly those of the twelfth century, with the utmost respect, and have also accorded the principal credit for the advance in military technique and the improved style of fortification to the king-dukes of Normandy. In 1869 de Caumont prefaced his description of a 'transition' in military construction to parallel that in religious architecture with the opinion:

> Ce fut principalement sous les successeurs de Henri Ier, sous Henri II auquel on dut un assez grand nombre de constructions, et sous Richard Coeur-de-Lion, que ces changements se produisirent. Ils coincident donc précisément avec la période durant laquelle s'opéra la transition du plein-cintre à l'ogive.[2]

Writing in 1962, M. François Gebelin makes a similar statement:

The great revival in military architecture was led, as one would naturally expect, by the powerful kings and princes of the time; by the sons
of William the Conqueror and their descendants, the Plantagenets,
when they became dukes of Normandy. These were the men who built
all the most typical twelfth-century fortified castles remaining to-day
... Louis [VII, king of France from 1137 to 1180] was no great builder
of castles ...[3]

More recently M. Héliot has mentioned the lead given by Henry I and
Henry II to castle-builders: 'En Normandie l'on modernisa systématique-
ment les forteresses royales à compter de 1120–1130 seulement, sous l'impul-
sion attentive des Henry I et II qui donnèrent un exemple largement suivi en
France et en Angleterre.'[4]

It was to Henry II also that the use of specialists for building siege-engines
was originally due in the West,[5] and to him are undoubtedly also due the
earliest English examples of scientific fortification, with straight curtains
flanked by projecting towers. Setting on one side for the moment the story of
the development of the keep from a square to a round plan (in which, it will
be seen, the kings of England took a much less conspicuous part), we should
enquire first whether there are earlier examples of flanked fortification on the
Continent.

For a start, we find that M. Raymond Ritter points to the castle of Carcassonne (Aude) as the earliest example of scientific fortification in France;[6] but
his date of about 1130 seems to depend on the authority of the local historian
Poux,[7] who appears to accept every mention of a *palatium* of the Trencavel
family in the documents of the period as evidence for the existence of a castle.
No explicit mention of a castle in fact occurs before 1191.[8] The present fabric
of the castle of Carcassone is in fact very advanced in character even for the
latter date.

M. Gebelin, on the other hand, gives an architectural history of the castle
of Gisors (Eure) which ascribes to Henry I of England, in 1123, the building
of the main ward.[9] This is an irregular polygon with mainly straight curtains,
flanked by open-backed towers, and looks on an undated plan very much
like the sort of work that Henry II, the king's grandson, was putting up at
Windsor and Dover 40 or 50 years later. A more detailed examination,[10]
however, shows that the bulk of these towers are additions, and the original
work has a wandering, uncertain trace quite unlike the work of Henry II.
The latter is thus seen to be the prime mover in the introduction of scientific
fortification in Western Europe.

As far as England is concerned, the first moves in the direction of scientific
fortification of the enclosure are represented by the upper bailey of Windsor,
and the inner ward of Dover. These were probably begun in the late 1160s;
in 1171–2 we hear definitely of money applied in the work on the wall round
'the King's houses of Windr',[11] and at Dover there was a huge expenditure in

the years 1168–80[12] much of which is attributable to the inner ward. Both of these lines of defence were made up of straight curtains, joining a series of rectangular towers of moderate size, looped for archery and boldly projecting from the curtain. Standing as they do on irregular earthwork, the towers are inevitably fairly numerous,[13] but apart from their arrowslits the latter represent little advance on the towers of an earlier period; in particular, they were either completely open at the rear or else their arrangements there seem to have been sketchy. At Dover, pairs of towers were built close together to protect the gates. At Orford (Suffolk), built 1165–75, the ward round the new great tower was of similar type, as shown in Norden's drawing of about 1600.[14] The inner ward of Portchester, probably made early in Henry II's reign, is a rectangle built in a corner of the Saxon Shore fort, with Roman walls forming two sides, and a rectangular tower — apparently open at the rear — projecting diagonally on the interior angle; a square gatehouse flanks the long south side.[15]

This last is a less satisfactory example of royal castellation, if only because of its uncertain date; but where the king led, his subjects followed. Framlingham (Suffolk) is an impressive example of a ring of lofty walls and open-backed towers, probably built by Roger Bigod, Earl of Norfolk, in the reign of Richard I (the castle had been destroyed by Henry II in 1174–5 for the rebellion of his father, Earl Hugh Bigod).[16] The refortification of the Bishop of Winchester's motte at Farnham (Surrey), which had also been slighted by King Henry, took on a similar form, with rather shallow rectangular towers rising from a massive polygonal revetment.[17] It seems likely that little enfilade shooting was possible; certainly this was the case at Framlingham. The towers of this castle project so little that they only flank their curtains at parapet level, and with single loops; and this is so in spite of the provision of numerous openings for direct shooting all about the castle.[18]

The shape of the flanking towers underwent a number of rapid changes; King Henry himself built a polygonal tower on the outer line of defence at Dover (the Avranches Tower, which is semi-octagonal).[19] It was not to have been expected in a period when the keep was moving from a square plan to a round one that round flankers would be long in putting in an appearance — the more so when we remember that Roman bastions, many of which were still in existence, were almost always round. In fact we soon find round mural towers, though at first of rather experimental shapes. Thus at Conisborough (Yorkshire, West Riding, now part of South Yorkshire) an inner ward of entirely Norman detail is flanked by small solid half-round buttress-towers;[20] while the curious 'shell-keep' at Berkeley (Gloucestershire), equally Norman in its dating-features, and ascribed to a date about 1184,[21] has three small half-round, open-backed towers on the perimeter of its revetted motte; there were probably more originally. Typical 'drum-towers' of the finally accepted type — large, hollow internally, and closed at the gorge — are found at Chepstow in association with a conspicuous Transitional gateway[22] and at Pembroke (the Dungeon Tower), in connection with, and sharing some detail with, the great Transitional keep. Both of these may be dated between 1190 and 1200. Helmsley, regularly flanked with round and half-round towers, belongs to the year 1200 or thereabouts.[23] From this time onwards there was to be no turning back; a regular scientific system of defence established itself, based on enfilade from towers almost invariably round.

The importance of scientific defence must not be overstressed; a well-sited castle was hard and dangerous to attack whether its defences were up-to-date or not.[24] We cannot imagine that an old-fashioned castle such as Richmond would necessarily have fallen an easy prey to thirteenth-century siegecraft. In fact the principal means of defence of any castle, early or late, simple or sophisticated, was of the simplest character — a heavy missile, typically a stone, hurled by hand from an embrasure of the parapet. The supply — in England at least — was plentiful; the material was cheap; no particular skill was needed in the operator; standing on even a modest castle-wall, 'he had in his hand one of the most awful engines of nature ... gravitation' (Chesterton). Accounts of sieges and contemporary pictures of sieges all confirm this very natural fact; occasionally the lord or constable is shown hurling javelins — a more knightly weapon, though scarcely more effective — but the shower of stones from the battlements which greeted an assailant was the main weapon against any assault on a fortified place. If it was the *only* weapon in use, then the typical earthwork trace — curvilinear, approximating to a circle — was ideal; a flanked castle had no advantages in the matter of defence by hand-thrown missiles. The clue to the rise of the new species of fortification is plainly archery; only with arrows and bolts could one enfilade a curtain of any length. The old style of fortification gave the minimum facility for shooting; but, from the very first, the new model was full of arrowslits.

There can be little doubt that the weapon whose employment called for such radical changes in the design of the castle was the crossbow.[25] Until the introduction of the longbow under Edward I — when in fact a technique of archery permitting a highly practised man to draw a bow of great strength was brought into use outside the region of South Wales in which it had originated — the simple bow was of little use in war. It is well known that the Norman host at Hastings included archers, one of whom, in the late stages of the battle, *may* have hit King Harold in the eye; but it is also clear that they achieved practically nothing else, and that the Saxons did not even trouble to bring any bowmen to meet them. The helplessness of the short-bow against armour is very evident; the Crusaders, encountering the formidable Turkish horse-archers, are repeatedly compared to porcupines, so thick did the arrows stick in their armour; but usually without doing them any harm. In the wars of King Stephen's reign we hear something of archers; they did well at the Battle of the Standard against the naked Galwegians, but did not stop David I's armoured Normans; and when the hateful Geoffrey de Mandeville

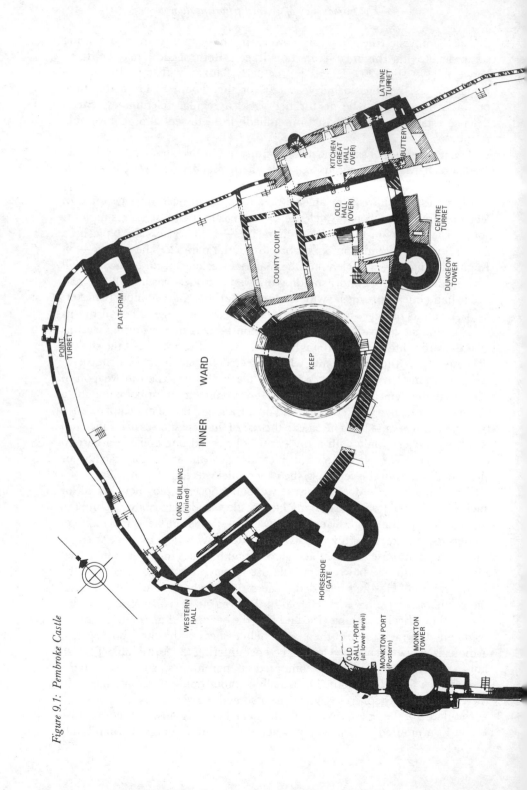

Figure 9.1: Pembroke Castle

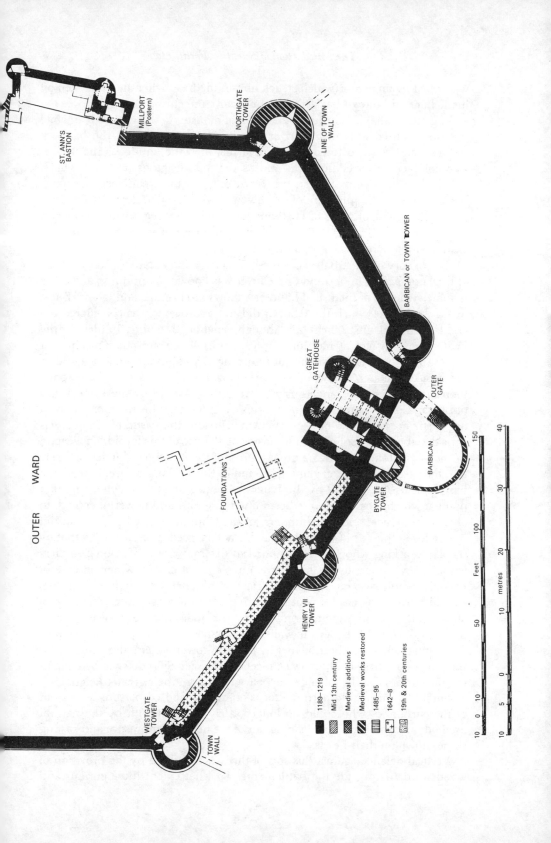

OUTER WARD

ST. ANN'S BASTION

MILLPORT (Postern)

NORTHGATE TOWER

LINE OF TOWN WALL

BARBICAN or TOWN TOWER

GREAT GATEHOUSE

OUTER GATE

BARBICAN

FOUNDATIONS

BYGATE TOWER

HENRY VII TOWER

WESTGATE TOWER

TOWN WALL

1189–1219
Mid 13th century
Medieval additions
Medieval works restored
1485–95
1642–8
19th & 20th centuries

Feet
150   100   50   0   10
metres
40   30   20   10   5   0   10

was killed by an arrow (which struck him in the head when he had taken off his helmet and drawn back his hood of mail), the chroniclers gloat over the trifling means that had brought this terrible monster to naught.[26] Meanwhile the unarmoured area of a warrior's body was decreasing as the hauberk sleeves were lengthed to cover the forearms, then the hands; as the helmet was enlarged to cover the face; and as the mail leggings (*chausses*), which appear in the Bayeux Tapestry as worn only by the wealthiest Normans, became standard equipment. The bow, as is well known, does not figure in Henry II's Assize of Arms of 1181, and was plainly not regarded as a weapon any longer. Yet Henry himself had for a number of years been building castles with loopholes — not, we may suppose, for the short-bow.

The history of the arbalast or crossbow is long and confused. In the shape of the large *balista*, on a stand or a cart, it was known to antiquity, and there is some evidence of the use of hand-crossbows at Hastings and later.[27] But it was a weapon of which the Church did not approve; it was considered too cruel for use against Christians, though sanctioned against Infidels in the East, where, in fact, it had long been in use. This reservation meant that there would be a steady stream of returning Crusaders who had learned in the East to use a crossbow, or — more dangerously — to control crossbow-men in action: more dangerously because these would be the princes and nobles and professional captains. Of this class, Richard I is the most famous; his death at the hands of a crossbowman before the castle of Chaluz was considered a judgment on him for fostering the use of this forbidden weapon in the West. John, too, was a great patron of the crossbow.[28] It seems likely that the weapon had been gaining ground in Europe long before; indeed, the ban upon its use, passed by the Lateran Council in 1139, may well mark a point at which crossbows were becoming numerous and powerful enough to attract the notice, and the thunders, of the Church. The Church's ban did not go for nothing; but notoriously it did not succeed. It seems likely that by the 1160s a king who was accustomed to dealing with professional soldiers would know where to lay his hands on plenty of crossbowmen in case of need; he would also have reason to fear that his enemies could do the same. In which case, his castles could be subjected to a most dangerous type of attack: if the enemy were to bring up to close quarters a siege-tower or 'rolling belfry', it could render the wall-walk untenable, even to men in armour. Such an attack would best be met by flanking-towers, themselves pierced for the crossbow; these could at once meet the deficiency in defence by enfilading the curtains, and challenge the belfry itself from their greater height.

Similarly, they could permit attacks on evilly disposed persons at the foot of the curtain — who could no longer safely be dealt with by the natural method: an armoured man leaning out of the nearest embrasure and casting stones down on their heads.

Vertical defence against this sort of threat was helped by the provision of wooden hoards outside the battlements. To what extent these curious and probably rather unsatisfactory structures merely covered the movements of people leaning out of the embrasures, and to what extent they supplied an actual passage leading round the castle outside the parapet,[29] it is difficult to say; in England no example survives, and the French example at the castle of Laval (Mayenne) may well not represent normal medieval practice.[30] Nor is it clear whether most hoards were permanent or semi-permanent, or whether they were merely got out in emergency at a threatened point. The whole enquiry is a very specialised one, which can hardly be followed very far here. Nevertheless, we have some evidence in the shape of the surviving arrangements for fitting hoards to walls and towers; in most examples this consists of a single row of square holes along the foot of the parapet, almost as if their purpose was merely to let water run off the wall-walk. If the object was simply to get out in emergency a lightly built screen, this was the handiest arrangement possible; but there was no question of much structural strength in most cases: the holes are generally small, rather widely spaced, and pierced only in the thin parapet. One cannot imagine a man's weight being lightly entrusted to any floor carried on so flimsy a set of joists. Elsewhere we find more solid arrangements — larger holes, or a second tier of holes below the first, so as to carry struts; even in some cases stone corbels. These suggest something more substantial than a mere screen, but they are rare on the whole. The references to hoards in the *History of the King's Works* are vague and uncertain, and further confused by allusions to *brattices*, which seem to be more or less the same thing. This is another use of the word *bretasche*,[31] and if there is any difference between 'hoarding' and 'brattishing' we should expect to find the latter representing something more substantial. As to hoarding, we commonly find it being fitted in emergency;[32] though in the peaceful year 1235–6 the walls of Sherborne (Dorset) were carrying hoards, which were doing the fabric no good, and which were accordingly ordered to be struck.[33] Well into the late Middle Ages we find references to this form of defence, and representations of it in French pictures in particular; but from the later work of Edward I and James of St George, his master-builder, English castles commonly have neither holes nor corbels for hoarding.

The alteration of the keep from a standard rectangular plan to an equally standard circular one makes a much longer and less connected story than the metamorphosis of the bailey. Most of this story belongs to France, and it is in France that the most recent and thorough study of this development has appeared: M. Héliot's paper *L'évolution du donjon dans le nord-ouest de la France et en Angleterre au XIIe siècle*.[34] The influence of other nations in the process seems to have been slight, though some round keeps of early date are reported from Germany. As mentioned, the Crusader East has little or no connection with the story.

The forms taken by keeps in the course of this process of evolution are very numerous, but they can be resolved into three main categories: towers with complex curved plans, towers on polygonal bases, and plain round towers. We may also add a few apsidal towers, round at one end and rectangular at the other, in England and Wales, and a small number of round towers with a beak on one side, formed by extending the circle of their ground-plan along two converging tangents, thus adding a great triangular buttress against the exposed side of the tower. The keep of Château-Gaillard is the most famous example of this type, which appears to be confined to France.

Neither of these classes is particularly important in the story of the keep and its evolution; even the three main categories are only part of a complicated, half-understood progress from a simple cuboidal shape of keep like that of Rochester to something close to a perfect cylinder — Châteaudun (Eure-et-Loir)[35] or Pembroke. They are neither entirely consecutive nor completely concurrent; they overlap in time, and the reign of the rectangular keep overlaps them. We may, however, place the complex, plainly transitional forms early in the narrative, and end it with the triumph, in the thirteenth century, of the simple round tower — though even then we must not forget that other forms could still be built, like the quatrefoil Clifford's Tower at York, erected in 1245–62, or the last great medieval keep of England, the Yellow Tower of Gwent at Raglan (Monmouthshire, now Gwent), which is hexagonal in plan, and was built in 1430–45.

The inherent defect in any rectangular keep lay in the 'dead ground' at its angles. Here it was hardly possible to see what an enemy was doing, and quite impossible to interfere with his activities. The angle-turret of a Norman keep was thus an obvious target for an enemy who was skilled in mining, though we do not hear of any such operation succeeding before John's attack on Rochester in 1216. Many years before this, dissatisfaction with the existing type of keep had led to a number of experimental forms in France — forms which hardly represent by themselves any continuous process of evolution; the later examples indeed show little or no advance on the earlier ones. Of these, Houdan (Seine-et-Oise), probably dated 1110–25, is the most important.[36] Externally it is a massive circular tower with four boldly projecting round turrets, symmetrically placed — one thinks at once of a tower like Longtown (Herefordshire) with its three buttress-turrets. But the plan reveals that Houdan is something very different; its interior is square (with some of the angles cut off) and the four turrets are on the corners of this square, leaving the segments of the main circle in front of the sides. Thus what we have is a square 'Norman' keep in which externally the square has been made round, both on the main body of the tower, which is now a circle, and on the turrets, which from being rather more than half-squares had become semicircles or rather larger segments. Certainly no dead ground was left around such a tower; everywhere an enemy could be observed from the walls, and, if at the right range, could be attacked from them; and this observation or attack could come from two or three places on the battlements. Amblény (Aisne), built in about 1200, is similar, but with the turrets greatly increased in size,[37] so that it is likely to have been modelled on Étampes (Seine-et-Oise) rather than Houdan. The Tour Guinette at Étampes, dated on archaeological grounds to 1130–50, forms in plan a perfect quatrefoil of four massive semicircular towers joined together.[38] It is the finest example of these transitional forms, though not the latest. The Tour de César at Provins (Seine-et-Marne), dated to 1160–80, is an extraordinary affair; the corners of its square structure are cut off above the base, and on the oblique sides so formed are set small half-round turrets which at their summits are separate from the main structures. While these certainly covered the dead ground on the angles, they had little else to commend them; they are cramped and fragile, and enjoy a relatively poor field of fire. No other keep followed the model of Provins, and M. Héliot is inclined to look for its pattern among a group of contemporary church-steeples.[39] The twin donjons of Niort (Deux-Sèvres), most likely datable to 1170–5, are simply square towers of the Norman type, but with the angle-turrets now circular; each donjon has one stair-turret, but the other turrets are solid; in the middle of each face is a buttress, serving little useful purpose, but also rounded in plan. Once again the dead angles could be watched, if not very effectively, from these small turrets.[40]

There are two other French examples of this kind: Romefort (Berri) and Mez-le-Maréchal (Loiret).[41] M. Héliot is inclined to note in this group as a whole a movement towards defence by enfilade, rather than a simple elimination of dead ground in front of the defences. On this explanation the whole series would appear to be disappointing; arrowslits are few, and the whole defence in every case was conducted from the tower-head, exactly as in an ordinary Norman keep.

There is nothing comparable to this series in England; the familiar examples of Orford (Suffolk) and Conisborough (West Yorkshire) have rectangular and trapezoidal turrets respectively, while of the smaller round keeps we can hardly count those with one functional turret, like Skenfrith (Monmouthshire, now Gwent) which has a small round projection housing the stair, or Chartley (Staffordshire) where two small turrets, close together, plainly defended the doorway. Only Longtown (Herefordshire) with three very small round buttresses disposed symmetrically — one protecting the stairwell — can be suggested as a poor English relation of the Houdan family. It is dated on architectural grounds to 1180.[42]

There remain the two major classes: polygonal and round towers; and here the contrast between French and English practice is remarkable. M. Héliot is able to cite only one early polygonal tower in France: the lower part of the keep of Gisors (Eure), ascribed to 1096–7; it is said to have been raised and its buttresses added under Henry II, about 1160–77. This seems a very early date, but, in any case, 'cette tour célèbre ... n'a guère fait école à ce qu'il me semble'.[43] The fine polygonal keep of Châtillon-Coligny (Loire), with its shallow buttresses, the only other French example cited, is dated 1190–1200.

Round French keeps, on the other hand, are very numerous. The question of their date is plainly a matter for argument; many of them have been attributed to improbably early dates, as is only too common in any country when no firm dating is available. It must be admitted that antiquarianism is a very natural and pardonable fault in antiquaries, but they should be mindful of the advice — attributed to the late Sir Goronwy Edwards — that those seeking to date anything on stylistic grounds should remember the sundial and its inscription: 'It's later than you think'.

Nevertheless, there is a sufficiently impressive number of French round donjons which belong either certainly or probably to the twelfth century — and some of them fairly early in that period — for it to be very clear that the round keep had firmly established itself in France long before 1200.[44] In particular, King Philip Augustus (1180–1223) and his masons made a speciality of erecting round keeps wherever they undertook the building or the modernisation of a castle.

The picture in twelfth-century England was very different. Here round keeps were few indeed; apart from the case of Longtown, already mentioned, there are apparently only three examples. Of these the earliest is the extraordinary tower of New Buckenham (Norfolk), of which only the base remains, with very little surviving detail. It can almost certainly be connected with a move to this new castle-site from the neighbouring Old Buckenham, where the owner, William d'Albini, set up a priory of Austin Canons in about 1145.[45] Its diameter is very large — 74 feet (22.5 m) — and it has the unique feature of a cross-wall dividing it into two roughly equal parts. It has thus been suggested, not unconvincingly,[46] that it is simply a Norman keep built on a round plan for lack of proper freestone for its angles, just as there are many round church-towers in this flint country of East Anglia. Certainly it is a very primitive-looking structure, and seems to have exerted no influence whatever on the development of the keep in England.

The second example is Conisborough, built in the later twelfth century, evidently by Hamelin Plantagenet, Earl Warenne and bastard brother of King Henry II, who owned the castle from 1164 to 1202. The detail — some of which is very rich — is pure Norman; the keep is basically the same sort of structure as an ordinary round keep, with one large circular chamber on each of the four storeys, and a few small rooms in the huge thickness of the walls; but the six great trapezoidal buttresses which rise above the body of the tower as small turrets form a feature which has only one close analogue: the keep of Hamelin's own castle of Mortemer (Seine Inférieure).[47]

The third of these English round keeps was built very close to the end of the twelfth century. In 1189 Isabella de Clare, heiress of Pembroke, married the distinguished warrior William Marshal, who became earl in her right. Her lands had been in the king's hands since 1176; the detail of 'the monumental donjon of Pembroke' is Transitional, with Norman and Gothic forms combined, and it is plain that William built his bride a new and splendid

Plate 1: Benton Castle; the smallest enclosure castle in England.

Plate 2. Castell Crugerydd, a motte and bailey at the head of a high pass in Radnor Forest. (By permission of the National Museum of Wales.)

Plate 3: Dover; the great keep, with the towers of its forebuilding in the background. It is surrounded by Henry II's inner ward. In front the outer ward, then the protective banks of the ancient stronghold. (By permission of English Heritage.)

Plate 4: Pickering; the motte, with a fragment of shell keep, and the wing wall. (By permission of English Heritage.)

Plate 5: Château-Gaillard; the unique inner defences.

Plate 6: White Castle; typical thirteenth century defences (though in fact the curtains are of the twelfth century).

Plate 7: Harlech; a masterpiece by Edward I and his master-mason, James of St. George. This is an aerial view from the North-West.

Plate 8: Nunney, licensed 1373; a powerful line defence compressed into a single lovely tower.

Plate 9: *Deal Castle from the North, looking down Deal beach towards Walmer. All the parapets are modern. (By permission of English Heritage.)*

keep soon after their marriage.

Unlike Buckenham and Conisborough it is a straightforward example of a round keep, and a very fine one: four storeys and a garret under the domed vault which roofs the whole structure and carried something like an inner and higher battlement on the tower-head. The base is strongly battered, the parapet has the holes for a fairly substantial hoard. The original entrance is at first-floor level,[48] but there is no forebuilding; this was to be the normal arrangement for round donjons. A remarkable feature of the tower was a generous provision of loops; already these are genuine shooting-slits, though their narrow recesses permitted very little traverse. They are used not only on the tower-head, where they would be useful, but on all three of the main floors. Finally, Pembroke is rather a grim tower from the point of view of domestic accommodation, and in particular no attempt was made to accommodate the hall of the castle in it, though it is one of the very largest of round keeps. This, too, was to be a standard feature of the type: round donjons contained only the lord's private quarters.

The backwardness of England in this matter of round keeps is remarkable, and the reason is not far to seek: the kings gave no lead. In the defence of the bailey, Henry II had been the great pioneer; in the evolution of the keep he seems to have experimented uncertainly with polygonal forms while still building a conventional keep like Newcastle, and finally to have given up in disgust and ended by building the keep of Dover. It has to be admitted that the Tour du Moulin at Chinon (Indre-et-Loire), which appears to be a small round keep, is attributed to this king, with considerable circumstantial detail, by the author of the local guide.[49] We are also told that he raised in height, if he did not build, the polygonal tower of Gisors, and in England he was responsible for three polygonal keeps. Of these the very large Orford has three big rectangular turrets and a small forebuilding;[50] it is a structure of amazingly elaborate plan, and reflects great credit on its architect,[51] but evidently it did not attract any imitators. Henry's other two keeps of this sort are simpler. Chilham (Kent) is an octagon in plan, much smaller, and with only one square turret (which contains the stair). Tickhill (South Yorkshire) of which only the foundations remain, had no turrets; its plan is a plain regular endecagon, with flat buttresses on its angles. The dates given to these towers by the *History of the King's Works* are: Orford 1166–72; Chilham 'in the 1170s'; Tickhill *c.* 1179–82; the authors also tell us:

In England no cylindrical tower-keeps appear to have been erected by the Crown before the reign of Henry III ... Though Château Gaillard proves that Richard I understood the principle of the cylindrical donjon, he built nothing of the kind in England, and John's only keep (at Odiham in Hampshire)[52] still shows an imperfect appreciation of the new idea. Now much ruined, it is octagonal in plan and measures some 40 feet across internally, with buttressed walls 10 feet thick ...[53]

So far as is known it was the last polygonal keep to be built by an English king.[54]

More might be said here; the phrases 'Richard I *understood* the principle' and 'an imperfect *appreciation* of the new idea' suggest that the difficulty was an intellectual one. This is surely wrong; we are dealing with highly intelligent kings. They probably understood very well the advantages of the new idea, but also its disadvantages, and were not converted to the latest doctrine. The new model had its defects, as M. Héliot points out: 'Bien disposé pour la défense, le tracé circulaire se prêtait mal au logement des seigneurs et des barons, à plus forte raison des princes.'[55]

Nor was it entirely a matter of creature comforts; the hall would be the dormitory of most of a castle's staff, and particularly of its fighting-men — a tactical point of some importance. Among Norman keeps, only a few little horrors like the Castle of the Peak, Clitheroe and Goodrich did not contain a hall; but among round keeps, only the freakish New Buckenham is ever likely to have had one; the splendid towers of Conisborough and Pembroke had no room for halls, and still less had their smaller, later and poorer relations. The polygonal towers may well have been intended to combine the advantages of the old and new systems, which they will not have done very successfully.

There are other royal towers of polygonal plan to be considered. The tower on the lofty motte of Oxford was decagonal in plan, and according to some authorities furnished with flat buttresses on its angles.[56] Its date cannot be satisfactorily determined.[57] The castle of Harestan or Horston (Derbyshire), appears to have been built in 1199 or immediately afterwards;[58] little remains of it, but at one end of the site is a large rock which seems to be the position of the keep. Here there survives a portion of plinth, forming two straight faces set at an obtuse angle, which is capped by a buttress.

Few subjects' castles were built with keeps of polygonal plan. Mitford (Northumberland) was simply a Norman keep with one side projecting to form a blunt salient. The excavation of the motte at Richard's Castle (Hereford) revealed the butt of a massive tower of octagonal plan and twelfth-century detail. As originally built, the corners were capped with pilaster buttresses.[59]

The very few other polygonal keeps in England and Wales are of much later date. By the thirteenth century the round keep represented standard practice; and here we have to note, nearer home, a case of the same antiquarianism in dating which has already been noted in France. Of our round towers, the two finest are Conisborough and Pembroke, the latter Transitional in detail, the former pure Norman. There has been a tendency to generalise from these two, and date round keeps in general to the later years of the twelfth century, or — since the pointed arches in many of these towers cannot be ignored — very early in the thirteenth. Now this is an unwise manner of generalisation; a similar method of dating Norman keeps would have applied the eleventh-century dates of Colchester and the Tower of London to all the other towers of the type. In any new style we must expect the setters of the fashion to be the important men, and new features to make their first appearance in the greater castles.[60] Here royalty was averse to this particular new idea, and it appears in the castles of the next highest social stratum — the earls, for both Hamelin Plantagenet and William Marshal were of this rank.

Finally accepted in England, cylindrical keeps were never numerous by French standards. This is not surprising; by the thirteenth century the need for new castles, or for any castles at all, was much diminished over England as a whole, and a large proportion of those which were still in use had masonry defences already. Notoriously the greater number of round keeps is to be found in the disturbed area of South Wales and the March. (In North Wales the thirteenth century was the century of the two Llywelyns, and until its later years there was little opportunity for English castle-building there. The Scottish border was peaceful for most of the century; so was the Channel coast). The number of round keeps in England and Wales seems to have been about 40 — not much more than 2 per cent of the total of our castles. From the time of Henry III, the royal family became reconciled to the new style of keep, and Edward I and III both built round keeps.

Cylindrical keeps were also built by the Welsh princes,[61] and are found in small numbers in Ireland[62] and Scotland.[63]

Notes

1. The employment of the portcullis supplies an instance; this was an expedient known to antiquity, and used in early medieval work but only very sporadically: at the entrances to the keeps of Colchester, Rochester, and Hedingham; one groove of a gate attached to the keep (that of the forebuilding?) at Bridgnorth (Shropshire); and a single instance of grooves at a main gate (Castle Rising, Norfolk). These last are only 3 inches (7.5 cms) wide, and the portcullis that ran in them will have been remarkably flimsy.

2. *Abécédaire ou rudiment d'archéologie* (Caen, 1869), iii, p. 446.

3. *The châteaux of France* (trans. H. Eaton Hart, London, 1964; originally published as *Les châteaux de France*, Presses Universitaires de France, 1962), pp. 43, 47.

4. Pierre Héliot, 'Les châteaux-forts en France du Xe au XIIe siècle', *Journal des Savants* (1965), p. 506.

5. *Ibid.*, p. 512.

6. Raymond Ritter, *Châteaux, donjons et places fortes, l'architecture militaire française* (Paris, apparently 1953), pp. 40-3.

7. Joseph Poux, *La cité de Carcassonne, histoire et description* (2 vols. in 3, Toulouse and Paris, 1922 and 1931). The relative passages are from vol. 2, pt. 1, pp. 14-18.

8. Ibid., pp. 20-1 and n[1] to p. 21. The dating has been discussed by M. Pierre Héliot in *Annales du Midi*, lxxviii (1966), pp. 7-21.

9. *Op. cit.*, pp. 43-7. The work in question is plainly that mentioned by Robert of

Torigni, p. 54: '*Henricus . . . moenibus ambitum et turribus excelsis inexpugnabile reddidit*'; for the actual date, see p. 106.

10. Y. Bruand, 'Le château du Gisors; principales campagnes de construction'. *Bulletin Monumental,* cxvi (1958), pp. 243 65.

11. Pipe Rolls, 18 Henry II, p. 16; see W.H. St John Hope, *Windsor Castle, an architectural history* (London, 1913), pp. 19-24.

12. Allen Brown, *English Historical Review,* lxx (1955), pp. 366, 390; *History of the King's Works,* ii, p. 630. A total of over £7,000 was spent.

13. At least nine at Windsor, probably ten or eleven originally. At Dover there are 14, including two pairs of gate-towers.

14. *History of the King's Works,* ii, plate 47A.

15. Stuart Rigold, *Portchester Castle (Guide Book,* HMSO, 1965).

16. Pipe Rolls, 21 Hen II, p. 108; 22 Hen II, p. 60.

17. M.W. Thompson, *Farnham Castle (Guide Book,* HMSO, 1961).

18. F.J.E. Raby and P.K. Baillie Reynolds, *Framlingham Castle (Guide Book,* HMSO, 1938).

19. D.F. Renn, 'The Avranches traverse at Dover castle', *Archaeologia Cantiana,* lxxxiv (1969), pp. 79-92.

20. Solid round towers were built at any time when normal (hollow) round towers were being constructed; D.J. Cathcart King and J. Clifford Perks, 'Penrice Castle, Gower' *Archaeologia Cambrensis,* cx (1961), pp. 98-9, n[70].

21. Lord Berkeley, 'Excavations at Berkeley Castle', *Bristol and Gloucestershire Archaeological Society,* lx (1938), pp. 308-339. While this paper is confusing, the conclusion seems to be drawn correctly from it.

22. J. Clifford Perks, 'The architectural history of Chepstow Castle during the Middle Ages', *Bristol and Gloucestershire Archaeological Society*, lxvii (1946-8), p. 318, 330-1.

23. Sir Charles Peers, *Helmsley Castle (Guide Book,* HMSO, 1934).

24. See, for example, Smail, *Crusading warfare, 1097–1193* (Cambridge, 1956), pp. 215-8.

25. The suggestion has been made (Hugh Braun, *The English castle* (London, 1936), pp. 65-9), that the higher curtains of this period were intended as a protection against the newly-invented trebuchet; but the latter had not in fact been invented by the 1160s. For its early history, see *Collected papers of Thomas Frederick Tout* (Manchester University, 1934), ii, pp. 217-20. Apart from a mention of *trabuchis* in a catalogue of weapons used at Cremona in 1199, which seems a doubtful authority, the first recorded use of the trebuchet was at the siege of Castelnaudary in September 1211 (*Le Chanson de la Croisade Albigeoise* (ed. Martin-Chabot, Paris 1960) p. 216). Its first appearance in Germany is recorded in 1212 (*Collected papers*, p. 219 n[6]), and though the name *trebuchet* ('tumbler') is a good French word, *Histoire des ducs de Normandie et des rois d'Angleterre* (ed. F. Michel, Paris, 1840), p. 188 says that few had been seen in France before 1217. The first English example was probably that being made at Dover in September-October 1224 by Master Jordan the carpenter (*Rotuli Litterarum Clausarum,* i, pp. 622a, 627a, 647a, 652b). In any case no practicable wall would be too high for a trebuchet to shoot over — or for that matter a mangonel; the latter engine, known since Roman times, had an unexpectedly high trajectory (Sir Ralph Payne-Gallwey, *The crossbow,* (London, 1930), pp. 281-3; my own experiments with small models completely uphold Payne-Gallwey's conclusions in this respect).

26. See Round, *Geoffrey de Mandeville,* (London, 1892), p. 221 n, in particular, the Ramsey chronicler's allusion to 'some twopenny-ha'penny archer' (*quidam vilissimus sagittarius*).

27. See Guy of Amiens, *Carmen de Hastingae proelio* (ed. Morton and Muntz, Oxford, 1972) lines 338, 411, also pp. 112-15; see also William of Poitiers, pp. 184-5.

28. Sir Charles Oman, *The art of war in the middle ages* (London, 1898), p. 558;

Payne-Gallwey, *The crossbow* (London, 1903), p. 46.

29. As shown in abundant detail in the drawings of Viollet-le-Duc (e.g. in the English translation by Macdermott (Oxford and London, 1860), pp. 61, 137), and the illustration at p. 475 of Camille Enlart, *Manuel d'Archéologie* (Paris, 1904) ii, p. 475.

30. Enlart, *op. cit.*, ii, p. 505; De Caumont, *Abécédaire ou Rudiment d'Archéologie* (Caen, 1869), iii, pp. 472-6.

31. *V. supra*, pp. 53-4.

32. *History of the King's Works*, ii, p. 674, for Hereford in 1173–4 and 1213; p. 745 for Mountsorrel, 1215, p. 826 Old Sarum in 1215.

33. *Ibid.*, p. 833.

34. Héliot, *Bulletin Archéologique*, new series, v (1969), pp. 141-94.

35. De Caumont, *Abécédaire*, iii, pp. 465-9, Héliot, *Bulletin de la Société nationale des antiquaires de France* (1968), pp. 225-47.

36. Héliot, *Bulletin Archéologique*, NS, v (1969), pp. 163-6; see also de Dion, *Bulletin Monumental*, lxix (1905), pp. 14-21; Harmand, *Bulletin Monumental*, cxxvii (1969), pp. 187–207. De Dion (p. 415) asserts that there was an identical donjon at Montchauvet, not far away.

37. Héliot, *op. cit.*, pp. 164, 166; there is a plan of this tower in *History of the King's Works*, i, p. 116; see also Lefevre-Pontalis, *Bulletin Monumental*, lxxiv (1910), pp. 69-74.

38. Héliot, *op. cit.*, pp. 166-7; also Héliot and Rousseau, *Bulletin de la Société nationale des antiquaires de France* (1967), pp. 289-301. M. Héliot cites Lefevre-Pontalis, *Congrès archéologique de France*, lxxxii (1919), p. 40 f.

39. Héliot, *op. cit.*, p. 167; Héliot and Rousseau, pp. 301-7.

40. Héliot, *op. cit.*, pp. 168-70, and authorities cited, also Héliot, *Revue du Bas-Poitou et des Provinces de l'Ouest* (1970), pp. 45-69.

41. Héliot, *op. cit.*, p. 169, and authorities cited.

42. The tower stands on a substantial artificial motte; there is a second motte-and-bailey very near (Longtown No. 2). In 1187 and 1188 (Pipe Rolls, 33 Hen II, p. 134; 34 Hen II, p. 214) we find among the Lacy castles both Ewias and a New Castle, which are probably Longtown No. 2 and Longtown itself. It would thus appear that the motte of Longtown was new in 1187; it would be a good many years before it could carry a strong tower.

43. Héliot, *loc. cit.*, p. 158. The allusion to Durham keep as having been built in 1099–1128 is unfortunate. The existing octagonal keep is a restoration of the work of Bishop Hatfield (1345–81). Its erection is recorded by Chambre, in *Historiae Dunelmensis scriptores tres*, Surtees Socy., ix (1839), p. 138. See also Pevsner, *Buildings of England* 9, p. 122; Armitage, p. 147. The keep (*arx*) mentioned in the time of bishop Ranulf Flambard (1099-1128), see *Symeon of Durham* i, p. 140, will have been the timber structure described by Laurence of Durham (*Surtees Socy.*, lxx, pp. 11-13, translation, Armitage pp. 147-9).

44. *Ibid.*, pp. 160-1.

45. Dugdale, *Monasticon*, vi, p. 419; see also David Knowles and R. Neville Hadcock, *Medieval religious houses* (London, 1953), p. 130.

46. Hugh Braun, *The English castle* (London, 1936), p. 49; Peter Westgate, *Buckenham Castle* (Guide-book, Norwich, 1937), p. 19.

47. Harold Sands and Hugh Braun, 'Conisborough and Mortemer', *Yorkshire Archaeological Journal*, xxxii (1934-6), pp. 146-59. There have been vague suggestions that the Yorkshire castle of Thorne had a similar keep, but this has not been excavated.

48. There is also a second doorway — an unusual feature — giving access by a bridge to the wall-walk of the adjacent curtain. This is at second-floor level.

49. Pepin, *Chinon* (Paris), pp. 73-8.

50. It would apparently have had about sixteen sides if the turrets had not been built.

51. Probably Ailnoth *Ingeniator*, for whom see Harvey, *English mediaeval architects* (London, 1954), pp. 16-17.

52. Built in 1207–14; *History of the King's Works*, ii, pp. 766-7.

53. Twelve metres across, with walls three metres thick; the figures are approximate. The buttresses were on the corners.

54. *History of the King's Works*, i, p. 77.

55. Héliot, *op. cit.*, p. 161.

56. Edward King, *Vestiges of Oxford castle* (London, 1796), pp. 8-9 and plate cxxvi; also Thomas W. Squires, *In West Oxford* (London and Oxford, 1928), pp. 69-71 and plates xxx-xxxiii.

57. *History of the King's Works*, ii, p. 772.

58. *Ibid.*, ii, p. 681.

59. Peter Edwin Curnow ad Michael W. Thompson, 'Excavations at Richard's Castle, Herefordshire, 1962–1964', *Journal of the British Archaeological Association*, 3rd series, xxxii (1969), pp. 112-14.

60. I first heard this rule put forward by Judge Perks; Dr Allen Brown expresses the same thought: 'Castles, like other good things, tend to work their way down in society from the top'; *Archaeological Journal*, cxxvi (1969), p. 141.

61. For example, Dolbadarn (Caernarvon, now part of Gwynedd) Dynevor and Dryslwyn (Carmarthen, now part of Dyfed); and perhaps Ystradfellte (Brecknock, now in Powys).

62. H.G. Leask, *Irish castles and castellated houses* (Dundalk, 1944), pp. 41-6.

63. David MacGibbon and Thomas Ross, *The castellated and domestic architecture of Scotland* (Edinburgh, 1887), i, pp. 73-8, 85-116.

10

The Thirteenth and Early Fourteenth Centuries

All the elements of scientific fortification evolved steadily throughout the thirteenth century, reaching at its end their highest English development in the great building campaigns of Edward I in North Wales. This is justly considered the zenith of English castle-building, after which no such glories were to appear again; in the shadow of its grandeur, the greater part of the fourteenth century is frequently seen as a period of decadence and decline — a character which it hardly deserves. Indeed, compared with this great programme of royal castle-building and the massive surge of baronial construction on the part of the Marchers that accompanied it, not only the ensuing period, but also the earlier thirteenth century, inevitably look unimposing.

Nevertheless, the early thirteenth century was a time of great activity, mainly in South Wales and the March, though there were still castles in central England which needed to be rebuilt or brought up to date. It is unfortunate that a surprising amount of the work of John and of Henry III — the latter being the greatest of our builder–kings — has vanished leaving no satisfactory trace, or is strangely difficult to date closely.

The general system of defence, by angle-towers enfilading straight faces of curtain, was already perfected, but that is not to say that its application in any individual case was a simple matter. For one thing, not till the last quarter of the century, the period of Edward I's great castles, do we find any significant desire for symmetry, such as produced castles like Harlech and Beaumaris. Even on a new site, on level ground, the application of the new principle could produce an awkward trapezoidal plan like that of Skenfrith (Monmouthshire, now Gwent); and there were few new sites, and those mostly not on level ground. Strong positions, like those of Beeston (Cheshire) and Montgomery, were almost inevitably of irregular shape, and often not too roomy.

But perhaps the greatest problem in this period lay in fitting up earlier earthworks in accordance with the new ideas of defence. In Wales and the March there are a number of cases where the old site was simply abandoned; but in England in general there were likely to be objections to this course: it would probably involve obtaining the king's consent, as a new site was being fortified; at the same time the original castle was likely to contain buildings which it would be wasteful to destroy; also the older site might be too good to abandon for any of a number of reasons.

Baileys were comparatively tractable; the curvilinear plan, with possibly a certain amount of engineering, could be turned into some sort of polygon; many baileys had one or more sides which were more or less straight already. At the worst one or two flanking-towers projecting from the curving wall of the bailey left it appreciably stronger. Ringworks, corresponding to a very compact and strictly curvilinear bailey, were more difficult to cope with. Few indeed have any surviving masonry, but something of what could be achieved on a site of this kind can be seen at Exeter or on the outer line of defence at Kidwelly (Carmarthenshire, now part of Dyfed); while an example of a small powerful thirteenth-century castle built on a ringwork has been found at Castell Bryn Amlwg (Bettws-y-Crwyn No. 2, Shropshire).[1]

The most intractable type of earthwork for this purpose was the motte, compact and almost inevitably curved in plan as it was. It could be treated in one of a number of ways: a single tower could be built upon it, or a ring of towers and walls could be built round its table-top. Both of these methods had been used in the late twelfth century: the one at Tickhill, where the polygonal keep stands on an enormous motte, the other at Berkeley and Farnham. Here the motte was revetted in both cases, and we frequently find revetments used in such circumstances — either vertical or at an angle closer to that of the earthwork, so as to form a steep apron of masonry. Finally, a number of 'shell-keeps', such as that of Pickering, probably belong to the thirteenth century. A single tower built on the motte would naturally be the castle's keep; there are examples at Longtown, Bronllys, Chartley and Hawarden (Flintshire, now part of Clwyd), all of which are round towers; there were others at Cambridge — also a cylindrical tower — and at Marlborough (Wiltshire), Caerleon (Monmouthshire, now Gwent), probably at Painscastle (Radnorshire, now part of Powys) and perhaps at Winchester; in these four cases the plan is uncertain. Clifford's Tower, the keep of York Castle, has a quatrefoil plan which recalls the alternative method of fortifying a motte, with clustered towers and short curtains about its perimeter.

This method was used very effectively at Clifford (Herefordshire), where the motte is protected on one side by a great fall of ground to the river Wye. On the other three sides there are five large half-round towers, two of them enclosing a gate. There is far more tower than wall on this part of the perimeter, and this is a feature of good work of the earlier thirteenth century. The same sort of proportion is to be seen at the inner ward of Beeston, and an even denser packing of round towers is found at the exposed northern end of the outer envelope at Dover, the so-called Norfolk Towers. Indeed, the extreme form of such a defence is to be seen at Richard I's inner ward of

Château-Gaillard, begun in 1196, which is in effect a continuous series of round tower-faces. Very much like Clifford, and the work of the Clifford family, is the immensely impressive Fountain Court at Skipton (North Yorkshire); here again there is a precipice in the rear, and the curved front is almost completely taken up by six very large round towers — two of them, enclosing a gateway, are apparently rather earlier — rising from a stone *talus* which completely conceals the slopes of the motte. This formidable structure appears to have been built in the first quarter of the fourteenth century,[2] but it has the full power and majesty of the Edwardian style. Elsewhere, the final shape of the inner enclosure at Alnwick (Northumberland), which appears to stand on a lowered motte, has taken the form of a cluster of towers, though much of the fabric is of modern date. Sandal (West Yorkshire), which is now dated to the middle of the thirteenth century, had two smaller round towers and a pair of others forming a gatehouse to flank its circle of walling, aided in this by an outer gate or barbican, between two round turrets, projecting far down the slope in front of the main gateway.[3] At Lewes two of a series of splendid polygonal towers of the thirteenth century survive, added to an older, very strong 'shell-keep'. At Carmarthen in 1275 it was reported[4] 'there is a certain castle in which there is a certain good "*dungio*" made out of five little towers'. Three at least of these small towers are still to be seen on the perimeter of a stout wall — one might well call it a 'shell-keep' — revetting the motte part of the way down. The superstructure has vanished; the whole was probably the work of William Marshal the younger, Earl of Pembroke, begun in 1223.[5] The small motte of Castell Coch (South Glamorgan) was completely altered by the building of three massive round towers down its slopes — two of them having the great square spurred base common in South Wales in the late thirteenth century — and the ranges of building joining them; but one segment of the perimeter was left recognisable as part of a motte, its defences being very curious. The slope of the earthwork, evidently somewhat steepened, is revetted to form a formidable talus; at the top is a stout wall with a row of arrowslits at inner ground level, from which the defenders would be able to sweep the face of the talus.

At Hereford and Builth (Brecknock) the descriptions suggest a central tower with a ring of smaller towers around it[6] — a combination of the single tower and the tower-cluster methods of defence. The tower of Hereford was built by Henry III *before* 1240;[7] Builth was one of Edward I's first great series of castles, begun in 1277. Unfortunately neither is standing today; at Builth masonry is gone, down to ground level, though excavation may yet recover the plan, or at least part of it; at Hereford the motte, with everything on it, has been destroyed.

The finest solution to the problem was that which was applied at Pontefract (West Yorkshire). Here an enormous round tower was built on the motte; apparently on the side of the bailey this was left as a simple cylinder, but towards the exterior its base is extended downwards in a mighty talus.

Rising out of this and flanking the outward face of the tower are three massive turrets — one could rather say towers. The base, which alone remains, shows late thirteenth-century detail, and the tower is likely to have been built by the great Earl of Lincoln, Henry de Lacy (1272–1311). It was considerably raised by John of Gaunt in 1374,[8] and its final appearance, of which we fortunately have a good picture,[9] was immensely imposing; 'the Dungeon cast ynto 6. Roundelles, 3. bigge and 3. smaul, is very fair,' Leland said of it.[10]

As money became available for the work, outer wards were frequently walled in this period, with defences commonly weaker and less systematic than those of the main ward, though the progress of military science, and sometimes the increasing resources of a family of owners, may give us the curious effect of outer defences that are stronger or better designed than those inside them. As in earthwork outer baileys, the purpose was either to accommodate under some kind of fortified cover the less essential parts of the owner's property, or simply to delay a besieger by denying him ground near the main defences. But there is one kind of outer defence which calls for particular notice, and in England it is largely confined in time to the period under discussion: this is the characteristic outer defence of a *concentric castle*.

The meaning of this expression requires a little consideration. A fully concentric castle is one with two complete envelopes, one inside the other; but in fact there is more to it than this. Castles like Kenilworth and Farnham, where the small inner ward stands in the middle of a large outer enclosure, are not truly concentric fortresses. The two lines of defence should be close together, with the inner overtopping and dominating the outer; generally the command of the inner parapets is sufficient to permit archers on them to shoot down to the counterscarp of the ditch over the heads of their comrades on the outer wall.[11] The two lines of wall were meant to be held together as a single line of defence; it is most unusual for there to be a ditch between them. Nor was the narrow outer ward generally used for any but a military purpose; no buildings stood in it, only towers and gates on its walls. In most concentric castles the double line was carried all round the perimeter, but at Rhuddlan (Flint, now part of Clwyd) the outer ward is greatly widened on one side to give access from the river by way of a water-gate. At Denbigh, Kidwelly (Carmarthenshire, now in Dyfed) and Goodrich (Hereford), the concentric defences are used on only part of the circuit, at Conway on the short ends of the site, and at Carew (Pembroke, now part of Dyfed) on one very exposed side only.

An enemy assailing a front of defence of this sort could have met with a great volume and diversity of aimed shooting,[12] as well as hand-thrown missiles from the embrasures of the outer line of walls. If he actually penetrated the outer defences, the troops meeting him there would have been helped by plunging fire from their comrades on the massive walls of the inner ward behind them. The outer ward's narrowness, in addition, gave the

Figure 10.1: Location of concentric defences (after C. J. Spurgeon)

defence every opportunity for sealing off a penetration by means of retrench-
ments — as we know was done at Carcassonne in the great siege of 1240 —
or of delivering a counterattack from either side, or from both sides at once.
Even if such an outer ward, at the foot of the main defences, had finally to be
abandoned, it would have afforded the poorest sort of lodgement for the
enemy — a long narrow corridor, every inch of it within stone-throwing
range of the inner battlements, and under the enfilade of the great towers on
the angles, a strip of killing-ground with much of the ultimately sinister

111

character of an artillery-fort's ditches. Some shelter might be found in the towers of the outer line, if there were any, but these were certainly not designed for the purpose of protection from the rear.

Multiple lines of defence of this sort represent a very ancient expedient, but in masonry construction they are not particularly common, though they are widely distributed, from Syria to Spain. Considerable use was made of concentric defences in the larger castles of the Crusader East; if we are looking for an ancestor for this type of defence, it is surely to be found in the magnificent Land Wall of Constantinople. Exceptionally, this wonderful defended front, erected in the fifth century AD, had three lines of wall: a simple breastwork and parapet on top of the vertical revetment of the scarp of the great ditch; behind it a moderately strong line of walls and towers; and, inside again, another such line, of enormous strength. Concentric defences of later date normally did without the outermost of the three lines. At Carcassonne, where there is now a very formidable outer envelope, there was clearly an outer line of some sort — the *lices* — at the time of the siege of 1240. At Dover Castle there was something similar from an earlier date; at the north end of the defences the two lines of walls and towers, very close together, with the great keep close behind again, form a most imposing triple front of defence. Part of the outer envelope was built as early as the reign of Henry II, and much of it was in existence when this part of the defences was assaulted in 1216.[13]

At our largest example of a perfect concentric castle, the Tower of London, the outer perimeter falls into two parts: the two southward sides of the great irregular hexagon, on the bank of the Thames, carry a series of towers and gates; but on the other four sides there are no original towers whatever — a surprising feature indeed. The two sides with towers, formerly believed to have been begun by Henry III,[14] are now known to be the work of Edward I, built like the rest of the outer envelope in 1275–85.[15] King Edward, indeed, was the great patron of the concentric style of defence, at the Tower, at Leeds in Kent,[16] and at four of the eight great castles built to secure his conquest of North Wales; but he was not the pioneer of this style in his kingdom. If we disregard Dover, our first concentric castle is the very important stronghold of Caerphilly (Mid-Glamorgan), begun in 1268, and again in 1271, after the Welsh had interrupted the building, by Gilbert II de Clare, the 'Red Earl' of Gloucester, and his unnamed master-mason. These were builders of surprising originality, innovators of the first order. The central citadel of Caerphilly is a small, compact, concentric castle, roughly square; its modest dimensions were reflected in King Edward's North Welsh castles. The inner line of defence is powerful — the curtains are of moderate height, but the angle-towers are tall and strong, and the two gatehouses very formidable; but it is the outer line that is remarkable. In most other concentric defences it is as if the triple fortifications of Constantinople had been reproduced with the low outermost line omitted; here at Caerphilly, if there

112

is in fact any question of a direct copying from the Byzantine land-wall, it was the second line of defence that was omitted. The outer envelope indeed was something more than just a breastwork, but it was a very low wall, with no towers except those at the gates, where there are two small pairs of round towers, originally open at the rear. Some degree of enfilade was obtained by extending the line of walls outwards in a salient curve to form flanking bastions on the corners. An outer defensive line of this modest sort would, of course, have been relatively easy to force, unless it was protected by formidable obstacles, such as the wide artificial lakes at Caerphilly certainly were; but any enemy who penetrated it would have been in a most hideous situation, utterly exposed to all the missiles of the defence — a fatal predicament, like that of a man on a raft under the broadside of a man-of-war.

King Edward and his masons were inclined to vacillate between the traditional form of concentric defence and the novel plan of Caerphilly type. At the Tower both styles are used, as we have seen; the two parts of the outer ward were separated by cross-walls with doors in them. Of Edward's Welsh concentric castles, Aberystwyth, begun in 1277, was of the conventional type; enough remains of its defences to show that the outer ward was strongly defended with fairly large round towers. The numerous small square turrets on the line of the outer ward at the contemporary Rhuddlan seem to represent a hesitation between the merits of the two systems; they permitted flanking of the outer line, but the earlier examples were small postern-gates, with only a narrow stair descending to the floor of the ditch; when this type was abandoned, the turrets were built as nothing more than solid buttresses at ground level, though they were evidently corbelled out above to make some kind of fighting platform.[17] Harlech, built after the final conquest of Gwynedd in 1283, represents a complete acceptance of the Caerphilly system. Its companions — Caernarvon and Conway — occupy long narrow sites, unsuitable for concentric defence — except that at the ends of the rocky ridge of Conway there are two small platforms, covering the entrances by land and water, and flanked only by little open turrets. This might suggest that the Caerphilly formula had triumphed; but Beaumaris, where the outer ward carries an imposing array of round towers, indicates a return to the older and more cautious approach before 1295, the year in which the castle was begun on a conspicuously level site. Harlech, indeed, represents the highest development of the concentric system in England: the masterly manner in which the great towers of the inner ward are used to enfilade different elements of the outer defence, and in particular to give cross-fire in front of the outer gate, has no equal elsewhere.

In subjects' castles after Caerphilly, the system was used with comparatively little skill; frequently the outer ward was added as something of an afterthought — as also occurred at the royal castle of Leeds in Kent. At Denbigh and Goodrich the outer wards form terraces at the foot of the main walls on the least approachable sides; at Goodrich the terrace was used from

Figure 10.2: The Welsh castles of Edward I

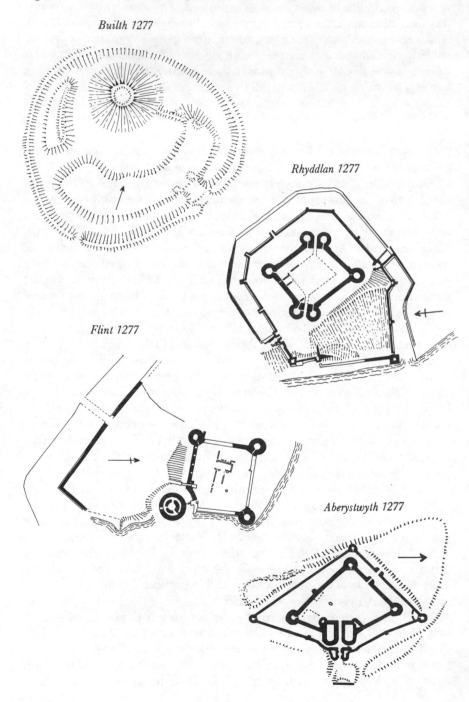

Builth 1277

Rhyddlan 1277

Flint 1277

Aberystwyth 1277

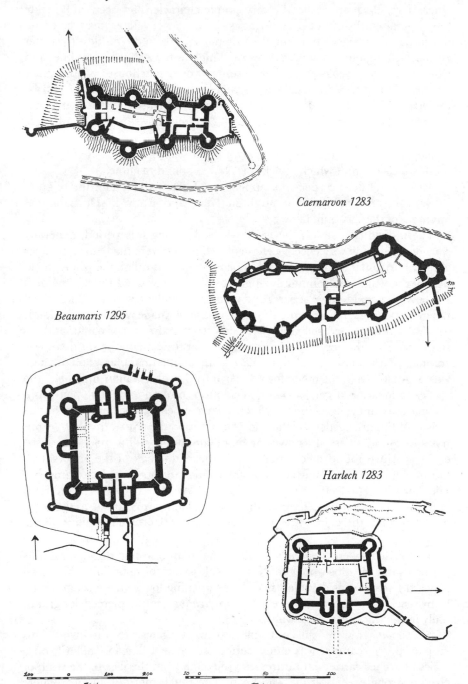

Conway 1283

Caernarvon 1283

Beaumaris 1295

Harlech 1283

the beginning for housing stables and other encumbrances. At Kidwelly, where a small square castle of a very simple character had been built inside the original earthwork (a partial ringwork), a new envelope was erected on the earthwork line, surrounding the original square on three sides; the outer curtains (though not their towers) were as high as those of the inner line; and when it is also revealed that there are no proper gatehouses on the inner defences, but a very imposing keep-gatehouse on the outer line, it will be understood that the defensive arrangements of Kidwelly are somewhat eccentric. Perhaps the most effective — certainly the simplest — of these minor concentric defences is at Carew Castle (Pembrokeshire, now part of Dyfed), where there is a simple, straight outer wall, with a small gatehouse, on the one side from which attack was almost bound to come.

This sort of defence does not appear much in England after the reign of Edward I; only at Queenborough in Kent and Raby in Durham was anything of the sort built later.

The individual parts of the castle evolved during this period, generally starting as already very effective elements. *Arrowslits* were made to allow for a greater horizontal traverse; instead of being pierced through the whole thickness of the wall, they commonly open out of a wide vaulted recess, in which the bowman could move at ease, and enjoy a far wider arc of fire. The actual tapered opening, ending in the slit itself, was often made with a *plunge*; that is to say, its floor sloped steeply downwards, so that the archer could land his shaft almost at the very foot of the wall; and at the base of the slit there was commonly a widening, called an *oillet* — most often circular, though there was a great variety of other forms. To improve observation and help the archer to look for targets, a *cross-arm* is found from an early date pierced in the masonry at eye-level in many loops. This appears to be largely a characteristic of English castles; by the end of our period the cross-arm often terminates in round oillets of its own, or more commonly still is made to consist entirely of two round oillets attached to the main shaft of the arrowslit. A fourth oillet was commonly added at the head of the opening, for symmetry's sake, for it was perfectly useless for shooting. We find arrowslits in the form of a cross, with round openings at the end of all four arms, as late as the reign of Henry VIII; there are some at St Mawes castle (Cornwall), built in about 1540–3.

The *curtains* were generally built straight and strong throughout this period; some of those built in North Wales were of enormous thickness. Edward I made considerable use of loops opening low in the curtain, either from recesses at courtyard level or from *fighting-galleries* pierced longitudinally in the thickness of the walls.

Machicolations were still unusual, except at gates. In the two forms employed, the parapet was either supported, as at Château-Gaillard, on a series of arches carried on buttresses projecting from the face of the wall, or else on strong corbels at the wall-head. The much more usual form where the parapet rested on corbels seems likely to be evolved from timber hoarding.

Apart from flying arches, springing from the inner flanks of the round towers of a typical gatehouse, so as to leave a wide chase for dropping missiles in front of the gates, there are very few English machicolations before the time of Edward I. His most ambitious work of this kind is represented by two complete rows of corbels (their parapets now fallen) along the tops of the short end curtains of the castle at Conway. At Beaumaris there are remains of machicolations over the outer gate and at the end of the spur-wall, called Gunner's Walk, which protected the dock.

As the perimeter defences of castles became more and more forbidding, so the necessity for strengthening the entrance became the more compelling, and gateways were designed to contain a formidable series of obstacles and forfeits to await an attacker. Space had to be found for machinery and fighting-positions, and it is not surprising to find that the *gatehouse* became a very big structure; its most common form was that in which the actual gate is flanked by two half-round towers, often elongated to the rear to enclose a prolonged entry-passage. This imposing structure had room for all the things which were needful at the gate of a fortress: porters' lodges, guardrooms with their prison accommodation, portcullis chambers over the gate, and positions from which an enemy attempting to force an entrance could be harassed from above or from the side. Such an assailant would be obliged to run the gauntlet of a whole series of defences, which might include any or all of the following: a drawbridge — perhaps more than one; arrowslits from the towers permitting a cross-fire on the approach; machicolations over the gate itself; portcullis; heavy gates with massive jambs, and holes for a powerful bar; murder-holes in the vault overhead,[18] and arrowslits in the walls of the passage. Portcullises and gates tended to multiply; from the first years of the thirteenth century, any gateway intended for serious defence was equipped with a portcullis, and by the end of the century any strong gate would probably have two of them.

Of these twin-tower gatehouses, perhaps the smallest and simplest example is the little gate — hardly more than a doorway, flanked by two little solid turrets — of the inner ward at Longtown (Herefordshire). This seems likely to be early in date, though it has a pointed archway and grooves for a portcullis. For datable examples, the earliest would appear to have been the long-since blocked north gate of the outer ward at Dover, attacked by the French in 1216. There were two gate-towers, of which they brought down one.[19] Among subjects' castles, by the 1220s the gatehouse of the small, powerful inner ward of Beeston (Cheshire) was formed by two big half-round towers flanking a strongly defended passage, the whole carrying a large upper room extending the whole width of the gatehouse. Well before the middle of the century — its arrowslits are of a primitive form — the great gate of Pembroke Castle could serve as an example of a powerful gatehouse: a massive rectangular block of building, three storeys high, with the entrance-passage pierced through it at ground level, flanked by lodges and with a portcullis chamber overhead. There were two portcullises, as well as numerous accessory defences. As the approach to the gateway is from a flank, the semicircular tower-face on this side was dispensed with, but in place of it, a large round tower — the Town Tower or Barbican Tower — which stands on an angle of the castle-walls a short distance away from the gate, is joined to the body of the gatehouse on all levels above the ground floor, so as to be essentially part of the defences of the entry.

An unexplained feature of this great gate is a curious projecting defence, a sort of balcony, looped and battlemented, carried on an arch supported by the stair-turrets which flank the inner end of the gateway-passage. This enigmatic structure suggests an attempt to protect the gate from attack from the rear; but there are no doors or portcullis at the inner end of the passage. The latter sort of defence is found at some castles; a fairly early example is at White Castle,[20] where there are jambs for a pair of gates at the rear of the gatehouse of the *outer* ward, closing against the interior of the castle — an arrangement which seems strange at first, but is clearly intended as a precaution against a casual penetration of the prolonged loop of the outer defences by a few men, getting in by surprise or treachery and attempting to open the gates to their friends before they were hunted down or shot. If the lodge-doors were inside the gateway-passage, such desperate foes would be unable to carry the gatehouse without breaking in these rear gates — which would probably have been beyond them in the time available.

From this it was a short step to turning one of the larger gatehouses into a self-contained strong point, with portcullis and gates at front and rear, lodge-doors inside the passage, and any other entrances to the building — from the wall-walk or elsewhere — strongly defended. The massive bulk of a three-storey gatehouse with two large, round-fronted towers flanking the passage naturally afforded a large amount of space for accommodation, and such a building begins to have a good deal of the air of a keep, particularly if there is no conventional keep in the castle. Though a number of our earlier writers realised this fact, it was the eminent Scottish antiquary, the late Dr W. Douglas Simpson, who gave to this sort of structure the name of *keep-gatehouse*. The first known gate of this sort is the East or Great Gate of the inner ward of Caerphilly, and to judge from the general character of that castle — whose design shows amazing inventiveness — it seems likely that the type first appeared there. The Great Gate, though much damaged, and subsequently rebuilt, still shows grooves for a heavy portcullis and jambs for a pair of doors at each end of its gatehouse-passage; on the second floor a single huge room — a hall — extends right across the whole width of the building; the doors on to the wall-walk on either side were each defended by a small portcullis. Nothing could represent a more unequivocal assertion that the gatehouse was also intended as a keep. (The other gate, at the far end of the small ward, was perfectly conventional, though very strong.)

At Tonbridge (Kent), another Clare castle, there is a fine gatehouse which is almost a duplicate of the Caerphilly gate; here even the doors of the lodges, opening into the gateway passage, had portcullises. There is another, much damaged, at Llangynwyd (Mid Glamorgan).

This gate was obviously made by the same master-mason who built Caerphilly, but another close copy, at the de Camville castle of Llanstephan, is not likely to have been. Here there were portcullises at front and rear of the gatehouse passage, but the absence of any access from the vaulted basement to the upper floors[21] would have left the defenders in a curious situation when both ends of the passage were closed; it would appear that the princi ple of the keep-gatehouse was not fully understood here.

The Caerphilly type of gate was copied in several of Edward I's North Welsh castles — copied closely enough to incorporate the large projecting round stair-turrets which are a feature of Caerphilly[22] though scarcely a necessary element of a gatehouse.

Aberystwyth, begun in 1277, has the remains of such a gatehouse, and there is another at Harlech, which dates from after the conquest of Gwynedd in 1283, and two at Beaumaris, begun in 1295 — a unique arrangement. It is, however, true that the inner ends of the gates of Beaumaris were never completed, and perhaps it is more significant that the grooves for the inner portcullis at Harlech are blocked at first-floor level, so that the inner end of the entrance-passage would have been protected only by a pair of gates and a small 'murder-hole'. It may be that Edward's great master-mason, James of St George, was not over-enthusiastic about this English speciality; Aberystwyth was laid out by Master Henry of Hereford, and at Harlech Master James may have been constrained by his royal master to build — as he certainly did build — something very like a copy of Caerphilly. Incidentally, both here and at Beaumaris there were to have been three portcullises in each gate when finished — the extra one being towards the front of the gate. Another huge gatehouse, intended to have been equipped on the same scale, but never finished, is at the castle of Llangibby (Monmouthshire, now Gwent), but probably the only keep-gatehouse in which three portcullises defending the entry were ever actually hung is the fine example at St Briavel's (Gloucestershire), the king's castle of the Forest of Dean. This probably dates from 1292–3; the doors of lodges and stairs, opening out of the passage, were each equipped with portcullises of their own. There are two smaller keep-gatehouses, with their flanking towers semi-octagonal instead of half-round, at Llanblethian (South Glamorgan) and Carreg Cennen (Carmarthenshire, now part of Dyfed). The former is at a Clare castle, said to have been 'recently begun' in 1314;[23] Carreg Cennen, though latterly a royal castle, is not adequately documented, but its detail is so closely similar to that of Llanblethian that it is almost certainly of much the same date.

Even in these small examples, the keep-gatehouse was an impressive structure, but it could be developed even further. The main gate of Denbigh

Castle is now sadly ruined, but its plan is plain enough; behind the two great polygonal towers which flank the gate there is a third, obstructing the entrance-passage, which takes a half-turn to the right to get past it. There were portcullises in both parts of the passage, and an octagonal gate-hall at the angle between them was originally vaulted; most of its detail has gone, but it has very much the air of a death-trap or 'killing-ground'. Something similar, but probably even more complicated, was planned at the King's Gate of Caernarvon, but never completed; only the outer gateway, of formidable strength, and some beginnings of an inner passage were built.

The keep-gatehouse did not have a long vogue; with its large openings to front and rear, it may be doubted if such a structure was really robust enough for a prolonged defence, independent of the remainder of the castle. As for its very numerous defensive arrangements, particularly the winches for its portcullises, they must have interfered with its use as a dwelling-house. Though a brilliant conception, this class of building was plainly not to everyone's mind.

One of the last true keep-gatehouses was the very fine example at Kidwelly ascribed to the early fourteenth century, and much rebuilt in the early fifteenth. The enormous gate of Dunstanburgh (Northumberland) was built in 1313–25, but it has been so much altered, and so badly damaged, that it is difficult now to say whether it was a keep-gatehouse or not.

Some gates with rear defences are found at a much later period, at such places as Bodiam (East Sussex), Tynemouth (Northumberland) and Hever (Kent), but none of these could function as a keep-gatehouse in the true sense.

Less ambitious forms of entrance are found beside the powerful twin-tower gatehouses of which much has been said here; the very occasional plain opening in a curtain (perhaps slightly thickened to form a platform from which the portcullis could be worked) was really only fit for posterns, but it is found in the surprisingly slight main gate of Kidwelly and in the original forms of the gates of Carew and Manorbier (both in Pembrokeshire, now part of Dyfed). The older type of gate in which the entry passes through the basement of a single rectangular tower is found occasionally, as in the later form of Manorbier, and probably that of Carew; as already mentioned, an archaic example of this class was built at Trematon (Cornwall). At Aberystwyth (Cardigan, now Dyfed) a minor gate is pierced axially through a solid-base half-round tower.

A stranger class of gate is the type where the entrance opens in the *flank* of a round or half-round tower. This type is not common; its oriental origins, and the attribution of most of its examples to the great William Marshal I, Earl of Pembroke, have already been discussed.[24] Outside Pembroke territory the flank gate did not appeal to English builders, and seems to be rare in Europe as a whole. Its principal advantage — the double turn or flank approach which it enforced on an enemy attacking the entrance — was more generally obtained by the use of an oblique barbican in front of the main gate.

Barbicans, indeed, were extensively used in this period; the word is a vague one, meaning little more than some kind of outer protection to a gate. Indeed, though many of them have perished — being commonly lightly built, possessing no domestic uses, and being very handily placed for the purposes of stone-robbers — enough remains to show that they partook of an enormous diversity of forms. They could function to double the main gate with an outer obstacle, to guard against surprise, to narrow the approach, to force assailants to change direction during an attack, or to draw them under fire from the main works of the castle — all these or any combination of them. They could also be used as forming-up areas for a sortie, and this would seem to have been a principal element in the employment of some of those which contained a substantial area, in particular a group of large semicircular barbicans, built with their backs against the main defences or on the counterscarp of the ditch.

Most barbicans were on a less ambitious scale; they could take the form of small outer gates, of detached towers or platforms to defend the far end of the bridge, or parallel walls to protect the drawbridge. Not until the fourteenth century do we find anything in the nature of a 'standard' form of barbican.

Towers were of the essence of the system of defence. Generally speaking, they were large, round (at least on their outer faces) and hollow, containing living quarters on their upper stages. Even when they are merely half-round or D-shaped in plan the rear is generally closed with a stout stone wall; only on town walls and a few outer defences do we get the open-backed towers which were probably meant for timber and wattle-and-daub rear walls.

As to their size, they reach a maximum with such enormous examples as the towers of Caernarvon, of which the largest, the Eagle Tower, is some 70 feet (21 m) in diameter — a normal large tower would be about half that amount in diameter. In general, the towers of the Edwardian conquest are the largest in the country; as this applies not only to the king's own foundations, but to baronial castles such as Denbigh and Chirk (Denbighshire, now part of Clwyd), it will readily be understood that the Edwardian period is the zenith of the English Middle Ages in the matter of the size of towers. Nevertheless, even as early as the 1220s, towers were built at such castles as Chartley (Staffordshire) and Whittington (Shropshire) with diameters of 40 feet (12 m) and over.

A strictly circular trace for the salient part of the tower was almost invariably used, but at the end of the period polygonal plans became fairly common, particularly octagons and semi-octagons. (There are a few earlier examples of this sort, such as the gate-towers of Carrickfergus and Grey Mare's Tail towers of Warkworth (Northumberland) which are ascribed to a date early in the thirteenth century.) Square or rectangular towers are few, and generally serve some very minor role, like the handsome little tower of the Spur at Manorbier, which contains latrines. It is thus a surprise to find a whole series of square towers, some fairly large, on the outer line of defence at Rhuddlan, begun in 1277 — but only on the outer line, and only at Rhuddlan. During the fourteenth and fifteenth centuries rectangular mural towers were to recover much of their former popularity, especially in the north, but in the classical fortification of Edward I's age they found little favour.

Certain complexities of plan appear, particularly at the end of the thirteenth century and at the beginning of the fourteenth, and especially in South Wales; round towers are found standing on square or rectangular bases — as at Cardigan (an early example begun c. 1240), Goodrich (Herefordshire), Carew and Newport (Pembroke, now in Dyfed), Castell Coch (South Glamorgan) and the Constable's Gate with its supporting towers at Dover; the finest single example is Marten's Tower at Chepstow. At the same time we find round towers on polygonal — normally semi-octagonal — bases at the great gate of St Briavel's (Gloucestershire) and the Pembroke-shire castle of Picton; also octagonal or semi-octagonal towers on rectangular bases, in a number of cases: on the defences of the dam at Caerphilly, at the gatehouse at Carreg Cennen (Carmarthenshire, now part of Dyfed) and at one or two smaller gates, like those at the bishop's castle at Llandaff and the priory of Ewenny, both in Mid-Glamorgan. The alteration in shape is normally brought about by means of triangular spur-buttresses on the angles, dying away at the top into the cylindrical or prismatic body of the tower. Towers of this sort were built well on into the fourteenth century, as at Newport and Caldicot (Monmouthshire, now Gwent), the gatehouse of Llawhaden (Pembrokeshire, now part of Dyfed), and probably the Water Tower at Kenilworth (Warwickshire).

Inevitably less important in scale, small towers and turrets are found from the period of the Edwardian programme onwards, carried in whole or in part on corbels; early examples are the northern turret of Manorbier (Pembro-keshire, now part of Dyfed) and the one complete outer gate of Beaumaris. Generally, these corbels are not used to enclose machicolations.

As at any other period, a few solid towers are found; generally these are very small.[25] The normal mural tower has three storeys — one rising above the curtains. The inner rooms generally form a figure very close in plan to that of the tower itself. Vaulting is unusual, except sometimes for the basement, though at Manorbier one tower has a vault at roof level [26] and another over the first floor; the half-round tower at Lincoln, called Cobb Hall, has a complicated vault, but most are very simple. Most towers were large enough for their chambers to make comfortable living quarters, equipped with fireplaces and latrines in the thickness of the wall; a fully developed tower has commonly a set of latrines, one above the other, at one inner corner, and a newel-stair at the other; frequently these form turrets annexed to the main tower, and the stair rises above the roof to form a watch-

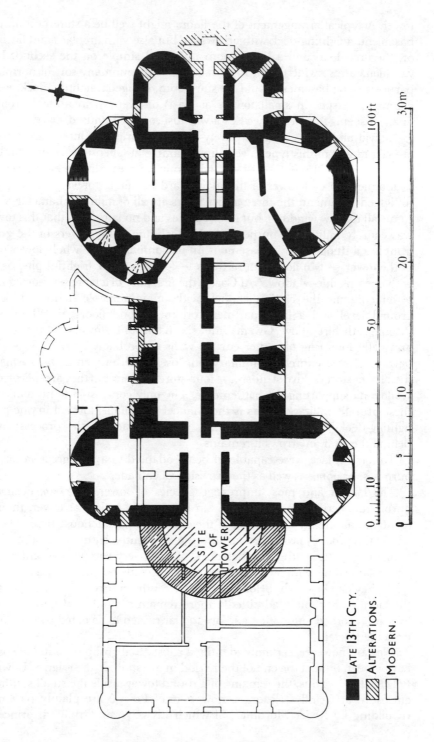

Figure 10.3: Picton Castle

LATE 13TH CTY.

ALTERATIONS.

MODERN.

SITE OF TOWER

100ft

3,0m

tower. A typical arrangement of the floors might well be a storeroom in the basement, a fighting-deck with arrowslits, but also with fireplace and latrine, on the first floor, and a living-room pure and simple on the second. But variations are so wide that it is misleading to mention any sort of norm; in particular, the basement could be storeroom, dungeon, fighting-deck, well-chamber, cesspit (in small towers at least) or even an inhabitable room; finally it seems that in many cases it was just so much unused space.

Individual towers can be of purely military character. Outer-ward towers are commonly of this type; a very fine example at Chepstow[27] had a timber rear-wall, but is three storeys high, with four big arrowslits on each level. At Manorbier the east tower of the main ward has four storeys, including an unlighted basement; the three upper floors are all of military character, with some tall narrow windows, but no fireplaces and no latrine, so that this tower was entirely military in purpose. At Harlech one of the towers of the great front has a dungeon in its basement; in its companion the whole lower part of the tower — two floors out of three — forms a single frightful pit-prison, with one tiny flue-window.[28] At Carew the first floor of a large semi-octagonal tower contains the castle's chapel, with an inhabitable fighting-deck at ground level and a fine apartment on the second floor. At Whitecastle (Monmouthshire, now Gwent) the six half-round towers added to an unusually lofty ring of earlier curtain-walls — probably in 1267–77 — are devoted almost entirely to military purposes, with numerous arrowslits in their lower storeys. Five of the six are four-storey towers, but they are mere stone scaffolding supporting the battlements. The only concession to humanity in these brutally military towers is the chancel of a chapel formed in one pure fighting-deck, which was not in any way disarmed in the process; even behind the altar an arrowslit remains.

Towers, in fact, were capable of being adapted to a very great variety of purposes, or none, as well as the provision of enfilade.

The largest and most impressive species of tower, the *keep*, occurred during this period most commonly in the form of a circular tower, though mention has already been made of the experimental gatehouse type of keep, and of the process, prolonged far into the thirteenth century and beyond, of equipping mottes with stone defences, often of very complicated character. At the same time, with a very few exceptions already noted,[29] round keeps, so far as they can be dated, belong to the thirteenth century — in a few cases to the fourteenth; though admittedly there remain a number of towers which have no recorded foundation and are too far ruined to be dated convincingly from their detail.

We can, however, certainly identify a substantial group of round keeps as having been built at the end of the period in question, in the reign of Edward I (1272–1307). Thus, the remains of a round tower inside the small southern enclosure at Cefnllys (Radnor, now part of Powys) are plainly part of a rebuilding by Roger Mortimer, of which Llywelyn ap Gruffydd, prince of

Wales, was complaining in 1273–4.[30] The reconstruction of the castle of Cambridge, whose weakness had been painfully exposed by the Montfortian rebels from the Isle of Ely in 1267, was undertaken between 1284 and 1299, and included a big round tower upon the motte. Of Edward's Welsh castles, Builth had a great tower, now vanished, on its motte, and Flint has an enormous unfinished round tower, with its own ditch, at one corner of the main ward; both of these were begun in 1277. Of baronial castles, the keep of Hawarden (Flintshire, now part of Clwyd) is dated to this period by its opulent architectural detail, and the big round tower of Llandovery (Carmarthen, now in Dyfed) was probably a keep, and almost certainly belongs to the same reign. Morlais (Glamorgan) is clearly the castle involved in the quarrel between the Earls of Hereford and Gloucester in 1290. It has the remains of two very large round towers; of these the one at the upper end of the site has a magnificent vaulted basement; Clark's plan of 1859 shows that it was entered by some species of forebuilding or barbican, with grooves for a portcullis, and was thus plainly a keep.

Other plans of keep are found besides the plain round form. Clifford's Tower at York, built on the huge motte of this very important castle between the surprisingly late dates of 1246 and 1272, is a quatrefoil in plan, with a rectangular porch for the entry. The singular tower called the Lord's Tower at Llangibby (Monmouthshire, now Gwent) consisted of a great circular projection, having a rectangular latrine-turret, the whole joined asymmetrically to one end of a large rectangular building with round turrets at the far corners. Apsidal keeps are of Welsh rather than English origin, but there is one at Roch (Pembrokeshire, now part of Dyfed) whose proprietors were English.

Of other forms, there is a small number of rectangular towers, like Penhow and Dinham in Monmouthshire, now Gwent. Simple rectangular keeps are more common in Welsh castles: both castles at Dolwyddelan (Caernarvonshire, now part of Gwynedd), of which the later and larger is plainly thirteenth century in date; Dinas Brân (Denbigh, now in Clwyd), Castell Mor Graig (Glamorgan), Castell-y-Bere (Merioneth, now part of Gwynedd) and Powis (Montgomery, now in the county of Powys). Welsh also, and only represented by their foundations, are two very powerful towers at Llanhilleth — a very large round tower with a central pillar, and a square tower with square turrets projecting from the middle of its faces — the same extraordinary plan as Trim (Co. Meath, Southern Ireland), Warkworth (Northumberland) and Castle Rushen in the Isle of Man. Probably neither of the Llanhilleth towers was ever completed. The belated Norman-type keeps have already been mentioned.[31]

The thirteenth century was a time of considerable intellectual activity; it also had its share of warlike occasions, and it is hardly surprising to find at least two important weapons appearing in the course of it, for in its earliest years the great trebuchet made its entry, and during the later years, under the patronage of Edward I, the longbow came into prominence. Both of these weapons call for discussion, as does their effect on the design of castles (though this, it will appear, was not particularly important).

The use of stone-throwing engines in sieges dates back into remote antiquity; two sorts survived into the early Middle Ages: the mangonel and the petraria (*perrière*).

Of these, the name mangonel (a word which means no more than 'an engine') is normally attached to a type of stone-thrower evolved under the later Roman Empire; here the arm which casts its stone ball, either from a spoon-shaped end or from a short sling, was powered by a massive rope spring, stretched horizontally across a powerful groundframe. The petraria (which means simply a 'stone-thrower' and can sometimes appear as a mere generic for all these classes of engines) seems to be of Oriental origin; the name 'Turkish *perrière*' appears. Here the principle was quite different, with an enormous pole-sling pivoted overhead on a lofty trestle. The longer end of the light and springy pole carried a small sling; at the other end were a number of attachments for ropes to be pulled on by the members of the detachment, after the fashion of bellringers. Both of these engines were fairly formidable, but each had certain defects: on the mangonel the enormous tension of the rope spring put severe strains on the frame and the throwing-arm, and repairs are likely to have been frequent; the perrière would only work with a very large crew.

It was from the perrière, however, that the trebuchet seems to have evolved; it was, in fact, a very large perrière with a disproportionately long sling and the 'bellringers' replaced by a massive counterpoise, a chest full of stones, or preferably lead, pivoting on the butt end of the throwing arm. A windlass was needed, as in the mangonel, to haul the latter down, and the rate of fire was inevitably slow, but the engine was immensely powerful and evidently very reliable (there was virtually nothing to go wrong with so simple a machine). Like any very heavy engine, it posed difficulties as regards transport; but as the wooden structure would come to pieces, it was the massive projectiles which would give the most trouble. Stores of these are to be found in a number of castles — spherical stones of the most careful manufacture, from 17 to 20 inches (42 to 50 cm) in diameter. The movement of any large number of these would be troublesome.

The trebuchet makes its appearance at much the same time as scientific fortification, but it is difficult to find any link between the two processes. One has been suggested, by Braun in 1936.[32] According to this argument, the loftier 'new' curtains of the period were built to keep out the projectiles of this novel weapon. In fact, some early curtains were quite adequate in height by later standards; it is the use of enfilade from the projecting towers which characterises the new defence. The consideration of dates and such figures as are available is also fatal to Braun's hypothesis. Thus, apart from a rather dubious mention in the 1190s, we first hear of a trebuchet at the siege of

Castelnaudary in 1211, and for the rest of the decade it is remarked every-where as a novelty. In the meantime, the 'new' walls and towers had been going up at Windsor and Dover since the 1160s. Nor is the idea of protection against the new weapon very convincing when one realises that of the older engines the mangonel at least had an extremely high trajectory, while the great power of the trebuchet enabled it to send its projectiles far higher than any castle-wall could ever be built.[33]

The longbow represents a method of coping with armour, against which the common short hunting-bow was useless. It was not enough to use a stronger bow; the means had to be found to draw it. Human muscle had either to be assisted mechanically, in which case the result was a crossbow,[34] or developed by technique and continual practice to give a greatly increased performance in action. This is the recipe for the longbow. Its origins are familiar; at the end of the twelfth century Giraldus Cambrensis describes certain archers whose shooting was immensely powerful. His actual anecdotes deserve nothing but contempt; 'drawing the longbow' was for centuries a synonym for economy with the truth, and Giraldus himself was a considerable liar; but as the father of British topography he has a far more honourable title, and there is no doubt that these famous bowmen came from Gwent in the southern Welsh March. The longbow appealed to Edward I and his commanders, and its use spread far outside its homeland. Notoriously it was a better battlefield weapon than the crossbow, but by the same token it was inferior as a sharpshooter's weapon, and the crossbow retained its primacy in sieges throughout. The only feature of fortification which could reflect the use of longbows in defence is the large proportion of long arrowslits, opening out of lofty recesses, which could be used for the tall weapon; at the same time, these were very convenient for crossbow shooting as well.

The longbow could be useful in defence when a number of besiegers showed themselves in the open, rushing a gate or preparing an escalade with ladders; here a mere handful of archers could bring a fearsome shower of great war-arrows about their ears. But its greatest usefulness appeared when the garrison marched out from behind their walls, either to deliver a formal sortie, to take the field as part of the army, or simply to assert the castle's mastery over its territory by eliminating hostile positions there or hunting down foragers and freebooters; then it would be, as always, a powerful field weapon and an essential support to the heavy-armed.

Notes

1. Professor Leslie Alcock and others, 'Excavations at Castell Bryn Amlwg', *Montgomeryshire Collections*, lx (1967-8), pp. 8-27.

2. Built by Robert de Clifford, lord of Skipton, 1310-14, and a member of the

same family who built Clifford Castle. The authority is his descendent, the Lady Anne Clifford; see Williamson, *Lady Anne Clifford* (Kendal, 1922, reprinted 1967), p. 415.

3. See *Medieval Archaeology*, xiv (1970), pp. 177-8. The main part of the structure is here dated c. 1230, the inner gate c. 1230, and the outer c. 1280. Hitherto the whole had been dated 1328 and later.

4. (Public Record Office) Chancery Inquisitions Miscellaneous, file 33, no. 31; quoted *History of the King's Works*, ii, p. 601; and *History of Carmarthenshire* (ed. Sir John E. Lloyd), i, p. 276.

5. *Brut y Tywysogyon (anno 1223)*, Red Book of Hergest version (ed. Thomas Jones, Cardiff, University of Wales Press, 1955), p. 225; *Annales Cambriae* (Rolls Series, 21), p. 75; *Roluli Litterarum Clausarum*, ii, pp. 46, 556, 134a, 140a. The earl spent over £800 on the royal castles of Carmarthen and Cardigan; but the rapidity with which the latter fell into the hands of the Welsh in 1231 (see both *Brut* and *Annales Cambriae*) and the heavy expenditure on the part of the Crown after its recovery in 1240 (see *History of the King's Works*, ii, p. 590) suggests that the bulk of this money was spent at Carmarthen.

6. For Hereford, see Leland (ed. Smith) ii, pp. 64-5, 'having in the utter Wall or Warde 10 Towers *forma semicirculari*, and one great Tower in the inner Ward'. For Builth, see *History of the King's Works*, i, p. 296, citing Public Record Office, E372/124, which lists the great tower, immediately followed by 'a stone wall with six lesser towers (*turriculis*) surrounding the castle' (*sic*, but the defences of both inner and outer baileys are separately mentioned). It is clear that in neither of these cases is the evidence for a ring of turrets round the great tower altogether convincing.

7. *History of King's Works*, ii, p. 674.

8. *John of Gaunt's Register* (Camden Socy., 3rd ser., xxi (1911), pp. 242-3).

9. A Flemish picture, previously attributed to Josse (Joos) de Mompers, the property of H.M. the Queen; see *History of King's Works*, ii, plate 51. The identification of the castle in this picture with Pontefract was the work of a Mr Ellis, Thoroton Socy., xxiv (1915-18 Miscellanea), pp. 1-5.

10. John Leland, *The itinerary of John Leland the antiquary in or about the years 1535-45* (ed. Lucy Toulmin Smith), i, p. 39. The small roundels were the corbelled turrets shown in the picture, the big ones the large turrets whose base survives. This description makes nonsense of the plan in Toy, *The castles of Great Britain* (London, 1953), p. 124, which in other respects is grossly inaccurate.

11. Something of the kind seems to have been provided for in one or two much earlier cases where the great tower stands close behind the main line of defence, as at Rochester (Kent) and Pembroke.

12. See particularly A.J. Taylor, in *Medieval England* (ed. Poole, Oxford, 1958), fig. 38.

13. *History of the King's Works*, ii, p. 633.

14. Royal Commission on Historical Monuments (England), *Inventory of the historical monuments in London*, v, especially the plan at the end.

15. *History of the King's Works*, ii, pp. 715-22.

16. *Ibid.*, ii, pp. 695-7.

17. The landward defences of this ward have clearly been begun at the gate on the north-west, and carried clockwise round the perimeter. On the first two curtains there is a series of loops which cannot now be used, and is discontinued thereafter. The four postern-gates are found on the same part of the defences, and on a small piece of the perimeter beyond this; the buttresses on the rest of the angles are again of two sizes, each found only on a single part of the defences.

18. These inner machicolations are sometimes mistakenly called *meurtrières* by our older antiquaries; but the French word means 'arrow-slits'. The name 'murder-holes' is Irish in origin, and probably correctly used in that country.

19. *Histoire des ducs de Normandie et des rois d'Angleterre* (ed. F. Michel, Paris, 1840).

20. Built 1267–76, probably towards the end of this period.

21. Both of these form a single great room.

22. At Caerphilly itself they contained long arrowslits for enfilading the rear of the gatehouse. Those at other castles were not generally equipped in this way. Pembroke seems to have been the original site of these stair-turrets.

23. See the Extent of Llanblethian, printed in *Archaeologia Cambrensis*, 5th series, vi (1889), p. 70, also pp. 73-4.

24. *Supra*, pp. 83-4.

25. For the occurrence of solid round towers, see *supra*, note 20 to Chapter 9.

26. This is a domed vault, obviously modelled on that of the great tower of Pembroke.

27. The south-west tower of the castle, on the westernmost ward.

28. Presumably this dreadful apartment was provided for breaking the spirits of the recalcitrant patriots of Meirionydd. For ordinary prisoners — in this royal castle, they would be mostly men accused of felony, who would have to be got out for their trials and probably again for execution — such a deep dungeon was hopelessly inconvenient; besides, there was already plenty of prison accommodation in the other dungeon and in the great guardrooms under the gatehouse.

29. New Buckenham, Conisborough, probably Pembroke and Longtown.

30. J. Goronwy Edwards, *Calendar of ancient correspondence concerning Wales* (Cardiff, 1935), p. 94. The prince was complaining of a 'new work' at this castle as a breach of the Treaty of Montgomery, 1267.

31. *Supra*, p. 73.

32. Hugh Braun, *The English castle*, (London, 1936), pp. 65-9.

33. An experiment with a model — not in fact fully charged in the counterpoise — involved the repeated clearing of an obstacle which stood 250 feet (75 m) high to scale.

34. The more primitive crossbows were cocked by the use of their archer's legs.

11

The Castles of the Welsh

The rulers of the Welsh princedoms, too, had their castles, but, in defence against a powerful enemy such as the king, they relied very largely on the difficulty — and, it must be admitted, the poverty — of their country. It is not surprising that castles should have played a very secondary part in their defensive strategy, and particularly in that of the lords of Gwynedd (Snowdonia); yet we find Dolforwyn standing siege by the royal forces in 1277,[1] and Dolwyddelan and Castell-y-Bere in 1283,[2] and we may be sure that it was against the king that native Welsh castles were of the least use. Welsh princes, however, had many less terrible potential enemies, English and perhaps more particularly Welsh, who could be held off by well-sited strongholds. Thus we find the motte-castle, alien institution though it certainly was, readily accepted by the native rulers; as early as 1111 Cadwgan ap Bleddyn was reconnoitring a site for one near Welshpool when he was assassinated.[3] In 1116 we hear of one at Cymmer in Merioneth, which is still to be seen, built by Uchtryd ap Edwin.[4]

By the end of the century, Giraldus Cambrensis notes two stone castles in North Wales, at Deudraeth and Carn Madryn,[5] and from this time till the end of Welsh independence we find a substantial number of stone castles built by the native rulers.

Thus, in the valleys of Snowdonia there are three small stone castles: Dinas Emrys, Dolbadarn and Dolwyddelan; the last stands close to an older site, itself stone-walled. To the north-east, Degannwy, though largely of English construction, was commonly in the hands of the princes of Gwynedd, who also held, southwards, the large castles of Criccieth on the coast and Castell-y-Bere, under Cader Idris — probably the largest and certainly the most princely of all. Further inland is the extraordinary structure at Cwm Prysor; while Carndochan, at the head of Lake Bala, must be a Gwynedd castle, possibly never finished. Finally should be mentioned the set of castles which Llywelyn ap Gruffydd — Llywelyn the Last — built to defend the limits of his conquests: Ewloe (Flint), almost in sight of Chester, and built in about 1257;[6] Dolforwyn, in the Severn Valley, facing Montgomery,

Figure 11.1: Dolwyddelan Castle

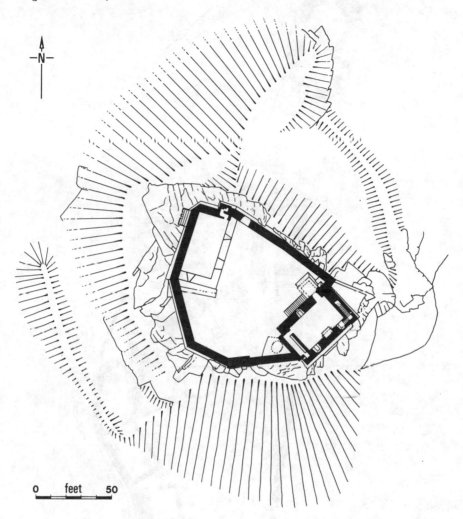

which was being built in 1273 to the considerable consternation of Edward I's council of regency;[7] finally a castle in the lordship of Brecon, destroyed by the Lord Edward and the royalists in 1265, which is to be identified as Sennybridge (Brecknock).[8] Powys Fadog had its big and opulent castle at Dinas Brân; Powys Wenwynwyn had Powis Castle near Welshpool (though much, if not all, of the present structure is certainly Anglo-Welsh construction of Edwardian date or later). The princes of Deheubarth built stone castles at Dynevor, Dryslwyn, Carreg Cennen and Newcastle Emlyn (all in Carmarthenshire and so now in Dyfed)[9] and were probably responsible for the fragmentary stonework at Nevern (Pembroke) and Ystrad Meurig

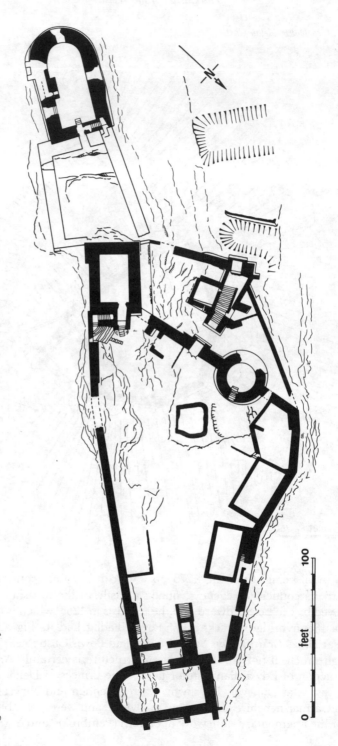

Figure 11.2: Castell-y-Bere

feet

0   100

Figure 11.3: Ewloe Castle

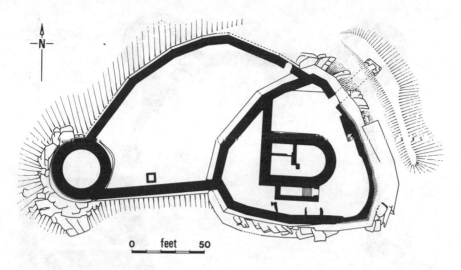

0   feet   50

(Cardigan, now in Dyfed). Even the petty Welsh lords of the south-east, overshadowed by the English power, began masonry castles at Castell Mor Graig and Baglan (Glamorgan) and Machen and Llanhilleth (Monmouthshire, now Gwent). Of these, only Machen has any history; only it and Baglan seem ever to have been finished. Castell Mor Graig stands on the very edge of Senghenydd, which was a cantref in the hill-country of Glamorgan, subordinated to the lords of Cardiff. Its features suggest a fairly advanced date in the thirteenth century; it has no signs of occupation, and its ditch — a very conspicuous feature of a Welsh castle, as a rule — is totally lacking on the most important (uphill) side. It is likely to have been built by the last native ruler of Senghenydd, Gruffydd ap Rhys, who was seized by his overlord, Gilbert the Red, Earl of Gloucester, in 1267, and consigned to prison in Ireland.[10] This is the sort of sudden disaster which would explain why a rather large and ambitious castle, of features which are not in any way English,[11] could have suddenly been abandoned. Sudden — and in this case repeated — abandonment may also explain the two very large towers whose foundations remain close to the motte of Llanhilleth. One set of foundations are those of a huge round tower with a round central pier to carry its floors; the other are those of a 'cruciform' tower, with a square body and square turrets in the middle of each of its faces. It would seem likely that these beginnings were the work of the later Welsh rulers of Gwynllwg, a little princedom known to have been destroyed in detail by its Marcher neighbours,[12] who drove its lords successively from Caerleon and from Machen; the end of the sad story is apparently unknown. The rulers of Afan, at the west end of the lordship of Glamorgan, were very Anglophile members of a Welsh dynasty, and evidently

Figure 11.4: Mor Graig Castle

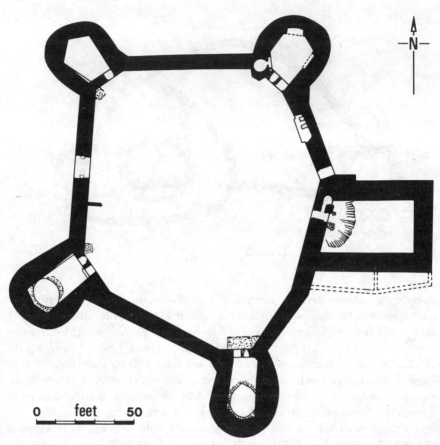

0 feet 50

built a strong square masonry structure of uncertain character at Baglan.

Between Edward I's victory in 1277 and his own rather criminal outbreak in 1282, Dafydd ap Gruffydd began a castle at Caergwrle or Hope (Flintshire, now Clwyd). Like its master, it was part-Welsh, part-English in character; it was never finished, but there were the beginnings of a huge round keep.[13]

While the Welsh stone castles are not a really homogeneous group, they have a great deal in common. It is not altogether difficult to identify an example from its plan and detail. There is no single distinguishing feature of a Welsh castle, but there are a number of usual characteristics to be noted. Thus, Welsh castles generally stand on rocky sites which dictate their plan; they are generally of irregular shape and small area. Flanking is seldom systematic, and generally poor. Ditches are commonly rock-cut and of formidable character, but gates are poorly developed by English standards; in particular, the portcullis is very rare. Only at the doorway of Dolbadarn can we be sure of one. Another architectural feature which seems to have been too much for Welsh builders is the 'corkscrew' newel-stair, so usual in English buildings; once again, Dolbadarn presents the only examples.

In these relatively small castles the keep is normally a dominating feature (very few have no keep), but Welsh towers, the keeps included, tend to have no more than two storeys. Some castles are all, or virtually all, keep, but most take the form of a tower with a single dependent enclosure; very seldom is there more than one ward. There is a very considerable use of rectangular keep-towers — not derived from Norman keeps — and, in the north of Wales, apsidal towers, in plan like an elongated capital D, are a fairly conspicuous feature — sometimes as principal towers, sometimes subsidiary. The arrangement, familiar in England, whereby sound building methods are confined to the keep, the enclosure being built in inferior materials, is not unknown in Wales. Finally, it seems clear that a number of Welsh castles were never completed; the Welsh, and not only the Welsh, were able to interfere with the slow process of an enemy's castellation in stone.

Generally, Welsh castles tended to be defective in scientific design, but well sited and strongly ditched; *Wallia pura* lacked skilled architects, but neither the keen eye of the prince, nor the strong arms of his subjects were lacking. Ornamental masonry is rare, yet at Llywelyn the Great's Castell-y-Bere fragments have been found of a splendid chapel; and Dinas Brân, to judge by the detail of its entrance and the quantity of freestone fragments lying about its enclosure, was an opulent structure.

The last years of Welsh independence seem to have been a period of vigorous castellation in Wales, not all of it due to Llywelyn ap Gruffydd. Mention has already been made of Castell Mor Graig (probably 1267), Ewloe (*c.* 1257), Dolforwyn (1273) and Sennybridge (1262–5). Dinas Brân makes its first appearance in 1270, and is unlikely to be much older. At Dolbadarn, which may be rather later, the round keep is very well developed; exceptionally, it has three storeys, linked by newel-stairs, and a portcullis at its first-floor door. This formidable structure might pass for an English addition, but the first thing the English did with Dolbadarn when they arrived there was to pull it down.

Before turning to the more troublesome topic of Welsh earthworks, we may notice the steady adherence of the Welsh to the keep, seen as the prince's quarters. (It is worth noticing that there are few traces of important domestic buildings away from the tower, except at the splendid Dinas Brân, where we can find the sites of hall and kitchen.)

Rectangular Towers: Gwynedd: Dinas Emrys, Dolwyddelan Nos. 1 and 2, possibly Carndochan in its original form, Castell-y-Bere, Dolforwyn. Powys: Dinas Brân; perhaps Powis (though the tower does not overtop the walls of the castle). Deheubarth: Nevern, probably Ystrad Meurig. Morgannwg: Castell Mor Graig.

Figure 11.5: Dinas Brân

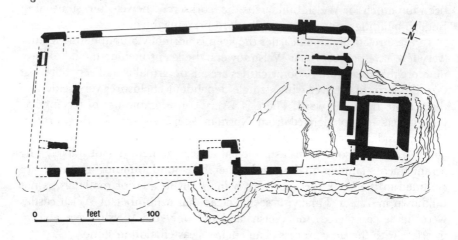

Figure 11.6: Caergwle (Hope) Castle

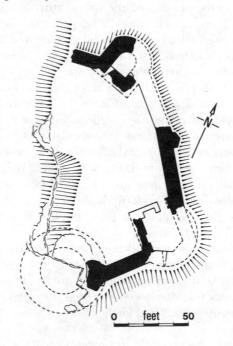

Apsidal Towers: Gwynedd: Ewloe, Carndochan, probably Sennybridge. (As subsidiary towers, Castell-y-Bere, also Dinas Brân in Powys).

Figure 11.7: Castell Carndochan

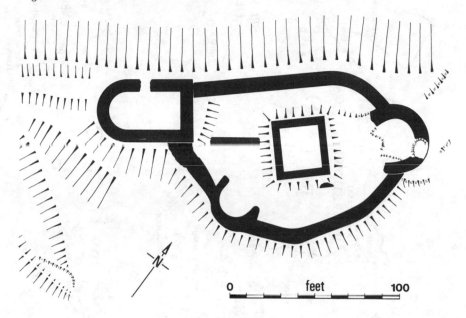

Round Towers: Gwynedd: Dolbadarn. Powys: Caergwrle (never finished). Deheubarth: Drysllwyn, Dynevor. Morgannwg: Machen, Llanhilleth No 2 (unfinished).

Other Plans: Llanhilleth No 3 (unfinished).

Apparently Keepless: Deheubarth: Newcastle Emlyn.

Uncertain: Gwynedd: Carn Fadryn, Penrhyndeudraeth. Deheubarth: Cardigan.

The recognition of Welsh stone castles, then, is not a particularly difficult task. The position is far more unsatisfactory for earthwork castles, in whose case historical record is more often than not absent.

The known Welsh earthwork castles are mottes, or much less frequently ringworks; usually they are small, and often without baileys. Unfortunately these are exactly the characteristics of known English castles — at least after the conquerors' bonanza that ended in 1094. In view of the early penetration of the Normans into virtually every part of Wales, it is thus almost impossible to say that any earthwork castle is Welsh in origin, in the absence of definite literary evidence to that effect; it is not good enough even to find it in Welsh hands when first recorded, unless it is definitely stated to have been built by a Welshman. Such evidence is unusual; there are only some nine cases in the

Figure 11.8: The castles of Wales

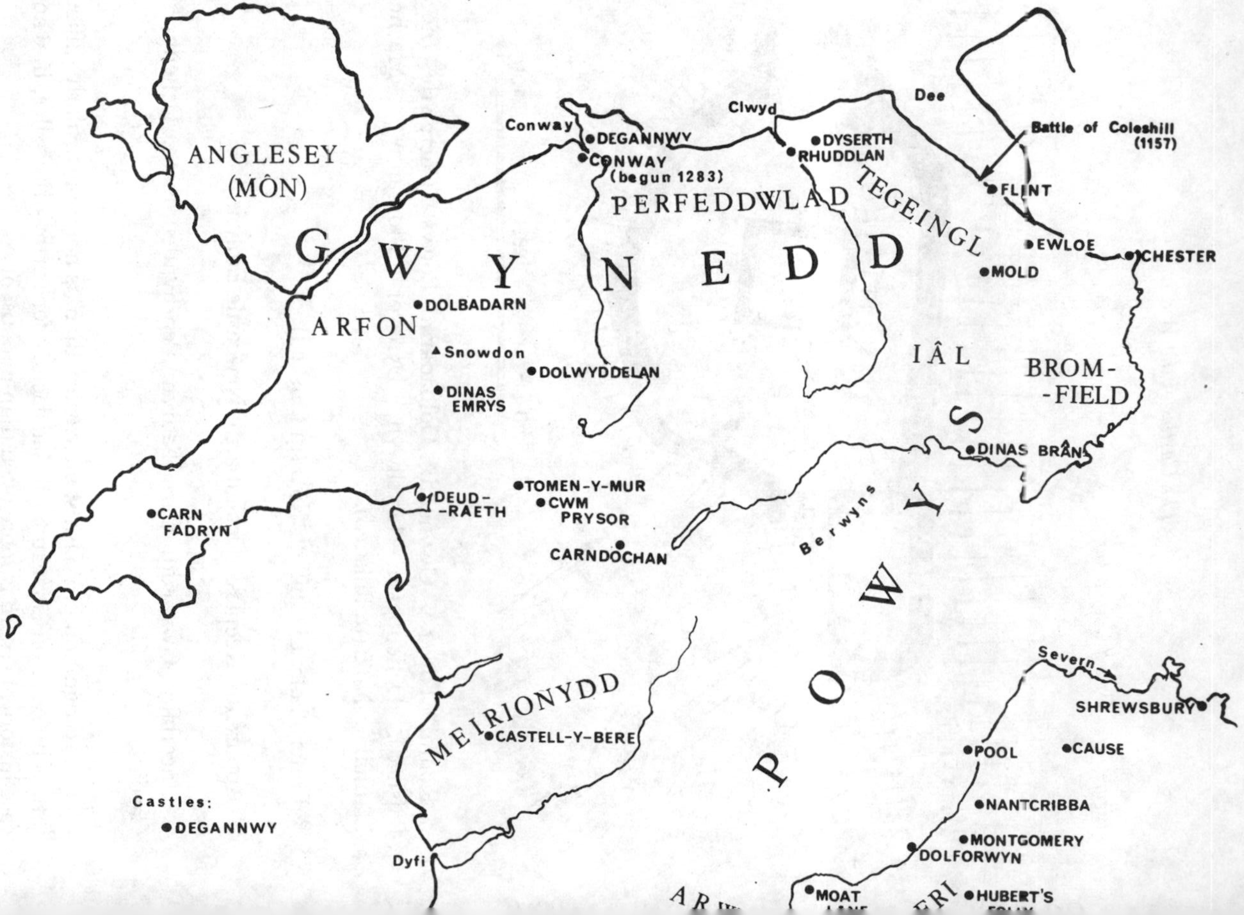

Castles:
● DEGANNWY

ANGLESEY
(MÔN)

G W Y N E D D

ARFON

● DOLBADARN

▲ Snowdon

● DINAS
EMRYS

● DOLWYDDELAN

● CARN
FADRYN

● DEUD-
—RAETH

● TOMEN-Y-MUR

● CWM
PRYSOR

● CARNDOCHAN

MEIRIONYDD

● CASTELL-Y-BERE

Dyfi

Conway

● DEGANNWY
● CONWAY
(begun 1283)

Clwyd

● DYSERTH
● RHUDDLAN

PERFEDDWLAD

TEGEINGL

Dee

● FLINT

Battle of Coleshill (1157)

● EWLOE
● CHESTER

● MOLD

I Â L

BROM-
—FIELD

P O W Y S

● DINAS BRÂN

Berwyn

SHREWSBURY

● CAUSE

● POOL

● NANTCRIBBA

● MONTGOMERY

● DOLFORWYN

● HUBERT'S

● MOAT

Severn

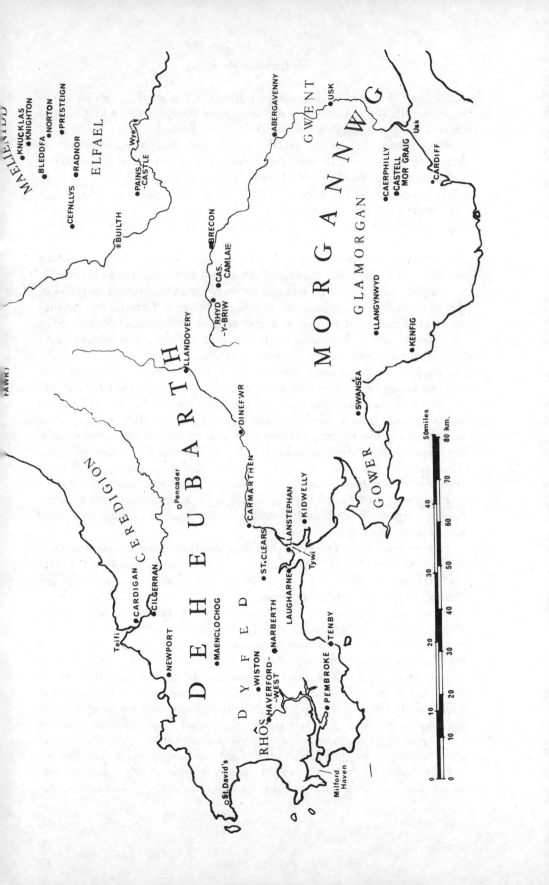

chronicles.[14] Many more, including a number which are definitely known to have been in Welsh hands at some time, were probably never English, but there is no means of telling original Welsh from English.

Place-names indicating Welsh occupation and administration — Maerdref or Faerdre, Maerdy, Llys, Faenor — give us no clue to the nationality of any proprietor, least of all the builder of a castle on the site.

This makes it all the more difficult to explain the enormous variation in the density of castles from one part of Wales to another. The starting-point of any such enquiry must be the relation drawn between castles and commotes (the small, practical units of Welsh administration, formed by subdividing the larger *cantrefs* or hundreds) by the late Sir Goronwy Edwards in his seminal lecture 'The Normans and the Welsh March'.[15] He shows that in Ceredigion (now part of Dyfed), during its Norman occupation in 1110–36, there was a remarkably close correspondence between the numbers of castles and of commotes in the province; and in general each commote contained its own castle. Here we have what might be called the ideal arrangement for an area of Welsh population in Anglo-Norman hands. Welsh lords, it is plain, did not use so many castles; they were less accustomed to them, and were commonly on better terms with their vassals; not that patriotism of the modern sort, such as earlier historians attributed to the Welsh population, is anything but anachronistic in considering the twelfth century, but xenophobia is a far earlier and more fundamental human characteristic, and the Anglo-Normans were certainly interlopers. To take an extreme example, there were six commotes in Môn (Anglesey) and three castles, all of them completely unconnected with the pattern of Welsh lordship; indeed Beaumaris was not built before 1295, and is in the same commote as Aber-lleiniog; both are English castles, built to protect a landing from the sheltered waters inside the Lavan Sands.

Although in *Wallia Pura* generally the proportion of castles to commotes is higher than this, it is not high enough to allow for a castle as the *llys* (head) of each commote, still less for extra foundations called into existence for changes of site and similar exigencies.

Heavy concentrations of castles occur where not only was the lord English, but a considerable body of his tenants were Englishmen, settled in manors, some at least of which needed the protection and control which a castle could afford. For example, the remarkable group in the Vale of Montgomery[16] lies mostly directly east of the Dyke, but the names of the individual castle-sites are even more purely Anglo-Saxon than one would have expected, the repetition of the suffix 'ton' throughout the group indicating that these little castles were stationed at small English settlements. It is possible to apply a similar test to groups of castles in other, less unequivocally English areas; for example, the closely set line of small castles which runs eastwards across northern Pembrokeshire (now Dyfed) to a point close to the East Cleddau river and the county (and *cantref*) boundary — ten castles in some 14 miles: Castle Morris, Letterston, Wolf's Castle, Little Newcastle, Puncheston, Castlebythe, Henry's Moat, New Moat, Maenclochog, Llangolman. The names make it clear that part of this series at least followed a line of Anglo-Flemish vills along the southern slopes of the Prescelly, though one or two suggest a different origin.[17]

It is a different matter when two or more earthwork castles are found in the same commote, in an area where there had been no English settlement. Changes in site are not likely to explain these extra castles; normally these involved abandoning an earthwork for a new masonry castle. There is a single case where it is likely that one Welsh motte-castle has been abandoned in favour of another; this is the commote of Iâl (Yale) in the princedom of Powys and the county of Denbigh (latterly Clwyd). Here there are two fine earthworks, of which Tomen y Rhodwydd (Llanarmon yn Iâl No. 2) is generally taken to be the castle mentioned in history; it is a very fine motte-and-bailey, but its companion — also a powerful motte — bears the administrative name of Tomen y Faerdre, and must have been at one time the head of the commote.

But more explanation is needed for the thick concentrations of earthwork castles in the valleys of the Dee, the upper Severn, the Tanat and the Teifi. Setting aside changes of site, and siege-castles (of which there is no recorded example in Welsh history), we can see that the lord of a commote could need an extra castle for strategic reasons, or to control some borough or trading centre. The trouble is that this sort of explanation can only cover a small group of sites; a strategic castle, from its very nature, is likely to be large and powerful, and to be recorded in history, while boroughs and commercial centres, like Llanidloes and Newtown in the Severn valley and Adpar on the Teifi, are likely to be fewer, and just as conspicuous and easy to identify.

The Severn valley's history is complicated; there are some 20 earthwork castles along the river, and these can hardly be apportioned between seven commotes[18] without some at least of the latter having a large allowance; Kerry (Ceri), for example, contains at least four castles, of which only Hubert's Folly (Kerry No. 4) has any history. The whole district forms a palimpsest of military planning, and the very numerous castles with no history may have served any of a number of different defensive purposes.

The upper Dee valley has a more straightforward history; if ever there was an English incursion (as the size of Bala motte seems to suggest) it was early, short and not noticed in the chronicles. The only recorded castles are Bala, Llandderfel (Crogen), Rûg (Corwen No. 1) and a castle of 'Dernio' (sc. Edeyrnion, and hence probably the same as Rûg). None the less, earthwork castles lie thick on the ground. The commote of Penllyn Is Treweryn contains two castles (Llanfor Nos. 1 and 2); Penllyn Uwch Treweryn, three (Bala, Llandderfel and Llangower); Edeyrnion another three (Corwen Nos. 1, 2 and 3; though Nos. 2 and 3 probably belong to the obscure subdivision of Glyndyfrdwy, which gave its name to its master, 'Owen Glyndourdy'.

In the Tanat valley group the motte at Sycharth (Llansilin, Denbigh) is in Cynllaith, motte and commote being again historically connected with Glyndŵr. The two motte-castles of Llanfechain and Llanfyllin (Montgomeryshire, now Powys) were clearly the strongholds of the two commotes of Mechain, above and below the Wood, but this leaves Mochnant, which straddles the old border between Denbighshire and Montgomeryshire (now Powys), and contains four castles.[19] In fact, Mochnant was latterly divided into Is Rhaiadr and Uwch Rhaidr — below and above the Waterfall — but not before 1166, by which time we generally suppose motte-castles to have been somewhat out of date.[20]

It is in the valley of the Teifi, however, that the most surprising examples are to be found. On the north bank, Iscoed, at the mouth of the river, was divided in 1200; it contains six castles, of which only the two in Llandygwydd parish call for any explanation.[21] Gwynionydd, further up the north bank, was also divided into two, but this hardly explains why it has nine castles, all earthworks.[22] Of these, Castell Hywel (Llandysul No. 1) alone has any history, though the name Castell Gwynionydd, for Llandysul No. 3, suggests — not very convincingly — that it may at some time have been the *llys* of its commote.

On the south bank, the two commotes of Emlyn, particularly Emlyn Is Cych on the west, could be regarded as regions of English influence; in Is Cych indeed, the principal castle of Cilgerran shares the territory only with Clydey, an earthwork with no history and some remains of clay-laid masonry — probably the seat of a Welsh vassal. The much more Welsh Uwch Cych, to the east, contains, in addition to its principal stronghold — a Welsh foundation — of Newcastle Emlyn, a motte at Cenarth, which seems to have been an important place at some time, and three others, even less known to history.[23]

Further up the river, Mabudrud forms part of Cantref Mawr, the unassailable heartland of the southern Welsh kingdom, where English power and English influence were the minimum: but there are six motte-castles in the commote.[24]

It is impossible to identify the supernumerary castles with any work of the Marchers or their vassals, or with strongholds of the princely rulers of entire commotes. It seems to be necessary to consider another Welsh class of some pretension. Under the great princely families, Welsh society admitted no nobility, but the word *uchelwyr* is commonly mistranslated 'noblemen'. In fact the *uchelwyr* were only *patresfamiliarum*, heads of free kindreds; but it is surely these who must be most seriously taken into consideration in connection with castles which are not otherwise explicable. This class of men had increased in regard and importance down to, and beyond, the Conquest of Wales.

There is, not surprisingly, very little supporting evidence. In the parish of Llanfihangel Aberbythych (Carmarthen, now in Dyfed) it appears that there was formerly a motte called Castell Y Rhingyll.[25] The *rhingyll* was a court officer of a Welsh jurisdiction; *anglice*, he appears as 'bailiff', 'beadle', 'serjeant' or 'summoner', but he was always chosen from among the *uchelwyr*.[26] If we are to take this at its face value, it is a strong piece of evidence, but it is subject to a number of doubts: the alleged motte no longer exists, the word *castell* is used in Welsh topography with no great degree of exactitude, and the antiquity of the name is quite uncertain. A stronger piece of evidence occurs when we hear, in 1315, of a Welsh undertenant building a *forcelettum* (a small castle) at Blank Mouster[27] in Glamorgan. This could well refer to the recently destroyed motte of Whitchurch No. 2.

But the most striking example concerns Owain Glyndŵr. Admittedly, he was much more than a mere member of the *uchelwyr*, being lord of a whole commote — Cynllaith — and of a more uncertain part of Edeyrnion, and of princely descent appropriate to these estates. One of the two mottes in Glyndyfrdwy has long been called 'Owen Glendower's Mound';[28] more importantly, Cynllaith contained his ancestral seat of Sycharth. Here there is a motte; Owain resided there, and an eulogy of his dwelling was written by Iolo Goch.[29] Sir John Lloyd paraphrases this:

> The attractions and comforts of Sycharth are portrayed by the bard with much loving detail. It has a moat for girdle, with a bridge which gives access to the lordly gatehouse. On the green hillock within are the timber houses, with lofts which rest on pillars . . .[30]

In fact, this very important proprietor, in the last years of the fourteenth century, is discovered living in a wooden house on a typical motte. No doubt similar, if less luxurious quarters would have served for the *uchelwyr*; what was good enough for him would have been good enough for them.

It seems probable that most of these subordinate earthworks belong to a period a good deal later than we normally associate with the building of mottes — that is to say, after the important date 1154 in England and the early years of the thirteenth century in Wales. There is nothing unnatural in this; the numerous Irish mottes, in so far as they can be ascribed to the Anglo-Norman adventurers and their imitators, must be later than 1169, and in Denmark mottes are to be found as late as the fourteenth century. Both Sycharth and Blank Mouster are fourteenth-century sites.

The question of the dating of the unrecorded castles is one which can hardly be given any fully convincing answer. One particular matter for concern is whether they belong to a period before or after the Edwardian conquest. *Ex hypothesi*, they do not appear in any text, and we can say no more than that it is very likely that they belong to the period after the conquest, when the *Brut Y Tywysogyon* is silent rather than relate a history of disasters, and when the princes were departed. It must be emphasised that these earthwork castles of the Teifi country are all of very much the same size

Figure 11.9: The Edwardian conquest of Wales

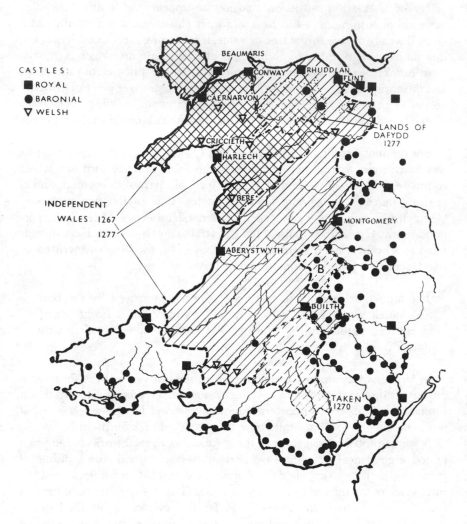

and strength, so that it is unlikely that any of them were ignored by the chroniclers merely on account of their unimportance.

If we can accept the theory that a substantial number of Welsh mottes were built after 1282–3, we must envisage a group of backwoods country gentlemen entrenching themselves against the mischances of the time, for Wales was conquered, but not pacified, before the time of the Council in the Marches; the disappearance of the princes may well have led to an increase in casual violence. Thus it appears that some of the gentry made use of a type of defence which had become obsolete for purposes of serious warfare. There is nothing unlikely or absurd about this; indeed, one may salute their prudence in usefully reintroducing an old means of defence to cover a new necessity.

Notes

1. *Brut y Tywysogyon* (ed. Jones) Peniarth MS.20 version, translation (Cardiff, 1952), p. 118; *Red book of Hergest* version (Cardiff, 1955), p. 265; *Calendar of ancient correspondence concerning Wales* (ed. Edwards, Cardiff, 1935), pp. 30-2. The siege appears to have been a serious one, lasting a fortnight, and the castle appears to have been a good deal knocked about.

2. For Dolwyddelan, see Morris, *Welsh wars of Edward I* (Oxford, 1901), pp. 190-1: for Bere, *Littere Wallie* (ed. Edwards, Cardiff, 1940), pp. 189-90, 192-3; *Nicholai Triveti Annales* (ed. Hog, London, 1845), p. 307; *Oseney and Wykes* (ed. Luard, Rolls Series, 36.4) pp. 292-3.

3. *Brut, Peniarth MS 20* version, translation, p. 35.

4. *Ibid.*, pp. 45-6; *Brut, Red book* version, p. 47; *Brenhinedd y Saesson* (ed. Jones, Cardiff, 1971), pp. 135-7; *Annales Cambriae* (ed. Williams ab Ithel, Rolls Series, 20), p. 36.

5. *Giraldus Cambrensis* (Rolls Series, 21.6), p. 123. These will be Penrhyndeudraeth (Merioneth) and Carn Fadryn (Caerns.). Both of these are represented by foundations, apparently of rather ramshackle stone structures.

6. Hemp, *Y Cymmrodor*, xxxix (1928), pp. 8-9, 18-19.

7. *Calendar of Close Rolls* (1272-9), p. 51; see also *Calendar of ancient correspondence concerning Wales* (ed. Sir J.G. Edwards, Cardiff, 1935), p. 86, and *Littere Wallie* (ed. Sir J.G. Edwards, Cardiff, 1940), pp. 23-4.

8. Fragment of a Battle Abbey chronicle, in Bémont, *Simon de Montfort* (Paris, 1884), p. 379.

9. All four of these castles were given English additions, Edwardian or later; Carreg Cennen was completely rebuilt.

10. G.T. Clark, *Cartae et alia munimenta quae ad dominium de Glamorgancia pertinent* (2nd edition, Cardiff, 1910), iii, p. 860.

11. The combination of a rectangular keep, round towers and apparently no gatehouse, is wildly un-English in character; the crude latrine is a Welsh feature, but the good flanking supplied by the towers is rare in Welsh work, and the eccentric shape and detail of the round towers are unique.

12. James G. Wood, *The lordship, castle and town of Chepstow, otherwise Striguil* (Newport, 1910), pp. 76-7, 81-3, 85-6.

13. For the mathematics of this, see D.J.C. King, 'Two castles in northern Powys', *Archaeologia Cambrensis*, cxxiii (1974), p. 138.

14. Cymmer 1116, Cynfal 1147, Iâl and Llanrhystyd 1149, Caereinion and Aber Dyfi 1156, Abereinon 1168, Trefilan 1233, Garth Grugyn 1242.

15. *Proceedings of the British Academy*, xlii (1956), pp. 155-77.

16. D.J.C. King and C.J. Spurgeon, 'The mottes in the Vale of Montgomery', *Archaeologia Cambrensis*, cxiv (1965), pp. 68-86.

17. Castlebythe, in spite of a name of Welsh origin, stands in a very English site; Maenclochog has a Welsh name and perhaps position, but appears as English in 1215 and 1257 in the Brut. Only the remote Llangolman seems not to be of English origin.

18. Both these figures are approximate; the exact number of castles depends on the distance one goes from the river, and the number of commotes depends on the rather vexed question of the subdivision of Cydewain (see Owen, *Pembrokeshire*, iv, pp. 586-7, 608-9).

19. The three mottes in the parish of Llanrhaiadr-yn-Mochnant, which stands astride the old border between Denbighshire and Montgomery. Nos 1 and 2 are in Is Rhaiadr (Denbigh). The fourth castle is Pennant (Montgomery). All three are now in Powys.

20. For example, Dr Radford, in Programme, *Cambrian Archaeological Association*, meeting (1962), p. 14: 'I do not think that mottes were being built as late as 1176' — a statement acceptable for most of England, but not Wales.

21. The other four are: Old and New Cardigan, Blaenporth (mentioned 1116) and the motte of Adpar — the Bishop of St David's commercial site.

22. Bangor, Llandyfriog, all three castles at Llandysul, Llanfair Orllwyn, Llanfair Treflygen, Llanwenog and Llanwnen.

23. One at Llangeler, two at Penboyr. (This commote lies in the former Carmarthen).

24. Four in Llanfihangel a'r Arth parish and two in Llanllwni.

25. Royal Commission on Ancient and Historical Monuments, *Inventory for Carmarthen*, p. 127.

26. Rees, *Historical Atlas of Wales* (London, 1951), p. 25.

27. *Calendar of Close Rolls* (1313–18), p. 161.

28. Corwen No. 2, Merioneth; for the tradition, see Lloyd, *Owen Glendower* (Oxford, 1931), p. 15 n l.

29. See Iolo Goch's eulogy of Sycharth, in *Archaeologia Cambrensis*, 5th series, xi (1894), pp. 240-1.

30. Lloyd, *Owen Glendower*, p. 27.

12

The Fourteenth Century

It is a common and natural experience in historical studies to find that, while an individual century makes a convenient period for consideration, its mathematical beginning and end are not convenient divisions for study; thus, the eighteenth century is generally more suitably terminated at 1789 or 1815 than at 1800. So it is here; the opening of the fourteenth century is spanned by the reign of Edward I, and the impetus of his programme of castle-building did not end with his life. At the other end of the century, English fortification had reached or was reaching a stage of such low activity that any one date is as good as another; there would be a good case for tacking on to the fourteenth century the small amount of fortification undertaken in the fifteenth, which shows comparatively little novelty or development. Only the greater prominence of fire-artillery makes for a difference.

The fourteenth century, from about 1310 to 1400, presents a number of features of significance. In the first place, owing to the wars of Edward I, Wales and the Welsh border were pacified to a very large extent, while the Scottish frontier, hitherto much quieter, became bitterly disturbed. However, this disturbance did not for most of the time constitute any very serious military threat, and the country as a whole enjoyed almost unbroken peace as far as significant operations were concerned, while the building activity of earlier centuries had established sufficient major castles to have dealt with any serious emergency. Many, it is true, needed repair, and some were in fact repaired, mainly in the north or on the Channel coast.

On the other hand, at a lower level the country was not by any means peaceful; there was some very bad government in the course of the century, which encouraged the evilly inclined of all classes to disorder, and left the wealthy to their own devices to protect their property; the continued development of the 'contract army' encouraged the growth of those private contingents which were to develop in the next century into the gangs of chartered rascals which were so fatal a threat to public order. There was also extensive agrarian trouble, reaching its climax in the Peasants' Revolt of 1381. On the south coast French raids were frequent, while in the north the forays of the

147

Scots (and of English borderers, too often their accomplices) were unceasing.

We have thus a century of second-rate castles; in the north many are not even second-rate; the need for defence drove individuals of relatively slender means[1] to erect minor *fortalicia*, wooden 'peels', and single towers (the latter in enormous numbers).

Even in southern England the large number of fourteenth-century castles represented only by their earthworks suggests that many were flimsily built. Only two major strategic castles were founded in the century: Dunstanburgh on the coast of Northumberland, licensed in 1315, and built in pursuance of the obscure and selfish policies of Thomas of Lancaster, and Queenborough on the Isle of Sheppey (Kent), raised in 1361–9 as a defence against French activity in the mouth of the Thames.

Gunpowder had been familiar since at least 1300, and guns of a sort since the 1320s; from about 1370 fortifications began to be adapted for their use.

Finally, England during this period became divided stylistically into two zones: north and south. The former comprised the six original northern counties — Northumberland, Cumberland, Westmorland, Durham, Lancashire and Yorkshire — which now evolved a Northern style of their own, while the remainder of the country continued with a normal development of thirteenth-century methods, based on flanking by boldly salient towers, generally round, but now sometimes square or polygonal. The Northern style was based on the use of towers which are uniformly square or rectangular, and of very little projection; in most cases an awkward oblique fire could be given by archers on their tower-heads, but no true enfilade would have been possible.

There is very little interpenetration of the two styles. In the south there are a few single square towers which recall the Northern 'pele-tower'; but this form of fortification is so obvious and elementary that there is no reason to look for any copying from foreign parts as an explanation for its existence in any of the countries where it is to be found; and these are almost all those in which fortification has been practised.

Invasions of northern England by the main European style of the south are naturally more frequent and more important. They are relatively common in the rebuildings of major castles, especially in Yorkshire and Lancashire. Nevertheless at Dunstanburgh the two systems are seen side by side: the enormous gatehouse, in breadth and in scale the largest thing of its kind in the British Isles, is plainly in the Edwardian tradition; but the other towers are all square, and one at least, the Lilburn Tower, would make a perfectly ordinary 'pele-tower' if it stood by itself. The towers added to the curtains of Knaresborough (North Yorkshire) in 1307–12 seem to have been half-round and solid. The great reconstruction of the main ward of Pontefract (West Yorkshire), largely ascribed to John of Gaunt in 1374, was carried out with square or rectangular towers, but these are placed to give good flanking, and the whole would look sufficiently normal in southern England.

The most characteristic castle-type of this period has been called the *quad-rangular castle*.[2] It is typically a compact hollow square or rectangle of build-ing enclosing a courtyard, its outer walls forming the defences. To consider first its southern form: this is seldom overpowering in height, but the front has typically an imposing symmetry, recalling Edward I's Harlech on a reduced scale, with an impressive gatehouse in the centre, flanked by towers at the ends of the front.[3] Almost always there was a tower at each angle; sometimes one in the middle of each of the other sides, as at Bodiam (East Sussex), the finest surviving example of the type; in this case one tower contains the rear-gate. In most fourteenth-century castles, defences and internal buildings form together a coherent unit, evidently planned as a whole, whereas thirteenth-century castles, even the best, look as if they had been designed as defences in the first place, and had had their houses put inside as an afterthought. The majority of fourteenth-century castles stand on low and level ground, so as to derive all possible benefit from wet defences; this would make such an integrated plan a simpler business.

Wet moats, indeed, form a major part of the defences of castles of the fourteenth century — and the fifteenth, for that matter — and this is particu-larly the case in the south. Here strong summit and foreland sites are not at all unusual, but they do not occur with such frequency as to be available to anything like every member of the class of minor proprietors who were build-ing most of the new castles. Even in the mountain zone many smaller castles of all periods had to be built on sites of little strength. In the mountain zone, moreover, it was generally advisable to avoid the valley floors — too liable to floods, and often completely overlooked from higher ground. But in southern England low and well-watered valleys, not hopelessly overlooked, are innumerable — ten a penny — and any of these would do for the site of a typical fourteenth-century castle. Wet defences, of course, were nothing new; earlier periods had gladly used them to defend low-standing fortifications, but in southern England in the late Middle Ages they became an almost universal feature in the defence of castles. There was nothing particularly surprising about this. If we need to look for any foreign influence, it will be that of the *Wasserburgen* of the lower Rhine and the Low Countries; but it hardly seems necessary to suggest any borrowings from outside the kingdom.

The wet defences are often most impressive, and the few quadrangular castles which have only dry ditches seem very inadequate. Farleigh Hunger-ford (Somerset) is unusual in standing on a site protected by strong falls of ground on three sides; the fourth was protected by a rather weak outer enclo-sure, and the main defences behind this seem to have been fairly powerful. Another quadrangular castle on a conspicuously dry site is Rotherfield Greys (Oxfordshire);[4] but to judge from its remains this was a castle of little strength; its plan was also somewhat irregular.

To revert to the normal *Wasserburg* type: its masonry defences — with the exception of one element — were generally not impressive; the towers were commonly tall, but of no great diameter, the curtains low and of rather moderate thickness; even at Bodiam walls and towers alike are pierced with domestic windows — heavily barred, of course — and there are no arrow-slits, even at parapet level. This fact may reflect the contempt of Sir Edward Dalyngrigge, as an officer of Edward III's army, for the normal defensive weapon of medieval fortification, the crossbow. Certainly there are gunholes in the gatehouse, as there are in many fourteenth-century fortifications, but they are not used anywhere in the perimeter. And assuredly the entrance was remarkably strong; a long wooden bridge ran across the artificial lake in which Bodiam Castle stands, parallel to the front of defence, and ending on a large octagonal stone pier or island — probably originally battlemented — which stands directly in front of the gate. Turning at right angles, the bridge then immediately reached the barbican, a regular little gatehouse with a light portcullis and two pairs of doors. Some distance behind comes the main gate; there were probably four drawbridges in the whole course of the approach. The gatehouse itself was very formidable; it is machicolated and has a number of gunports — two at least for heavy guns; its passage has grooves for three portcullises, and the intervening vaults were handsomely made, with ribs and bosses, each of which was circular, with a round machicolation in the middle — pretty and practical at the same time. This was a nightmare approach, as terrible as anything in Edward I's North Welsh castles, and yet it defends a stronghold which in all other respects is very much smaller, both in regard to its defences and to its strategic importance. In other castles of this type, there is a similar concentration of strength on the gatehouse. At Cooling (Kent) the perimeter defences, licensed in 1381, are rather stronger than those of Bodiam — with tall curtains generally unpierced by lights, and corner-towers with plenty of gun-ports. The main gate, protected by a large outer ward, was certainly very small, but it was reached across a long bridge, and had a portcullis and a number of gunholes. The perimeter defences of Scotney (Kent), a small castle of irregular plan, with a moated outer ward, were evidently weak; the one surviving tower is of two storeys only; yet there was an outer gate or barbican before the main gate. A similar concentration on the defences of the entry is to be observed in fifteenth-century castles of the same type. It would appear that the enemy was expected to come to the front door.

Nor was this supposition the mere piece of military stupidity that one could find oneself imagining if one was unwise: castles of the quality of Bodiam and Cooling, Scotney and Wingfield, Shirburn, Hemyock and Maxstoke, were not built to resist the siege-royal; the resources of their owners were not adequate for withstanding a powerful army, even had they had a really strong castle as a centre for resistance. Had Duguesclin mounted a serious invasion of England in the late fourteenth century, he need have feared no resistance from Bodiam or Cooling, still less from Scotney — unless indeed there had been an English army in the vicinity, when even such small castles might have been expected to put up a fight. A well-equipped besieger, with plenty of time, would have been able to fill or drain their moats, and so to choose his own point of attack; but even first-class castles would have been in danger from such an enemy. The type of opponent whom the ordinary fourteenth-century castle-builder was prepared to meet was likely to lack both time and equipment: raiders (as distinct from a serious invasion) from France or Scotland — dissident peasants, gangs of ruffians, violent neighbours — all would have had to attack the entrance or leave the castle unattempted. At Boarstall (Buckinghamshire), licensed in 1312, nothing remains but the gatehouse and a very formidable moat with steep sides; there is no actual trace of any masonry walling, and this has been the state of the castle for many years.[5] It is impossible to be sure in the absence of excavation, but it seems that the perimeter was only palisaded; this would be the ultimate in concentration on the strength of the entry. One exceptional castle of this period calls for note on account of its abnormal scheme of defence: this is Mettingham (Suffolk). Here there are the normal wide wet moats, and the normal powerful gatehouse; unusually, there are moated outworks, and what may have been an inner stronghold outside one corner of the main work; this, however, has been greatly altered. What is most remarkable is that, as far as can be made out, the square corner-towers had no projection at all, though they were higher than their curtains. The latter are tall rather than thick, and seem to have been equipped with a double row of great plain arrowslits below the parapet. This represents a remarkable reliance on direct shooting in defence.

As regards northern England, Ogle (Northumberland) was evidently a southern quadrangular castle built in the far north; the Northern type, however, is not found south of the Humber; Wressle (North Yorkshire), on the north bank, is the most southerly example. The peculiar Northern style has already been mentioned, and calls only for short treatment here. It was based on the use of square towers, and has more in common with Scottish practice than English. As well as an enormous number of single towers — all of forms based on the square or the rectangle — we find numerous keep-and-enclosure castles with square keeps, commonly reinforced by one or more square turrets, but bearing little relationship to Norman keeps. Next, there is a characteristic group of northern quadrangular castles, of which Castle Bolton (North Yorkshire), may be accepted as the finest surviving example, the equivalent of Bodiam in the south — though the broken remains of Sheriff Hutton show that this was even more formidable. There are numerous intermediate forms between the two main types: the regular, symmetrical keepless quadrangular castle like Bolton, and the irregular keep-and-ward castle of the type of Etal (Northumberland); but a common feature of all is that very little heed is given to enfilading arrangements, and the towers, as a result, have only slight projection. There are some exceptions; the bishop's castle of Rose (Cumbria) is well flanked, and elsewhere some few towers project boldly, but it is clear that flanking was generally little considered.

Another difference between north and south is the opulent character of many northern castles of the fourteenth century, particularly those of the quadrangular type. The typical southern castle of the period was built by the head of an emerging family — not infrequently a successful soldier like Dalyngrigge — and had modest, though comfortable and up-to-date domestic accommodation. Many northern castles, on the other hand, were robber-proof palaces built by established nobles; over most of England buildings of this kind would never have needed so much as a pretence of fortification, but these northern examples are not simply fortified by way of pretence. On the whole they are weaker than their opposite numbers in the south — certainly relatively to their domestic splendours. In any case, the southern castles are superior in terms of military science.

And yet the towering grey bulk of Bolton has an intimidating aspect which is by no means misleading. Its four big square corner-towers have only a very shallow projection, and the weakness of its flanking defence is hardly cured by the two little turrets in the middle of the longer curtains of its rectangular plan. There is no wet moat, and very little of any sort of ditch at all; the loops on the outer walls are not real arrowslits, and there are no gunholes. But the huge mass of building — three storeys high with the corner towers rising another two storeys above the curtains — has a massive strength; the walls are of respectable thickness, and the entry has a singular feature: the gate itself had two portcullises, and in addition every doorway into the buildings surrounding the courtyard was protected by a portcullis. The sides of the quadrangle are almost as grim as the outer walls. There was nothing perfunctory about the defences of Bolton.

Similar, if less powerful examples are to be encountered at Chillingham in Northumberland, Lumley in Durham, and Wressle in North Yorkshire, and there are smaller examples, like the very badly sited Danby (North Yorkshire). The mightiest of all, Sheriff Hutton, seems to have been slightly irregular in plan, and there are others that deviate considerably from the rectangular, such as Ford (Northumberland), Gleaston (Lancashire, North of the Sands) and Brancepeth (Durham). In Cumbria there is a local type of quadrangular castle with fewer towers, or with none at all; Naworth is probably the best example, but Bewcastle — a plain square of curtains, with no contemporary tower — is perhaps the outstanding case in its utter simplicity. These are defences in a poor region, and it is probable that many of them had their inner buildings made of wood.

These castles were generally keepless — though one of the towers of Ford was held in need,[6] and one tower of Gleaston was vastly larger and more important than its fellows. Gleaston, indeed, is more like a set of border towers (of which one is very large) tied together with a perimeter of walls than a normal castle. But the north as a whole was a land of square towers and square keeps, the latter being generally only more highly developed versions of the former; in addition, some of the older castles, such as Warkworth (Northumberland) and Knaresborough (North Yorkshire) have keeps of different patterns; while the very opulent quadrangular-type castle of Raby (Durham) has at one angle a fine big tower of pentagonal plan, Bulmer's Tower, which originally stood inside a ditch of its own. (Raby, in addition, has a low outer line of defence completely encircling the main body of the castle, which makes it an unusual northern example of a concentric castle.)

Kirkoswald (Cumbria) was very much a quadrangular castle of the Northern style, with the additional advantage of a wet moat; but one of its corner-towers was developed to form a powerful keep. Most keep-and-ward castles in the north, however, had rather shapeless enclosures, like Etal and Edlingham (both in Northumberland).

Edlingham, indeed, owes its irregular plan to a complex history of building, in which the bad times of the Scottish Borders played their part. It began as a civilian, but substantial, hall-block of the peaceful thirteenth century; then a perimeter with a gatehouse was added as times became worse, and finally a splendid tower for solar and keep. This is by no means the only example of the conversion of an unfortified building: Haughton and Aydon, both in Northumberland, are others. The first was twice raised and also reinforced to make so formidable a tower that it has never been called anything but a castle. At Aydon a fortified courtyard between a projecting wing and two stout lengths of curtain was added on the more accessible side of the house, and a large bailey outside that.

There was also a gatehouse-and-ward type, represented by Morpeth and Bothall (Northumberland) in the fourteenth century.

Even in the larger castles which were being repaired at this period in the north, such as Alnwick, Warkworth, Tynemouth in Northumberland, together with Carlisle, Cockermouth and Egremont in Cumberland, Brough and Brougham in Westmorland (all of these in modern Cumbria); the influence of the Northern style is apparent in square or polygonal towers in preference to round.

Not that this was altogether a northern feature; in the south the square mural tower was regaining ground, and polygonal towers were also far more common. Southern castles in the fourteenth century were not in fact confined to the quadrangular plan, any more than their companions in the north. Dudley (Staffordshire) was licensed in 1263, but was certainly being built in 1311,[7] and is generally considered to be essentially a castle of the early fourteenth century. Its building involved the reoccupation of the powerful earthworks of an eleventh-century motte and bailey, dismantled by King Henry II on account of its lord's complicity in the rebellion of 1173–4. Accordingly, the bailey was walled to form an irregular polygonal trace, with no flanking worth the name. Though the perimeter, on its towering summit site, was far from easy to come at, this was not at all a scientific plan. The gatehouse, which may incorporate some twelfth-century work, did not apparently flank the defences; it had two portcullises, and was subsequently strengthened externally with a typical late fourteenth-century barbican, with round turrets on its outer corners. The castle's most remarkable features were the defences of the motte; its summit was surrounded by a thick wall, carried down as a revetment. Inside this *chemise* stood a massive two-storey building with large round turrets — or rather towers — on its corners, and a portcullis to protect its doorway. Though much damaged, the essential features of this very powerful keep-complex are plain; other towers of the same form are found elsewhere.

Royal building continued on a more modest scale, and with domestic comfort as a principal object; but along with other work designed to strengthen the south coast against invasion, Edward III undertook the construction of the last great royal castle of medieval type — Queenborough in the Isle of Sheppey (Kent). Fate has generally showed itself harsh to our late-medieval castles, and of Queenborough, built between 1361 and 1371, nothing remains but possibly some maltreated earthworks. Fortunately we have a drawing by Hollar and a very detailed plan among the Hatfield MSS. These show us a concentric castle — literally and geometrically concentric, for its two lines of defence are both circular. The inner ward was formed by a ring of buildings around a courtyard; their outer walls were thick and high, with machicolated parapets. On this perimeter were six large towers, also machicolated, two of them forming the fronts for a big gatehouse, with portcullises at each end of its passage. The outer ward was wider than in Edward I's castles, and formed a plain circle, broken only by a large twin-tower gatehouse and a small postern-gate opposite one another, and joined to the inner ward by pairs of walls, with doors midway along them, so as to form corridors across the ward, and check the movements of any enemy who had forced either of the outer gates. As the main gate of the outer ward was on the side opposite to the inner gate, it was a most complicated and dangerous business to force an entry by way of the gates.

The circular arrangement suggests some sort of kinship with Henry VIII's artillery-castles, and the plan has certainly an odd resemblance to that of Deal; but a gap of nearly two centuries separates the two, and from what we know of artillery and its use in the fourteenth century it is wildly unlikely that a castle would have been specially designed for its employment as early as 1361.[8]

As for the elements of defence, these had for the most part been perfected in the thirteenth century, but there were still certain improvements and developments which could be made.

The employment of round towers was still usual, but less a matter of almost religious observance than it had been. Walls and towers were generally on a more modest scale, but this was simply because they formed part of less ambitious castles. Arrowslits could be plain or of a complex four-oillet pattern, or any of a number of intermediate forms. Some examples are very short, like those at Nunney (Somerset), but that even these feeble examples were intended seriously is shown by the manner in which two are directed to flank the doorway. From about 1370 onwards we find gun-ports, especially at gates.[9] Their earliest form is very much that of an arrowslit with a round oillet at the base, but the shaft of the slit becomes shorter and usually wider, and the oillet — which is of course the port proper — increases in diameter. At the outer gate of Cooling (Kent) there are a pair of simple round ports with no sighting-slit above, but this type of opening is only usual at a much later date than 1381, when Cooling was licensed.

Machicolations are more frequent, especially at gates, like those of Bodiam. Often, at as Cooling and Scotney and at the two splendid angle-towers of Warwick, towers were machicolated, but it is rare to find a whole perimeter defended in this way; the inner ward of Queenborough seems to have been, and Nunney certainly was; but Nunney is no more than a powerful tower.

It was at the gate, and especially at the outer defences of the gates, that fourteenth-century fortification largely exerted itself. This is not in the least surprising; the numerous small new castles needed strongly defended gates above everything, and over much of the country there were older castles, strongly sited, or with powerful defences, but with gates of obsolete type, which needed to be brought up to date.

As regards principal gatehouses, little improvement on their defences was needful, or possible; the Edwardian period had brought the gatehouse to a high state of perfection, and there was little to do but copy its details. Gatehouses tended to become wide and comparatively shallow, sometimes with turrets at all four angles, as at Boarstall (Buckinghamshire), sometimes reaching the extreme form of a plain rectangle with the passage running through the middle of the long sides, with lodges in the ends — a form found at Caldicot (Monmouthshire, now in Gwent) and Whorlton (North Yorkshire). It was rather in prolonging the entry outwards by outer gates or barbicans in which this period excelled.

Thus, even the very powerful gate of Harlech — the double gate of a concentric castle, be it remembered — was strengthened in 1323–4 by the construction in the ditch of two rectangular towers through which the entry passed,[10] and an elaborate system of drawbridges, so that there were four gateways in succession. Less spectacular, perhaps, but more subtle were the approaches of Bodiam and Queenborough, already described.

In a number of cases an outer gate, normally taking the form of a rectangle with small towers or turrets on its forward angles, was added in front of an older gate. This was particularly necessary at such a place as Lewes (East Sussex) where the gate had no portcullis; but barbicans of this type were also built at Carisbrooke in the Isle of Wight and Saltwood in Kent, and even at Dudley, where the original gate was strong and recently built.

With such an arrangement, it would be of the utmost importance to prevent an enemy bypassing the outer gate, and if this stood some distance in front of the main defences, it would need to be joined to them by a pair of walls enclosing the entry and the bridge across the ditch. Walls of this kind, projecting from the front of the main gate, had long been a common feature of defence. They may have been intended to protect the drawbridge from missiles from a flank, or to give cover to sortie-parties; they could easily have been adapted so as to close the gap between inner and outer gates.

From this process was evolved the formidable fourteenth-century complex of gatehouse and barbican. Here there are essentially two gates, inner and outer, the former being part of the main defences, the latter standing on, or close to, the counterscarp of the ditch. These are linked by side-walls enclosing the bridge or causeway across the ditch. The whole forms a splendid means of flanking, and also added a new terror to the entrance. The outer gate might be quite a weak affair, as at Alnwick (Northumberland), or extremely strong, like that of Warwick; in either case an assailant who forced it would find himself in a long narrow corridor — its floor probably made up in part by drawbridge-pits — overlooked by the main gate in front, by the wall-heads on either side, and by the top of the outer gate from behind. The outer gate either has no rooms at entry level, or else these do not communicate with the upper part of the building, which is reached along the top of the flanking walls from doorways in the front of the main gatehouse.[11] The very idea of venturing into a killing-ground of this sort must have been intolerable. As well as Warwick — the finest example — and Alnwick, there are barbican defences of this sort at Brampton Bryan (Herefordshire) and Tynemouth (Northumberland). The Bars (town gates) of York were of this form, though all have lost their barbicans except Walmgate Bar. The double-gate arrangement at Brougham (Cumbria) gives something of the same effect.

Keeps in the fourteenth century took on a variety of forms. In the north of the country the square tower predominated; even in the south the round keep so usual in the previous century was only represented by the new tower built on the motte of Southampton in 1378–80. Experimental forms were common. We have included the singular keeps of Llangibby and Pontefract as part of the Edwardian movement in defensive architecture, though they may well be held rather to belong to the fourteenth century in the narrow sense which we are using here.

The main group of fourteenth-century keeps is made up of rectangular towers — generally elongated in plan — with round or polygonal towers on the angles. Dudley has already been mentioned, and there are others at Stafford and Nunney (Somerset). At Stafford, a long narrow block with very salient octagonal towers at its angles, built on a motte, survives only as the foundations under a large 'folly' of 1800, itself now largely pulled down. This reoccupation of the ancient castle of Stafford was licensed in 1348; there is little evidence of any outer buildings of this date in the original earthwork bailey or elsewhere. In the same way Nunney (licensed in 1373), which has large round towers on its angles, had as its dependent work only a weak walled enclosure running up the valley slope outside the moat; the effect is not so much that of an ordinary keep, still less of a northern tower, as of a castle whose defences had been contracted so as to contain only the quarters of its lord. The tower was machicolated all round, and the one small door had a drawbridge; the moat is wide and wet, and stands where it can only with difficulty be drained; like Bodiam, which it does not otherwise resemble in the slightest, this was a powerful castle. Llanblethian (St Quintin's, South Glamorgan) may have had a keep of a similar kind, while the early square keep of Mulgrave (North Yorkshire), was fitted with round turrets at some uncertain date. The finest and most complex example of this sort of tower, however, is probably Edwardian; this is Picton (Pembroke), a massive block of building much altered to form a nobleman's house: its original character — a tower, not a small enclosure castle — is attested by its vaulted basement; on each corner it has a powerful round tower rising from an octagonal base; these are all of different sizes. There is a small double-towered gatehouse at one end, and old prints indicate that there was a half-round tower on the other. Versions of this type of keep are common in France, and there are a number in Ireland.

Of square or rectangular keeps in the south, Fillongley No. 1 (Warwickshire) was licensed in 1301, so that what appears to be a square tower in its ditched enclosure may be truly Edwardian in period; but the very large structure at Baginton in the same county is of fourteenth-century date, and so is the tower of 'Norman' plan at Hopton in Shropshire. The great tower on the motte of Fotheringhay (Northamptonshire), now vanished, was called the Fetterlock, so that its plan was presumably apsidal.

In some larger northern castles we find keeps which owe little to the Northern style. The five-sided keep of Raby (Durham) has already been mentioned; the octagonal tower on the motte of the bishop's castle at Durham itself (completely rebuilt in the nineteenth century) dated from the reign of Edward III. Warkworth in Northumberland was given an extraordinary keep, both powerful and palatial, in about 1400. This stands on the motte, with a widely battered base; its plan is square, with a square turret on the middle of each face;[12] all the salient angles are chamfered off; finally, there is a central turret over a ventilation-shaft. At Knaresborough (North Yorkshire), a great semi-octagonal tower was added to the castle in 1307–12. This is much damaged, and the rest of the fabric is in an even more fragmentary state, so that the contradiction between the very heavily defended entrance to the tower and the enormous windows in its rear is not easy to resolve; in fact the tower seems to have been designed to be held, along with a loop of very lofty walling (of which only a stump remains), enclosing a small courtyard into which the great windows opened. This appears to have been entirely an appendage of the tower, only entered from it; but even so, one may confess to doubts whether the tower, for all its massive strength, may be legitimately called a keep.

A similar doubt applies to the castle of Wardour (Wiltshire), licensed in 1392. This great block of building — a regular hexagon with a rectangular gatehouse projecting on one side — has a tiny central courtyard; can this properly be called a tower or an enclosure-castle?

There are other less certain indications of fourteenth-century keeps, as for example the North-East Tower of Farleigh Hungerford, which has vanished except for its foundations, but was far larger in plan than the other corner-towers.

Notes

1. In the survey made for Henry V in 1415 — *Nomina castrorum et fortaliciorum infra comitatum Northumbrie* (British Museum, Harleian MS 309, folios 202b-203b; printed in Cadwallader John Bates, *The border holds of Northumberland* (Newcastle-upon-Tyne, 1891), pp. 13-18); 32 out of 78 towers and several 'castles' have owners with no title of nobility, not even 'Chlr' (knight). Many are parsons.

2. See Harvey, *The castles and walled towns of England* (London, 1911), pp. 171-2. The alternate name for the type — 'The Lancastrian Castle' — would have been unfortunate, as most quadrangular castles were built before 1399, when the Lancastrian branch of the Plantagenets reached the throne.

3. See John Harvey, *Gothic England* (London, 1947), plates 61, 62.

4. Where a donkey in a treadmill is still used to raise the water-supply from far below.

5. It was palisaded in the Civil war (*Symonds' diary*, Camden Socy., (Old Series, 74), p. 231); even the plan of c. 1444 from the Boarstall Chartulary (*Victoria county history, Buckinghamshire*, iv, facing p. 10) appears to show the gatehouse only, and no walls.

6. Against the French under Montalembert d'Essé in 1549; Holinshed, *History of Scotland* (part of the edition of 1808), pp. v, 562.

7. The lord of this castle seems to have used questionable means to rebuild it; *Calendar of Patent Rolls* (1307-13), p. 369 for complaints.

8. But see O'Neil, *Castles and cannon* (Oxford, 1960), p. 6.

9. *Ibid.*, pp. 6-7.

10. The bases of these towers have recently been exposed.

11. At Alnwick and Brampton Bryan the wall-walk of the flanking walls can be reached by a stair from a door inside the passage, but even this may have been guarded by the pit of a drawbridge.

12. This extraordinary plan has parallels in the Irish castle of Trim (County Meath) and in one of the two towers, probably abortive, whose bases survive at Llanhilleth (Glamorgan); also at Rushen (Isle of Man).

13

The Fifteenth Century, and Early Artillery Defences

By the year 1400 the impetus had gone out of castle-building in England. The country had been one of the leaders in the design of European fortifications down to less than a hundred years previously; but now there was little to do but fill in the gaps in the system of second-rate castles which had been built up in the fourteenth century. The absence of invasion, or of civil war prolonged beyond a mere *coup d'état*, left the larger castles with little employment; even in the Wars of the Roses the object was not to conquer territory, but to seize the organs of government. A contestant in possession of these could only be resisted by an opponent who could defeat him in the field and seize the government in his turn. Had the royal castles been in good repair, the path of revolution would have been impossible. But the defence of private castles against the central authority was still impossible, weakly wielded though the latter now commonly was. The only practical defence of a private castle was that of Alnwick, one of the three Northumberland castles held by the Lancastrians in 1461–2;[1] even this was taken. The lesser emergencies, against which the second-rate castles of the fourteenth century had been built, were hardly less likely to arise, and called for much the same sort of precautions as before, but there were fewer families that could afford to build a castle. New castellation was only on a fraction of the scale that it had been in the fourteenth century.

In quality, moreover, there was a considerable falling-off; the degeneracy of the English castle, which earlier writers have supposed to have appeared at the beginning of the fourteenth century, becomes very plain in the fifteenth. In particular castles like Croft (Herefordshire), Caister (Norfolk), Hever (Kent) and Herstmonceux (East Sussex) are flimsily built, in a way that would hardly have suited the architects of Bodiam and Cooling, At the same time, there is little in the line of evolution or experiment; except for a greater use of machicolations, a fifteenth-century castle is much like one of the fourteenth. The exception occurs where we meet works specially designed for fire-artillery; but these are very few and at least one — God's House Tower at Southampton — could possibly have been built as early as 1380.[2]

But we must not overstate the case; there had been lightly built castles before, and these were meant seriously in military terms: Penard (West Glamorgan) comes to mind at once.[3] This dates from the thirteenth century.

Again, we must not take too low a view of fifteenth-century work in general. There is always Raglan (Monmouthshire, now Gwent) to consider; though a splendid dwelling, it was also a very serious military stronghold. As has been remarked, our late-medieval castles have generally been unlucky in their fate. Of fifteenth-century castles we may particularly regret the destruction of Lathom (Lancashire).

Nor was the Crown quite as inactive as one had been inclined to believe; the *History of the King's Works* records an unexpected amount of expenditure, and Edward IV at least appears to have been the builder-king whom Skelton makes to speak in his disturbing threnody:

> I made the Tower strong, I wist not why;
> I knew not to whom I purchased Tattershall;
> I amended Dover on the mountain high,
> And London I provoked to fortify the wall;
> I made Nottingham a place full royall,
>   Windsor, Eltham, and many other mo —
> Yet, at the last, I went from them all,
>   ... *Et ecce nunc in pulvere dormio.*

At Nottingham the base of an enormous semi-octagonal tower survives to show that this king's ideas were not petty; at Warwick an ambitious structure, unfinished, is ascribed to Richard III.

There is another warning to be given about the decadence of English castle-architecture in the fifteenth century: it is a purely English phenomenon. As to France, the splendour of French fifteenth-century castles is perhaps the main reason why our neighbour nation eclipses us in the field of medieval fortification; and it is the castles of the latter part of the century, after the final defeat of the English invaders, which are the finest.[4] Over Europe in general, castles were built well into the sixteenth century; this is true of Scotland, Germany and the Baltic countries. The big fifteenth-century castles of Spain are familiar, while as for Italy, the powerful *rocca* of the late fifteenth or early sixteenth century, with its squat flankers — square towers, roundels, even proper bastions — is a familiar feature of the Italian countryside.[5] Commonly it is heavily machicolated and pierced for guns of various calibres, like the splendid example of Senigallia (Marche).

This means that the decided decadence of the English castle in the fifteenth century must be due to strictly English phenomena; the likely nature of these has already been indicated. In addition, the expense of paying the excellent professional soldiers of the time, whose wages were high, weighed heavily on public and even private defence budgets. We must, therefore, refuse to follow either of two very familiar arguments — that the castle declined in England because of the demands of domestic comfort; or that it did so because of the growing power of fire-artillery. Other nations had guns; other nations aimed at a rising standard of comfort. Factors applicable to Europe as a whole cannot be called in to explain a condition peculiar to England.

Our surviving fifteenth-century castles are thus not of the first interest; they largely repeat fourteenth-century plans and methods; over most of England the main type was the familiar *Wasserburg* with the serious defences (apart from the moat) concentrated at the entrance. Herstmonceux could serve as a typical example; it is a large and palatial brick building, which had several interior courtyards, with towers on all four corners, a major gate and a postern-tower front and rear, and towers in the middle of the other two sides. So far the defensive arrangements were very much those of Bodiam; but between each pair of towers was placed a turret rising only to the level of the curtains. There are eight of these turrets, some of which have been used as window-bays by the later owners of the castle, who zealously pierced large openings in its walls. How strong these defences were originally must depend on a detailed study of their fenestration, which has not yet been made; but they do not appear to have been particularly powerful. Nevertheless, all round this rather modest perimeter extended a formidable moat, and at the inner end of the bridge there waited a very real and formidable gatehouse, of imposing bulk, machicolated and pierced for archery and artillery. This castle is frequently supposed to show strong French influence (see Platt, *The castle in mediaeval England and Wales* (London, 1982), p. 168). I had the privilege of visiting it with the Château-Gaillard organisation in 1966; this being the ninth centenary of the Norman Conquest, the French contingent was large, and of illustrious membership; but all with one voice asserted that they had nothing in France like Herstmonceux.

In Herefordshire, Bronsill, Croft and possibly the small and curious Treago followed this type. Croft is unimpressive, with its thin walls and slender corner towers; but with its moat filled in and its gatehouse destroyed it could hardly be otherwise. Bronsill, licensed in 1460, is represented only by foundations along its moat, and by one round tower of its gatehouse. It may never have been finished, for it is in several ways a castle to have left its mark on history. It was approximately square, of the Bodiam formula: two opposite gatehouses, face and rear; towers on the angles and extra towers on the flanks — eight projecting works in all. On its fragmentary gate-tower there is a round opening for a gun of some kind, and round three sides of its ditch there is still a wide, flat-topped bank which suggests some sort of defence against artillery. Kirby Muxloe in Leicestershire is a big brick quadrangular moated castle, built in 1480–4 and left unfinished after the beheading (it can hardly be called an execution) of its owner, William, Lord Hastings. There is a rectangular gatehouse with turrets at each corner, and there were to have been seven square or rectangular towers, of which one is complete. In front of the curtains — though not of the towers — there is a narrow terrace, fronted by a thin wall. Nowhere is there enough left to suggest its employment. Both the gatehouse and the one surviving tower were amply provided for the use of guns, apparently of fairly heavy calibre; the gatehouse has six ports and the tower seven, all on the lowest floor. The ports have a fair amount of internal splay, and are in general well arranged. In the tower the inner arches of the ports were blocked by a thin skin of brickwork which excluded draughts, rats, etc. in peacetime,[6] but could have been knocked out in short order when war was at hand; the ports in the gatehouse seem to have been left open, as more likely to have been needed without warning. The balance between domestic convenience and military strength was clearly well kept. This was to have been a splendid residence, but well protected against the more unimportant class of enemies, and with ample opportunities for hitting back at the more formidable sort of opponents with fairly powerful artillery. Caister (Norfolk) is a brickwork castle of considerable area, with wide moats around its main enclosure and two dependent wards. Its main gatehouse has been destroyed, and the curtains are of amazing fragility — in places as thin as 2 feet (61 cm). The flanking was largely by little buttress-turrets, with a couple of larger round towers, the bigger of which survives — a slim, lofty cylinder of five storeys with a turret-room above again; pierced with enfilading gun-ports low down, but also (and most exceptionally) having what looks like a sort of sniper's nest, with half-a-dozen ports, in the turret-room right at the top of the tower, which can hardly have been of much use. In spite of these military features, and of the continuous machicolations round most of the surviving defences, the impression is that of a degenerate and almost entirely specious castle. All the same, Caister was defended in 1469 against an irresistible superiority of force, and when it was yielded its commander did not give its weakness as one of the reasons for his surrender.[7]

Hever Castle (Kent) is almost the ultimate in front-gate fortification: it is double-moated, but three of its sides are of slight thickness and only moderate height, and now pierced with windows. Flanking is confined to the fourth side, where two little turrets stand beside a very powerful rectangular gatehouse.

Development in the exposed regions was not important; the Welsh March was shaken in the early years of the century by the rebellion of Owain Glyndŵr, but the existing network of defences was sufficient to contain this, and no new construction can be ascribed to this emergency. The few new castles in the border counties — of which Raglan is by far the finest — have nothing to do with border defence.

The north country also produced little of note and less of novelty. The building of towers went on apace, but Northumberland produced no castle in this century except perhaps Bywell, where only a gatehouse remains; it is suspected that the enclosure was never built. There is no fifteenth-century castle in Westmorland (now Southern Cumbria), and in Cumberland (northern Cumbria) Askerton may only have become a castle as a result of a rebuilding of 1485–1525; otherwise the only late castle was Rockcliffe, built between 1493 and 1522; though always called a castle, it was apparently a large tower. Witton-le-Wear is Durham's one fifteenth-century castle; it is an unimposing keep-and-enclosure castle; even Yorkshire only produced two weak quadrangular castles — Hornby and Snape — and a few fragments. Only in Lancashire, south of the Sands, was there a considerable group of castles of this date. Unfortunately little survives of this group: Lathom 'House' — in fact a strong castle with a keep and two wards — and Bury have vanished entirely, and little remains of Greenhalgh and Thurland.

The invasion-coast produced a number of chain-towers at Portsmouth, Dartmouth and Fowey, and some of the earliest blockhouses for guns; but we have lost what was almost certainly the finest work of this sort, the 'strong Castel quadrate having at each Corner a great Round Tower' which Leland mentions at Plymouth.[8] Nothing remains of it but part of its barbican; this is one of the worst casualties in the whole history of English fortification.

A few great towers of this period were added to castles in southern England. The splendid brick tower of Tattershall (Lincolnshire), for all its angle-turrets and two-stage parapet, was never a military keep, and its fairly numerous and low windows give us cause to question whether its addition left the castle weaker or stronger.

There can be no similar question in the case of Lord Hastings' Tower at Ashby-de-la-Zouche (Leicestershire). To what was probably something less than a castle was added this splendid machicolated tower, the resulting combination being rightly given the name of castle. Nunney is an earlier example of the use of a powerful keep with a feebly fortified enclosure, and the finest of our surviving castles of the fifteenth century appears to have been begun with a similar plan in mind.

This is Raglan; here the earliest parts of the building — dated to the second quarter of the century — include a powerful tower and weak gate, which was latterly walled up, being replaced by a powerful twin-tower gatehouse, part of a strong enclosure of irregular shape, flanked by a variety of polygonal towers. This remodelled plan seems to have been begun in about 1450. The keep — the Yellow Tower of Gwent — stood right outside this ward; it is a lofty tower of the unusual hexagonal plan, with four storeys surviving; its summit has been destroyed, but was presumably machicolated, and its basement was pierced for crossbows and fairly heavy guns. Round this stands a low hexagonal *chemise* or 'mantlet' — a concentric work with small turrets on the angles. Keep and *chemise* stand in their own wet moat; the perimeter of the rest of the castle is largely protected by a natural escarpment. The new gate opens between a pair of semi-hexagonal towers —

beaked to the front, and fallaciously suggesting an anticipation of the four-sided bastion of Vauban's days and earlier. The ward is very wide in relation to its length, and a large domestic block divides it lengthwise, into a service area and a private court; there is no military significance in this division, but it does mean that the rooms in the dividing block, which include the hall, chapel, buttery and long gallery, are sheltered inside the defences, except at the furthest end.

Apart from the beaked, polygonal plans of most of the towers, the general effect is that of a normal castle, built in accordance with general principles of medieval fortification, but also equipped for defence with guns. A similar castle, though a great deal smaller, is Berry Pomeroy (Devon). The site is on the top of a cliff, and the line of defence was comparatively short. There is a gatehouse with two semi-hexagonal towers, like that of Raglan, and a half-round flanker, St Margaret's Tower; the latter in particular has the appearance of a thirteenth-century tower, and can be taken for one by the unwary.[9]

It is remarkable that little French influence can be found in fifteenth-century English work. For example, the common French double drawbridge — a wide one and a narrow one side by side, with slots overhead for the arms of their counterpoises — was only copied in the Yellow Tower at Raglan; while the change in elevation of the normal castle, whereby the curtains were raised to the level of the tower-heads,[10] found no acceptance in England.

More needs to be said about the use of guns, and at least something about the guns themselves. The application of gunpowder to artillery dates from the early fourteenth century, beginning in the third decade and becoming widespread over Europe in a very short time. From 1345 onwards, as we learn from Tout's excellent paper on the subject,[11] guns and powder became a standard item of expenditure in the accounts of the English crown. The first guns were all very small, but not intended to be fired when held by hand; by the 1380s we hear of 'handgonnes', and by the same time of fairly substantial cannon. One group of English weapons is mentioned as having fired stones 24 inches in circumference;[12] they will therefore have had a bore of about 7.6 inches or 19 cm. One group of 'great cannon', however, averaged as little as 150 pounds in weight (68 kg). 'Small cannon' are mentioned, with average weights of 49 lbs and 43 lbs (22 and 19.6 kg).[13] Guns such as these are too heavy to have been fired manually or carried on the march; but they could easily have been moved about in action by one man, still more by the two or three that are likely to have formed their crews. It seems that this intermediate class of weapon is of great importance in the history of castles, but it has generally been rather neglected. Handguns are studied by historians of the infantry; guns large enough to have had a wheeled carriage attract the notice of gunners and naval historians, but this middling character of guns falls between the two stools; and yet it played an important part over a long period of history.

The handgun of the late fourteenth century and much of the fifteenth was a miniature cannon — a poor little weapon, small in the bore and short in the piece — mounted on the end of a long stock or pole, whose main function was to keep the treacherous little weapon away from the face and eyes of the gunner. As in the case of the contemporary crossbow, the butt was not held to the shoulder; in the case of the gun, it seems to have been passed either over the shoulder or under the arm.

Heavy guns were lashed or bolted down on sleeper-like beds of wood, crude stocks called 'trunks'. In a few cases these had small truck-wheels, as in the replica-carriage now supporting the great gun of Edinburgh castle, Mons Meg. In some cases guns were even laid on the ground.

It is clear that we may expect to find ports for handguns at shoulder-level, a port for a heavy equipment close to the floor. When we find, on the other hand, ports opening at waist-height, we may well expect them to have been intended for real guns, but of the lighter calibres. The oldest examples in England, for example, are apparently the ports in the arcade on the Western Shore at Southampton (Hampshire), made soon after 1360. At this time there were only light guns available; neither handguns nor 'heavies' had been developed. Accordingly, we find the ports set in tapered embrasures with level floors 'from 3 to 4 feet above the present floor level, which seems to be that of medieval times'.[14] Possibly the guns could have been laid on the floor of the recess, but in some thin-walled examples, such as the West Gate of Winchester, there was not room on the sill;[15] one is inclined to visualise a support like the trestle-table shown in the famous illumination (dated to 1326) in Walter de Millemete's MS *De officiis regum* in the library of Christ Church, Oxford, which is our earliest representation of a gun. But a support of this kind is not necessary; it would be natural to handle a portable gun which was too big to fire from the shoulder at waist-height, especially one with movable chambers. Some, no doubt, had stands of a fairly sophisticated nature, but others were meant to be laid and fired by hand. Even a 'small' gun of 50 lb weight — and many will have been far below that — could be effectively fired by a man supporting the breech-end (preferably by means of a wooden stock or some other projection) while the muzzle rested on the sill of the gunport or some other support; provided only that the gunner was not expected to receive the full recoil of the weapon himself. We must, therefore, look for means of recoil-reduction; and it is not hard to find them. Surviving guns of the sort with which we are concerned, and even some that seem small enough to have been fired from the shoulder, are frequently equipped on the under side of the muzzle with a projecting skeg or claw, of considerable strength, with the flat side towards the breech of the gun.[16] This was clearly intended to hook over something such as a parapet or a port-sill, and take the kick of the weapon when it fired. The German name for a handgun, by the time these weapons became reasonably practical, was *Hakenbuchs* — hook-gun. This intractably Teutonic word passed into French as *arquebuse*, and hence into modern English with the loss of the last letter only. (In contemporary English, the name was the euphonious word *hagbussh*.) In fact the arquebus was an ordinary gun, fired from the shoulder, having a barrel and a butt of normal size, and capable of some quite effective shooting; according to Sir Charles Oman, it won its first decisive battle at Bicocca in 1522. The armourers, however, increased the thickness of body-armour until the arquebus had to give place to the long and clumsy, but hard-hitting handgun called a 'musket'. There is little evidence that the arquebus, in its years of success, carried a hook under its muzzle; on the contrary, we hear of an *arquebuse à croc* as a heavier weapon of the wall-gun class. (We may notice in passing that the word 'musket' makes its first appearance as the name of a heavy, swivel-mounted weapon.)[17]

The use of the muzzle-hook may explain a curious feature of many gun-ports: the presence of a pair of square sockets in the sides of the recess, generally close to the actual opening of the port and about level with its sill. As these sockets are now almost invariably empty, it is clear that they were meant to carry a timber[18] — a stout wooden transom across the recess. An example of such a transom survives at the Dutch castle of Doornenburg. This would make a more suitable support for the hooked muzzle than the sill of the port itself. The subject of these transoms is one which has hardly been studied at all in English, and no apology seems to be due for offering no very systematic account of them here. They are certainly not confined to England. They do not seem to have come into use before the latter part of the fifteenth century, and appear as late as the reign of Henry VIII. Matters are complicated by the use of somewhat similar timber transoms or sills in heavy gunports, for example in St Margaret's Tower at Berry Pomeroy, built at the end of the fifteenth century, in the Lord's Mount at Berwick-on-Tweed, begun in about 1541, and in the battery at Norham (Northumberland), built early in the reign of Henry VIII. At Norham the guns were obviously meant to be really powerful, and here a stout timber sill was let into the floor and into the walls at the ends, about 4 feet (1.22 m) in from the actual opening of the port. At Edgcumbe (Cornwall), a Henry VIII block-house of either early date or archaic type, the transoms passed above the ports for the heavy guns. It seems clear that this sort of transom was meant to carry some sort of a breeching for the gun. It is also possible that some of the transoms to ports for wall-guns were meant to carry the swivel mounting that was developed at some time in the late fifteenth or early sixteenth century.

As to the actual openings of the ports, most early examples are of the inverted-keyhole type; the very earliest are simply ordinary arrowslits with a rather large round oillet at the base; the vertical slot became shorter in course of time, and acted merely as a sighting-slit. This type is of the widest distribution, being found from Scotland to Italy, from Spain to Egypt. In England it becomes less usual in the fifteenth century, being often replaced by a plain round opening, usually cut in a single ashlar stone; a couple of early examples are to be found on the famous outer gate of Cooling, licensed in 1381 — though Lord Cobham, its builder, survived until 1408. At Kirby Muxloe there is a separate small sighting-slit above each round opening. More rarely we find the oillet halfway down the slit; this seems to be a fifteenth-century feature at the earliest; it is to be seen in the gatehouse of Berry Pomeroy and the 'college' ward at Caister.

A type of gunport common in other countries is the *canonnière à la française*, known to a more prosaic generation of British antiquaries as the *letterbox* gunport. Here traverse is permitted rather than elevation; the narrow throat of the port, in the thickness of the wall, is circular; its outer opening a wide horizontal slot (whence the name). Variations occur; sometimes the ends of the slot are rounded, sometimes it is divided in the middle by a short mullion, to support the lintel. Later, and more importantly, the narrow slot is replaced by an elliptical opening, permitting a degree of elevation and depression. While these are 'French ports', they appear in other countries, in Germanophone Switzerland, in Italy, in Scotland;[19] but in England, significantly perhaps, the only examples are a pair of the narrower sort at Harbottle (Northumberland). Once again, we find the builders of our fifteenth-century castles showing a certain insularity, or at least insensitivity to French initiatives.

Latterly the ports for heavy guns were square, as at Berry, at Carisbrooke, and in the coast-defence towers of the south coast; wider ports, allowing for a substantial traverse, called for an arched head, as we find in the work of Henry VIII, and elsewhere around the Danish fortress of Hammershus, the battery at the rear of Somerset Tower on the Isle of Jersey, and the very formidable ports on the inner ward of Villa Viçosa in Portugal.

Sometimes ports are combined with loops; at Herstmonceux and in the Yellow Tower at Raglan there are round gunports under the sills of fine arrowslits with four oillets each. At Berry, in the basement of St Margaret's Tower there were three openings, of which the most developed is well preserved. Here there is a vertical slit with two round oillets opening symmetrically on it; the slit ends below in a massive stone sill, beneath which opens a single square port for a heavy gun. At each opening there are sockets in the sides of the recess for timber transoms; these vary in size, the thinnest being at the top. The middle hole was plainly for a wall-gun, as the lowest was for a heavy equipment; the topmost hole may have been for a hand-gun (used in a rather cramped posture) or an alternative port for uphill shooting with the wall-gun; there seem to have been no openings in this position in the other two loops.

The employment of guns from ports of all these kinds depended first on their siting, secondly in the amount of traverse allowed. The heavy guns, lying on the ground, were particularly restricted in regard to traversing; it is sometimes said of them (for example by Sir Charles Peers of Kirby Muxloe)[20] that they could only have fired straight ahead. In fact, even the worst examples — which certainly do not include Kirby Muxloe — permit at

167

least some lateral movement. At Raglan it is possible to see a certain amount of development; thus, the gunports in the basement of the Yellow Tower — partly because they are pierced through a great thickness of wall — are very narrow and permitted only the narrowest arc of fire. One port points towards the ward of the castle, and its sector of fire was thus only a few feet long, very narrow, and most unlikely ever to be occupied by an enemy. Matters were not improved when in due course the low mantlet-wall was built round the tower; if this stood head-high it would have completely masked the gunports; but since these do not appear to have been blocked as useless, it is possible that an embrasure of the parapet was left in front of each — not enough of the parapet remains for us to be sure; but at the best this would not have improved the field of fire. At much the same time the main gatehouse and the polygonal tower beside it were built; and their complex plan, pierced with a great number of gunports, rendered possible a most lethal crossfire anywhere close to the gate. At Kirby Muxloe the plan is altogether unfavourable for defensive fire, but the gunports are so well placed that there are very few positions around the surviving parts of the defences where one is not confronted by the saturnine gaze of a port.

In the early days of artillery the provision of ports is the most important development — indeed the only substantial development — due to the new weapon. As far as England is concerned, no other substantial alterations are to be noticed before the reign of Henry VIII. The fine big roundels of continental fifteenth-century work have no parallel in this country; still less have wholehearted artillery-castles such as that of Ham (Somme)[21] or the citadel of Schaffhausen in Switzerland.[22] The idea of defence by artillery caught on very early, but it was long before anyone concerned himself about protection against gunfire.

To an unadvised modern mind this must seem ridiculous; artillery was to prove fatal to the old systems of defence; why were not these immediately strengthened in a last desperate effort to stave off the inevitable? The fact is that, when dealing with a civilisation, a form of government, a type of machine, or a means of war which has since been overtaken by the processes of change, historians are apt to display 'what might be called a post-mortem attitude, to listen too anxiously for the first distant rumblings of the inevitable storm, to look with undue avidity for symptoms of decay' (W.L. Burn) until this tendency has become almost instinctive with the ordinary reader and writer.

In fact, the invention of the gun was of the utmost advantage in the first place to the defence; one can tell as much from the eagerness with which castle-builders everywhere found place for the new weapons. The whole mass of offensive siege-apparatus up to this time had been carpenter's work: pavises, cats or sows, rolling belfries, slinging-engines; and all were now exposed to new and more penetrating missiles on the part of the defence. The new weapons were quite small, and could be mounted anywhere where they were needed; even a castle's 'great guns' would not be the largest of their kind. A fair-sized gun could also discharge a shower of scrap-iron or the like, which could do a great deal of mischief to an attack on the gates, or to an escalading-party. One particular casualty was likely to be the great trebuchet, hitherto queen of sieges. It may be necessary to recall that this weapon consisted of an enormous wooden trestle on which pivoted a gigantic counterpoised pole-sling. It was virtually impossible for the attackers to screen such a weapon from direct fire, since its own range was limited, and the trestle might easily stand 24 feet (7.3 m) high. Worst of all, the main bearing — the most vital part of the whole machine — was at, or close to, its highest point. On the other hand, trebuchets used in defence could be screened behind the walls of town or castle, and would have been as effective as ever.

The options of the attackers being so restricted, it was natural that they should try to redress their position by battering down the walls with their own ordnance. In course of time, as is well known, this became a straightforward and easy task; but it did not take that form in the beginning. We are told of a few premature successes by artillery, like the capture of Berwick-on-Tweed in 1405,[23] due mainly to panic raised by the unfamiliar weapon; but by the 1450s it is generally concluded that guns were in a winning position, with the successes of Charles VII's artillery under the brothers Bureau, and of Mohammed II at the siege of Constantinople. All the same, these triumphs were won at the expense of enemies who were beaten from the start.

Certainly, breaking down stone walls with stone shot cannot have been a very rewarding business, and so little came of it when the projectiles were small that we find the size of guns dramatically increased and increased again. The result was that, before the gun as a weapon was much more than a century old, it had been launched into the first of those attacks of gigantism which occur at various points in its history. The English in 1384 were using guns of a bore of nearly 8 inches, as has been mentioned. These were already substantial weapons; 8 inches (20 cm) was to be the bore of the 'whole cannon' of the sixteenth and seventeenth centuries. Fifty years later, in 1434, the English besiegers of Mont-Saint-Michel abandoned two guns which are still preserved there; the one 19 inches (48 cm) in bore, the other 15 inches (38 cm). Still larger examples are 'Mons Meg' of Edinburgh and 'Dulle Griet' of Ghent, with the great Turkish gun from the Dardanelles, dated 1464, now at the Tower of London. Such monsters posed some difficult problems in logistics; they weighed much less than a big trebuchet, but the latter came to pieces for transport, and never involved such alarming axle-loads as a big gun. It was presumably to reduce these that some of the biggest fifteenth-century cannon were made to unscrew in the middle of the piece, so that the breech could be taken apart from the chase.[24]

Nor were these early guns pleasant or safe to use; the fact that the Church allotted gunners to the patronage of St Barbara, whose intercession is invoked on behalf of those facing the immediate bitterness of death, is sufficiently alarming in itself; early writers also insisted that gunners should be men of extreme piety — their souls could be required of them at every shot they fired. Nor is all this merely a churchman's view of gunnery; when Henry, Prince of Wales — the future Henry V — returned in triumph from his campaign of 1408 against Owain Glyndŵr's fortresses on Cardigan Bay, he brought with him the fragments of 'Neelpot' (Nieuport?) and 'Messager' which had blown up at the siege of Aberystwyth, and of 'The King's Daughter' which had burst in front of Harlech. The explosion of the 'Lion' at the siege of Roxburgh in 1460 killed James II of Scots. The built-up construction of so many of these huge guns, with an inner barrel of longitudinal bars held together by an outer casing of iron hoops shrunk on to it, reflects considerable credit on the technical skill of the smiths who used this method of construction, but it is impossible for an artilleryman of a later age to refrain from the comment that this was simply not the way to make a gun; the technology of gunmaking was exploring a blind alley. The introduction of iron shot was fatal to the built-up weapon. Far more effective than gunstones, they were also heavier and needed a more powerful charge. Only a cast gun, and one of very much heavier metal for its bore, would serve. As a result, we find a brisk reduction in the size and bore of guns (though less in their weight), until the largest current piece was the 'cannon royal' of 8 to 8.5 inch (20 to 21.5 cm) bore. As this could weigh as much as 8,000 lb (3,629 kg), it was not much lighter than some of the huge built-up guns of the previous century, and in fact the largest guns in general use in the sixteenth and seventeenth centuries were the demi-cannon, a short 30-pounder (14.6 kg) and the culverin, a long 17 pounder (7.7 kg).[25] Henry VIII — a sound judge in artillery matters — believed that giant guns had a moral value; but his own great gun 'Policy' was a wooden counterfeit.

There are not many artillery-works of medieval date in England, and those that there are cannot be described as highly specialized. The West Gate of Canterbury (Kent), for example, built in 1375–81 (probably by the great English master-mason, Henry Yevele)[26] is merely a good example of a town-gate; but it has at least 19 gunports of the inverted-keyhole kind. Another fine work on a town wall is that variously called the South Castle, the Spur, the Millhouse, and God's House Tower, at Southampton (Hampshire): a long rectangular projection at the south-east corner of the town. It served a number of purposes, including the control of the sluices of the moat, but also has eight gunports on the first floor. These were for wall-guns, and are of the usual inverted-keyhole form.

To the middle of the fifteenth century may probably be dated the curious little building misnamed Bow and Arrow Castle[27] on the Isle of Portland (Dorset). A small, compact, tower-like structure on an isolated rock, with an irregular plan, it has five small circular ports for guns of the wall-piece size.

There are virtually no internal features, and the whole suggests an infantry blockhouse.

The large artillery-work on the north side of Warwick Castle was begun by King Richard III (1483–5). It was never finished, and was hideously mutilated by a later age, but it evidently consisted of a large, roughly square block, half projecting from the line of the curtain, with octagonal turrets on its salient angles. There seem to have been originally seven round ports, some of them with sighting-slits, for heavy guns. There is no sign of any skill in their dispositions, or in the general plan of the work, which was certainly rather archaic for the 1480s.

Notes

1. The other two were Bamborough and Dunstanburgh, both royal castles.

2. For its dating, see O'Neil, *Castles and cannon* (Oxford, 1960), pp. 11, 14.

3. Its walls vary in thickness from 3 feet 6 inches to 2 feet 10 inches (1.07 m to 86 cms). One turret has walls only 1 foot 7 inches (48 cms) thick. The superb quality of its Mountain Limestone mortar has preserved this altogether flimsy castle in fair condition down to the present day; there may have been many similar castles less well built.

4. See Ritter, *Châteaux, donjons, et places fortes* (Paris, 1953), pp. 110-139. The list of splendid fortresses here set out makes it difficult to follow the suggestion of M. François Gebelin, in *The Châteaux of France* (trans. Hart, London 1964), p. 84, that this period can be written off as a time of decadence.

5. See, for example, Marinelli, *Le antiche fortezze di Romagna* (1938); Hale, in *Europe in the late middle ages* (ed. Hale, Highfield, and Smalley, London, 1965), pp. 466-94.

6. The basement of this tower was a habitable room with a fireplace and a window.

7. *Paston letters* (ed. Gairdner, London, 1904), v, pp. 56-7.

8. John Leland, *The itinerary of John Leland the antiquary in or about the years 1535– 45* (ed. Lucy Toulmin Smith), i, p. 214.

9. E.g. Sir Nikolaus Pevsner, *Buildings of England 5 (South Devon)*, p. 49, accepts both gatehouse and tower as of *c.* 1300.

10. See Ritter, *op. cit.,* pp. 69, 112-13 (with a long quotation from Viollet-le-Duc), p. 121.

11. 'Firearms in England in the fourteenth century', in *Collected papers of Thomas Frederick Tout* (Manchester, 1934), ii, pp. 233-76.

12. Hogg, *English artillery, 1326–1716* (London, 1963), p. 202, quoting *Issue Rolls of the Exchequer* (ed. Devon, London, 1837), p. 212. See also Tout, *op. cit.,* p. 256.

13. Tout, *op. cit.,* pp. 253-6. Weights cited are of the 'piece' only; wooden stocks and carriages are not included.

14. O'Neil, *op. cit.,* p. 7.

15. *Ibid.,* p. 12.

16. For these claws, see Wagner, Drobna and Durdik, *Medieval costume, armour and weapons* (tr. Layton; London, n.d.), part vii, plates 1-4, 6-7, 10, 12.

17. Lewis, *Armada guns* (London, 1961), pp. 30, 220-1.

18. In some Henrician ports, this was replaced by an iron bar.

19. See Viollet-le-Duc, *An essay on the military architecture of the middle ages* (trans. Macdermott, Oxford and London, 1860), p. 181; Châtelain, *Châteaux forts, images de pierre*

des guerres médiévales (Paris, 1983), p. 99; Sailhan, *Bulletin de la Société des Antiquares de l'Ouest*, 4th series, xiv (1978), p. 552, types IIIa, IIIb and IIIc. Cruden, *The Scottish castle* (Edinburgh, 1960), pp. 218-24, plates 41, 42; Caldwell, *Fort*, xii (1984) pp. 15-24; MacGibbon and Ross *The castellated and domestic architecture of Scotland* (Edinburgh, 1887), in particular the enormous number of gunports at Noltland (or Notland) in the Orkney Isles, ii, pp. 213-21.

20. Sir Charles Peers, *Kirby Muxloe Castle* (Official Guide, HMSO, 1917), p. 19

21. Albert Mersier, 'Le château de Ham', *Bulletin Monumental*, lxxviii (1914), pp. 232-315.

22. Viollet-le-Duc, *op. cit.*, pp. 190-9.

23. *Eulogium historiae, a monacho quodam Malmesburiensi* ... (ed. Haydon, Rolls Series, 9) iii, p. 408.

24. The Dardanelles gun is exhibited with the two sections separated. It should be emphasised that these guns were not breech-loaders, but simply screw-guns, taken apart for transport purposes.

25. The variation between individual guns was enormous, and the metric equivalents given here are far too exact.

26. Harvey, *Henry Yevele* (London, 1944), pp. 35-6.

27. To distinguish it from the Henrician Portland Castle. My own paper on this curious little place (*Dorset Nat. Hist. and Arch Socy.* lxix (1948), pp. 65-7) dates it a little more confidently than I should today.

28. *History of the King's Works*, iii, 381-2, and plate 29.

29. *Ibid.*, iv, 416-17.

30. Châtelain, *op. cit.*, pp. 60-1; Viollet-le-Duc, *op. cit.*, pp. 177-81; Salch, Burnouf and Fino, *L'Atlas des Châteaux forts en France* (Strasbourg, 1977), pp. 464-5.

31. Hoffsummer, *Étude archéologique et historique du château de Franchimont, à Theux* (Liège, 1982).

32. MacIvor, in Caldwell, *Scottish Weapons and Fortification, 1100-1800* (Edinburgh, 1981), pp. 124-5.

33. Salch and others, *op. cit.*, pp. 627-9. French defences against guns (*a facie saevientium saxivomorum*) appear to have been constructed even earlier than this; at Melun (Seine-et-Marne) in 1420, we are told that *muri quidam fossatorum laterales extrinseci elevantur in altum, ut eorum summitas medium moenium proximorum ... praecellat ... Antemuralia quoque, validis castris non disparia* [!], *per quae, et in quibus inclusi ... possent obsessurorum irritare proposita, per oppidi circuitum ... construuntur.* In other words, a stone-faced counterscarp covered more than half the height of the actual walls against battering, and there were robust advanced works to frustrate the knavish tricks of the besiegers; *Vita et Gesta Henrici Quinti* (ed. Hearne, 1727; written c. 1445).

34. See n[5], *supra*.

14

Henry VIII and Coast Defence

In choosing 1547 — the death of Henry VIII — as the terminal date in the history of the English castle, I have been often questioned, and even (somewhat absurdly) denounced.[1] There are good reasons for this choice of date; in any catalogue, such as *Castellarium Anglicanum*, it is far better to include too many examples than too few. Further, Henry VIII's defences of the south and south-east coast represent a programme of fortification which can only be compared with Edward I's North Welsh castles. Later than 1547, the Tudor programme of defences petered out among forts of acute bastioned or tenaille trace both generally weak and entirely un-medieval.

A further good reason for including the Henrician castles is less compelling today: until very recently, little study had been made of the post-medieval defences of the kingdom, and in particular, the earlier fortifications of the south coast. In *Castellarium Anglicanum*, speaking from as late as 1980, I commended to my readers a good picture-book by Mr Beric Morley;[2] there was nothing better to recommend. Many of the sites had been in the hands of the military or of some equally unsympathetic body, but almost all are now open to the public. A new generation of scholars has been interesting itself in artillery-fortifications, and an important series of papers in the periodicals *Fort*[3] and *Post-Medieval Archaeology* — both recently founded — together with the publication of vol. IV of the *History of the King's Works*, has left us better informed, perhaps, about this period than about any other in the history of our castellation.

The objections to including Henry VIII's strongholds in a catalogue and discussion of castles appear to be twofold: on the grounds of function or of structure; but in neither case at all convincing. To take the first, and surely the more significant objection: these are not castles, we are told; they are simply forts, serving only a military purpose. It has already been pointed out that a typical castle is a fortified habitation, but there are a great many atypical castles, in which the element of habitability is unimportant, as compared with the requirements of defence; and these belong to this category. At the same time, in some of the larger coastal castles, the captain's quarters can be as good as those reserved for the constable of any medieval castle; at Deal in particular the King could be accommodated not unworthily, if he came there in an emergency or for a tour of inspection. As to the structure of the Henrician castles, by medieval standards their profile is squat; their battlements, unpierced by loops, have rounded merlons and widely-splayed embrasures with sloping sills, to reduce damage by gunfire; and they are robustly built. But they remain examples of what Dr Colin Platt has called 'upstanding fortification'. They are structures of masonry, not of revetted earthwork, and do not use a bastioned trace (scarcely even a bastion) or a tenaille (star) plan. Their crenellation is of a latter-day pattern, but still they are battlemented buildings, and the battlements are of practical use, not ornamental. All in all, they constituted examples of what another modern authority, the eminent Dr Duffy, has called 'reinforced-castle fortification', the first reaction of the defence to the discovery that the new weapon could be dangerous. This was the case in particular with Henry's inland fortifications.

Coastal defences were founded before the time of Henry VIII, largely defending the narrow entrances of the main harbours on the western half of the south coast: the chain-defences of Portsmouth, Dartmouth, Plymouth, and Fowey, and a small but uncertain number of blockhouses. At Portsmouth and Plymouth the original arrangements have disappeared; at Fowey they consist of a pair of moderate-sized square towers, some way up the estuary. Fowey castle is a fragment; its mate, Polruan, has some modest arrangements for guns. Dartmouth preserves a more impressive system of defence: overlooking the narrows and the chain there is a powerful square tower with seven gunports, of which one, pointing up the harbour, could hardly have been used along with the others. These are very primitive, their guns would have needed to be laid more or less on the ground, and little traversing and less elevation was possible. But here the target would have come to the battery; it was designed against ships attempting to run the narrows at point-blank range, and constituted a real deterrent to attack. Additional artillery-works stand outside the narrows (Kingswear) and further up the harbour (Dartmouth No. 2).

Further east, the single round tower of Camber (East Sussex), later to be developed into a substantial castle, was built to guard the approaches to Rye and Winchelsea.

Henry VIII's earlier work was mainly in the north, and much of it has been destroyed. To a large extent it consisted of modernisation of existing castles, but where new building was undertaken this took the form of roundels of quite modest size, like those which were added to Carlisle, and the two which remain at Berwick-on-Tweed. At Norham three ports for heavy guns on wooden beds were pierced in the curtain; on the outer line of defence the thirteenth-century half-round towers were fitted up for defence by musketry and light guns; their round fronts were also cut back into the beaked, semi-hexagonal plan which has already been noted at Raglan and

174

Berry Pomeroy. This work was begun as early as 1509.

Two important single works in the north are represented only by fragments; both are in Northumberland, on the very border: the keep of Wark-on-Tweed, finished by 1519, and the Lord's Mount (Berwick No. 2), built in 1541. The first of these involved the remodelling of the defences of the motte; whether the massive revetment carried down to ground level was part of the original structure, or whether it dates from 1519, is now quite uncertain; the general plan was circular, more or less, with a straight face towards the bailey. The circuit of the table-top formed a terrace, with about a dozen embrasures for cannon, round a substantial tower of polygonal trace, which was certainly built under King Henry. According to a report of Lord Dacre to Wolsey, it was four storeys high, in each of which there were 'five great murder holes [gunports] shot with great vaults of stone, except one stage which is of timber, so that great bombards can be shot from each of them'.[4] 'Great bombards' seems likely to be very much of an overstatement; upper ports of this sort in other castles of Henry VIII's work are for light guns of the numerous classes mentioned in documents of the period.

The Lord's Mount at Berwick has suffered by being left outside the Elizabethan defences, and only part of its base remains; it was an enormous round tower, about 105 feet (32 m) in diameter, with walls 16 feet (4 m. 88) thick. There are still four ports (out of six) for fairly heavy guns, massively vaulted over; this is a most impressive fragment. The ports permitted considerable traverse, having both internal and external splay. The splaying of gunports is obviously a feature of great importance, and external splay in particular was used by O'Neil as a criterion of date in artillery-defences.

Coming to the final great programme of fortification of the last years of Henry VIII's reign, the most substantial single piece of work was in the north: the landward defences of the harbour at Hull. These have completely vanished; they consisted of a long ditch and rampart with three strong-points on it, two 'blockhouses' at the ends, and the castle midway. The former were artillery-works with apparently two storeys of ports, and a plan recalling the ace of clubs, the three conjoined projections having a curious pointed plan. The castle was rectangular, with a pointed projection to front and rear, and a central rectangular tower. The walls were of great thickness — 16 or even 19 feet (4m.90 or 5m.80) — but the ports seem to have been very narrow, allowing little traverse.[5]

The new Citadel of Carlisle (Cumbria) belongs to the same period; here again little is left, only the base of one of the two massive round towers which faced the open country. Between these there was a small rectangular tower of uncertain employment, and at the rear a third roundel — apparently open at the rear — to fire into the city. The surviving fragment[6] is less robust than other inland works of the period, but the walls are about 12 feet (3m.65) in thickness, and the great gunports have a large outward splay.

The emergency at the end of Henry VIII's reign was concerned with the

Reformation, or rather with the Henrician Schism in which it began:

> In 1533 the Act in Restraint of Appeals severed England from the Church of Rome. The better-known Act of Supremacy in the succeeding year, under which Henry VIII became Head of the Church of England, simply added insult to injury, but at least it left no doubt of the challenge to Rome. And Rome's reaction was formidable. In 1538 Pope Paul III brought about a diplomatic revolution by bringing together the perpetual enemies Francis I and Charles V in the Truce of Nice — a truce for ten years, plainly levelled against the schismatic King of England,[7]

against whom a Bill of Excommunication and Deposition was also directed — once more adding insult to injury. The ten-year truce in fact lasted only till 1542; but though the Continental threat was diminished, it was not ended. Indeed, its principal development was the formidable French attack on Portsmouth in 1545, when the *Mary Rose* foundered. Confronted by Henry's powerful fleet in the narrow and fortified waters of Spithead, the French had to achieve a decisive victory, and this was impossible in the then state of maritime skills. Elsewhere they made some landings, but the great armament achieved nothing of any significance.

The programme of fortifications, whose pace had been less hectic since 1542, continued beyond the attack of 1545 to Henry VIII's death two years later, and beyond it, though the corrupt governments of Edward VI's reign and Mary I's deluded approaches to disarmament — which cost her Calais — did not supply a good climate for defence.

The remains of these coastal castles are almost entirely confined to the south coast; the blockhouses at the mouth of Milford Haven and that at St Ives, noted by Leland, have vanished, and the castle of Holy Island (Northumberland) perched on Beblow Crag, which has dictated its irregular plan, belongs to a later date. The fortifications in the mouth of the Thames and those of the Essex coast have all vanished, usually replaced by fortifications of later date. These were almost all simple blockhouses, though East Mersea (Essex) shows on a map as a trefoil in plan, and can have had a central tower; unfortunately, it has been completely destroyed.

The defences of the invasion shore in the great programme of 1539–47 show a great deal of variety. The simultaneous use of temporary earthworks (bulwarks), of simple blockhouses, and of fairly complicated castles was probably inevitable, but the extreme variation between individual castles is very notable, and it clearly indicates that the whole series was essentially experimental, and not firmly based on any contemporary Continental practice.

Certainly no foreign castles have been discovered from which they can be supposed to have been copied. The only apparent exceptions are the elementary examples mentioned in the last chapter, with a single platform in front

Figure 14.1: Sandsfoot Castle

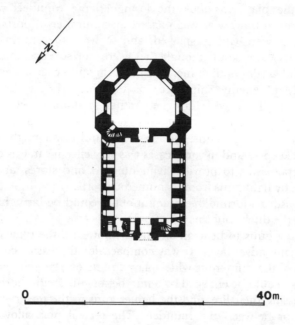

```
0                                              40m.
```

of a big rectangular tower on the landward side — Sandsfoot and Brownsea Island in Dorset[8] and St Andrew's Point in Hampshire (vanished) — which could have been modelled on the Tower of Belem at Lisbon. But this sort of fortification is so simple that one hardly needs to look for copying. Nor are they closely related to earlier English coastal defences such as those of Dartmouth. Even the blockhouses seem to have varied in plan, with the D-shape predominant, as at the vanished Tilbury (Essex) and the surviving St Catherine's and St Aubin's (Jersey). At Plymouth No. 3 the round end is replaced by a semi-octagon. The weak Edgcumbe (Cornwall) is square.

As to Henry VIII's bulwarks, it is worth noticing that not one of them has been discovered in our time, though those around Deal in particular can be fairly closely located.[9] Moreover, the indefatigable Stukeley got sight of three of the four at the Downs, one of which he drew as a plain circular bank and ditch, with traces of embrasures, on the line of the ditch linking the strongpoints along this very vulnerable piece of coastline.[10]

As to the castles, the variations between individual examples are so great that even the most cautious generalizations on the subject must be qualified. Commonly they take the form of a central tower, with a gun-platform or platforms attached to it. The platforms are generally open to the sky, so that the abundant smoke from their heavy guns could clear away as rapidly as

177

possible. Sometimes the guns fired from the parapet; sometimes the wall rose above their embrasures to form a wall-walk and battlements for musketeers. Commonly the platforms took the form of large roundels with several gunports. The central tower was pierced by a number of ports for smaller guns. All ports were widely splayed, and so were the embrasures of the parapets; walls were stout, though they were not so enormously thick as those of inland castles of the time. The main threat to coastal castles was the heavy gunfire of enemy ships, just as the ships themselves were their intended target. They were designed rather to damage and beat off an enemy fleet than to offer a prolonged resistance to bombardment or landing-parties, however strong. Thus, though the central tower might be made to function as a keep — and in some cases was very effective in this character — its main purpose was to provide living-quarters and stores, and to supply overhead fire by light guns from its numerous ports.

In a few castles a formidable amount of fire could be brought to bear on an enemy in the ditch; but this is not usual.

For bringing guns to bear on an enemy, however, the typical Henrician castle had many advantages. It was compact, for the easier control of fire, and the arcs of the numerous wide-splayed ports overlapped generously, so that any target could be engaged by a number of guns, with those in different roundels crossing their fire, and the lighter guns in the tower shooting over the tops of, or between the roundels. The typical port allowed a useful amount of elevation, and the ordinary roundel was compact enough to give reasonable scope for defence by a single gun, and roomy enough for use with a heavy gun in each port.

The weak point in any English defence against France or any power possessing the Low Countries was the Downs. The anchorage was sheltered inside Goodwin Sands, and Deal Beach was long and easy, a very vulnerable sector. Accordingly, here there was a defensive system far more developed than elsewhere: parallel to the shore a fortified ditch, with no fewer than seven strong-points on it: three powerful castles — Sandown, Deal, and Walmer — and four bulwarks to cover the intervals with their guns. Deal, in the middle, was the 'Great Castle'; Sandown on the north and Walmer on the south appear to have been identical, with a quatrefoil of artillery-works around a big circular tower; the roundels so big that there are virtually no curtains between them. Deal forms a sexfoil, and its central round tower is further surrounded with six small half-round projections, alternating with the outer roundels, and one storey lower than the tower itself, so that shooting could be carried on at once from the parapets of the tower and its turrets. All three castles had a fighting gallery at ditch-level with numerous small ports for light guns and musketry, which could have produced a fearsome crossfire in the bottom of the ditch. At Deal the ground floors of the inner roundels were pierced by another series of ports, this time for ordinary arquebuses, to sweep the castle enclosure and defend the keep.[11]

Figure 14.2: Deal Castle

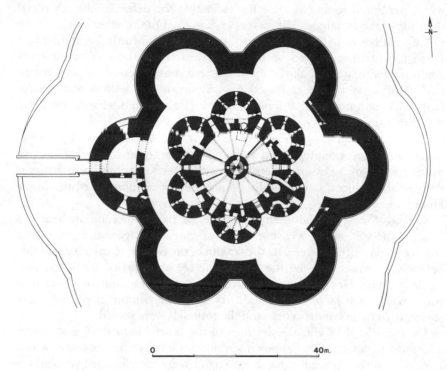

0   40m.

Westward from here, two castles, guarding weak points on the Kent and Sussex coasts, rather stand apart from the rest.

Sandgate (Kent) is unique in having a central keep (now turned into a Martello tower), a roughly triangular ward with three small round towers and curved curtains of no great thickness (5 feet 6 inches/1m.68), and a large platform outside all, shaped as a rough trefoil, with a curious half-round gatehouse. This castle was apparently designed by the questionably competent Stefan von Haschenperg; it looks as if he had known so little of artillery defences that he could only imagine them as an adjunct to normal medieval fortifications; thus he had first to build a rather poor little medieval castle, and then to construct a sort of bulwark round it. This was a roundabout method of producing a castle of the Henrician type.[12]

Camber (Sussex) started as a round blockhouse at the beginning of Henry VIII's reign (1512–14) only to end up in 1543, after a very complicated process of development, with an outer enclosure with four roundels and a gateway (which has since been rebuilt).[13]

The waters round the Isle of Wight were heavily defended. On the mainland, at the entrance to Spithead and guarding the approaches to Portsmouth, stands the formidable Southsea. Its platform is a long rectangle parallel to the shore, with right-angled salients in the middle of its long sides, which permitted some casemate fire enfilading the defences, though not at the ends of the rectangle. The tower was square. On the other side of Portsmouth Harbour, a blockhouse was built on Hasilworth Point (modern Haslar). It has disappeared; so has the next example, the small castle on St Andrew's Point, about halfway up the eastern shore of Southampton Water. Old plans show that it consisted of a square tower, with a semicircular battery in front; now all that remains of it or Hasilworth is a few fragments of masonry visible at low tide.

Further up Southampton Water stands Netley. A long block of platform, facing the shore, and interrupted by a single-storey square 'tower', it has very much the air of a cut-price Southsea; it was the contribution to national defence of a subject, Lord St John — not the last of subjects' castles in the Henrician system.

On the other side of Southampton Water, at its entrance, on the head of a long pebble-spit, stands Calshot Castle, a massive polygonal tower with a complete concentric battery. At the far end of the Solent, to the west, another pebble-spit almost blocked the arm of the sea and carried the formidable castle of Hurst. Here a polygonal tower stands in the middle of a polygonal ward, with three large roundels. In its exposed position, it needed more shelter than others of the series, and the roundels were roofed.

On the Isle of Wight, the defences of the 'East Medine' have vanished. The most important was Sandown, on the south coast; this, together with a later fort which replaced it, has been engulfed by the Channel. Its plan has been preserved, and shows an irregular structure with — remarkably — a

Figure 14.3: Netley Castle

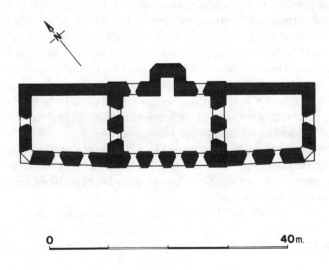

0   **40**m.

Figure 14.4: Calshot Castle

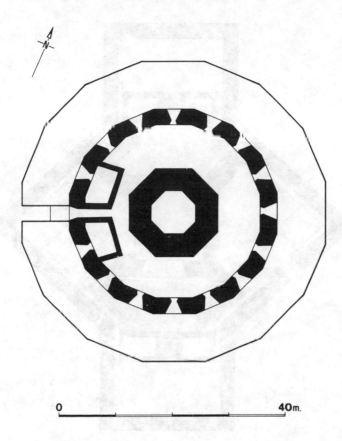

0   40m.

pentagonal bastion at one end of its landward face. This served only to flank that single side with the aid of a square tower at the other end: the twelfth century called into aid of the sixteenth.

At St Helens, on the east side of the Isle, there may have been a small fortification built in this reign, but little is known of it; it may have been a privately-built blockhouse. A similarly complete disappearance has overtaken the 'East Cow', at the mouth of the Medina river. The two 'Cows' were built together and Leland mentions both, the East Cow being the smaller of the two, but almost at once it drops out of memory and virtually nothing is known of it.[14] Its fellow West Cowes (Isle of Wight) has a curious plan,[15] also seen, on a larger scale, at Portland (Dorset). Here there is a central tower with wings extending on either side so as to form a long building, straight at Cowes but with a re-entrant angle towards the sea at Portland; this front is closed by the curved platform for heavy guns in each case.

Figure 14.5: Southsea Castle

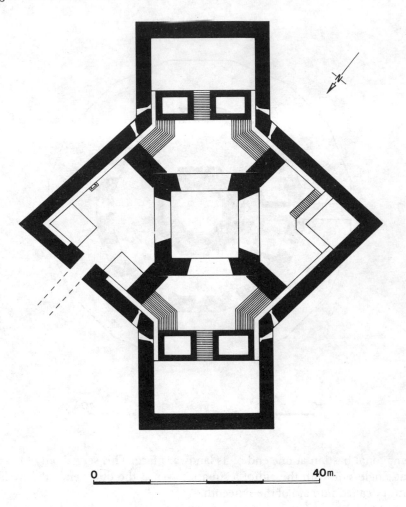

```
0                                          40m.
```

Opposite the Hurst, at the west end of the Isle of Wight, two small and
inadequate works had already been built, at Freshwater and Sharpnode; a
third, and by far a more powerful fort, the castle of Yarmouth, was begun a
few weeks after Henry VIII's death in 1547, and had therefore most likely
been 'devised' in his lifetime; but it differs from the others: there is no tower;
the whole is a square structure, with its inevitable weakness in diagonal fire.
The sea laps the north and west walls; the platforms on the north — vastly
altered for later artillery — are separated by a small courtyard from a line of
living quarters on the south. There is only one flanker, at the south-east,
where the two landward fronts meet; it is remarkable in itself, for though it is
built as a tower of three storeys, two of them original, and is not particularly

Figure 14.6: Hurst Castle

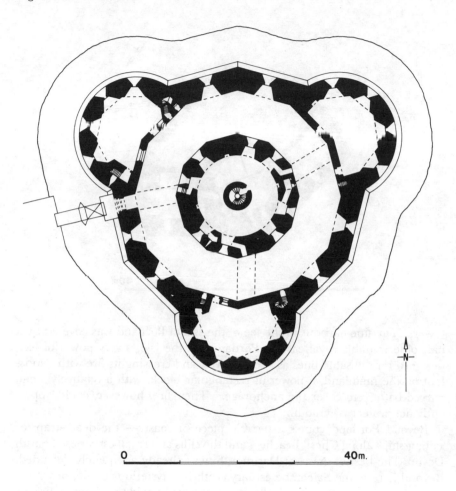

0   **40**m.

large, its plan and details are those of a typical artillery bastion of sixteenth–nineteenth century type; the two long faces meet in an acute angle, projecting thence to form *orillons* to protect the ports for light guns in the flanks.[16] It seems plain that Henry VIII's death is in fact our final date, and that Yarmouth belongs to the later age.

On the remainder of the south coast there was less castellation, and more of it was the work of patriotic or merely anxious subjects. The next castle is on Brownsea Island, at the mouth of Poole harbour, and it was the work of the townspeople of Poole. The harbour is a considerable sheet of water, but very shallow, and the island almost blocks the entrance; it seems likely that the Crown authorities thought little of its importance. The castle has been greatly altered; it consisted of an angular platform in front of a square

Figure 14.7: Portland Castle

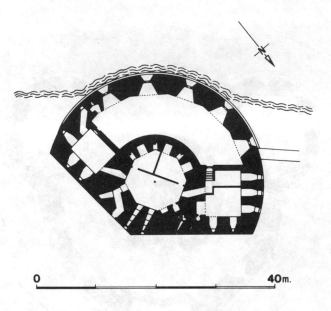

0   40m.

tower.[17] The fine harbour in the lee of the Isle of Portland was covered by a pair of formidable royal castles: Portland, on the Isle, a very powerful fort, designed on the same lines as West Cowes, and crossing its fire with Sandsfoot on the mainland, a powerful rectangular block, with a relatively small curved battery to cover the anchorage.[18] Their fire, however, could apparently not protect Weymouth.

Beyond Portland comes a terrible piece of coast — the death-trap for sailing-ships along Chesil Beach — and the cliffs and small estuaries of South Devon. The best of these, at Dartmouth, was already adequately defended. Beyond here is the Salcombe estuary, with its mysterious castle, of which, since it never appears in the Rolls, it can at least be said that it was a private venture. The harbour entrance is extremely rocky and dangerous, and the scanty remains of the castle occupy a rock ledge at its most awkward angle, under the foot of a towering cliff. It may be doubted whether guns could be depressed sufficiently to fire from the cliff-top into the castle; but a tall, protective *Schildmauer* was built across the rear of the site, with a powerful round tower at one end. It can only be said that this is more like a Henrician castle than anything else; and I am glad to find the learned authors of *The History of the King's Works* in agreement.[19]

The great port of Plymouth had multiple defences: its big 'Castel Quadrate' with probably rather primitive guns, on the end of the harbour-chain at the eastern end of the sea-front, with a string of blockhouses ending on the west, at the mouth of the Hamoaze. Plymouth No. 2 (The Devil's Point) was on the Devonshire bank and Edgcumbe on the Cornish side. Plymouth No. 3 (Winter Villa or Firestone Bay) is a very well-preserved example, on a semi-octagonal plan, with ports for heavy guns in its basement. But for all of these Lord Russell, acting as inspector of defences in 1545, considered the weakest points on the coast to be Weymouth and Plymouth.

The good, but narrow, harbour of Fowey received a 'castle' at St Catherine's (Fowey No. 2, Cornwall) by the munificence of one Thomas Treffry, a leading citizen; essentially it is only a normal apsidal blockhouse, but the foreland on which it stands is cut off by walls from the tower to the cliffs on each side, so as to give it some sort of enclosure. Leland, who was here in 1538, says it was finished in his time, but there is some reason to suppose it was later than this.

A final, splendid pair of royal castles flanked the entrance to Carrick Roads at Falmouth, the ideal port for sailing-ships, a huge and roomy anchorage.

> Before the gates there sat
> On either side a formidable shape[20]

— St Mawes on the east and lofty Pendennis on the west; but this entrance is wide, and these two majestic castles stand a mile and a quarter (2 km) apart, so that both have dependent outworks at the water's edge to reduce the range; even so, St Mawes stands in an overlooked position. Both have ornate round towers; St Mawes has three open roundels directly attached; Pendennis a large open battery concentric to its tower, as at Calshot, and an extended gatehouse building across the battery; both of these are later additions.

The business of all these castles was, uniquely, to deny possible anchorages and landing-places to an enemy fleet along the south and south-east coasts. The batteries which could achieve this needed defence on the landward side, lest they be overrun and silenced by a few boatloads of troops, scrambling ashore elsewhere on the coast. Many of the sites were hard to defend against this or any other sort of danger from the land; but all-round defence of some degree was indispensable; it was possessed not solely by the castles, but all the blockhouses and even bulwarks of which we have any information. The walls did not have to be of the strongest; neither from the land nor the sea would a castle be likely to be effectively battered. Sailing-ships could carry formidable guns, but they were neither very steady gun-platforms, nor stationary ones — except at the cost of becoming stationary targets. Galleys certainly could batter, creeping up into the shallows and using their big bowchasers; but galleys were brittle craft for a fire-fight with a stone castle, and the English Channel was not friendly water to them or their tactics. As to attack from the land, the castles could easily beat off a few boatloads of foot soldiers disembarked at some point on the shore near by;

while as for a serious siege by a substantial force — as the authors of *The King's Works* point out — this would have involved the failure of the castle (or rather of the defensive system as a whole). It would also have involved a deadly waste of time on the part of the invaders, devoting their energies to the siege of a peripheral castle while the forces of the invaded realm were gathering against them — and inviting battle with the sea at their backs, the immediate part of it still under fire from the castle's guns. A more likely form of attack would be by a substantial landing-party bringing up a few guns; but not much was to be feared in this case. Landing guns on the beach was a tricky business, and even a saker, about the lightest of battering-guns, with its little 5 lb (2.26 kg) ball, weighed nearly three-quarters of a ton, and could be relied upon to display to the full the maddening awkwardness of all guns on wheels. A limited detachment such as we are visualising had little time to waste before local forces closed in, and it is difficult to imagine substantial battering-pieces being brought up by them.

The fortifications of this period having no connection with the evolution of the defences of the succeeding age, it may well be asked, from what source were they themselves evolved? It appears that the answer may be disappointing to those who wish to trace a well-founded pedigree through every period; in fact, these castles seem to have been evolved in the brains of Henry VIII and his officers. In the first place, they vary so greatly that it is impossible to believe that there was ever any common ancestor; could Deal, Southsea, Portland, Sandsfoot, Hurst and Calshot be formed on any one model? Then, they are small in area, but independent; their supposed Continental ancestors will have been large works. In effect, almost all Henrician fortifications, even where they cover a long front — as at Deal beach or at Hull — are strong, but compact. Something similar was carried out around the city of Calais and the castle of Guines in its Pale, with strong works linked by long 'brayes'.

The whole, it is clear, was a great programme of experimental character, which cannot have any Continental system fathered on it. It is unfortunate that the theory, advanced a good many years ago, is still current, that the Henrician castles follow a German pattern, introduced to England by the Moravian architect Stefan von Haschenperg.[21] In fact, there is nothing particularly German about the employment of roundels; there are many in France, and some very impressive examples in Italy, the land of origin of the pentagonal bastion. As regards the highly ambitious designs for round bastions of Albrecht Dürer, an art-loving King like Henry VIII would surely not have needed any Haschenperg to draw his attention to them — though he had neither the time nor the resources to carry out such enormous works. As for von Haschenperg, he falls very short of a Master James of St George to King Henry's Edward I; he first appears in 1539, when the King is likely to have been recruiting everyone with any pretensions to be a military architect. Pretensions are precisely what Master Stefan had; in fact, he was a land-surveyor, who seems to have done a decent 'plat' of the Pale of Calais, but in May 1543 left the king's service with a flea in his ear. For his last two years he had been engaged at Carlisle; here and elsewhere, his work appears to have been sub-standard. He had no lesson to teach the English engineers of his time.

These castles clearly helped towards quenching the zeal of the Continental rulers for an English Crusade. They are of considerable interest for their own sakes, even though they have little relevance to any earlier or later scheme of defence, and though few of them ever fired a shot in anger, that is no uncommon fate for a good fortification.

Notes

1. K.J. Barton, review, *Archaeological Journal*, cxi (1984), pp. 357-8.
2. *Henry VIII and the development of coastal defence* (HMSO, 1976).
3. The annual publication of the Fortress Study Group; see, in particular: Malpas in iv (1977), pp. 1-3; Kenyon in vi (1978) pp. 24-5 and xi (1983) pp. 36-56; Andrews and Pinsent in ix (1981) supplement, pp. 6-7; Donnelly in x (1982) pp. 105-26.
4. *Northumberland county history*, xi, p. 54; quoting *Letters and papers, Henry VIII*, iii, part 1, p. 140.
5. *History of the King's Works*, iv, pp. 472-7; Cook, *Post-medieval archaeology*, v (1971), pp. 198-201.
6. D.J.C. King, *Castellarium Anglicanum* (New York, 1983), I, liii.
7. *History of the King's Works*, iv, pp. 670-3, plates 46, 47.
8. *Ibid.*, p. 467.
9. Elvin, *Records of Walmer* (London, 1890), pp. 157-8.
10. See Kenyon, *Antiquaries' Journal*, lviii (1978), plate 51.
11. The castles in the Downs are — rightly — very well written up; in particular, see Biddle, in *History of the King's Works*, iv, pp. 455-65; and Saunders, *Guide Book* to Deal and Walmer castles (HMSO, 1963).
12. I owe this explanation of the unusual plan of Sandgate to Judge Perks; it seems both ingenious and probable.
13. *History of the King's Works*, iv, pp. 415-47.
14. *Ibid.*, pp. 536-8.
15. *Ibid.*, pp. 535-9, especially Fig. 45.
16. *Ibid.*, pp. 553, 565-9.
17. *Ibid.*, pp. 465-8; *Royal commission on historical monuments, Inventory for Dorset*, ii, part 2, p. 280 and plates 158-60.
18. *History of the King's Works*, iv, pp. 466-70; *Inventory for Dorset*, ii, part 2; for Portland, pp. 250-2; for Sandsfort, pp. 336-8; for both, plate 146.
19. *History of the King's Works*, iv, p. 595.
20. John Milton, *Paradise Lost*, bk II, lines 648-9.
21. For his career see B.H. St J. O'Neil, 'Stefan von Haschenperg, an engineer to King Henry VIII, and his work', *Archaeologia*, xci (1945), pp. 137-55.

Appendix: A Note on Keeps

At this juncture, when we have covered the whole subject-matter of English medieval castles, it is time to consider keeps in depth. As to the name keep, it is greatly used, but is itself open to criticism; as to the keep — the thing itself — there are on record a number of statements of opinion which appear to call for comment or contradiction.

A serious criticism of the word 'keep' is that it is not a medieval term. The proper English word is dungeon, but that has too long been contaminated with the secondary meaning of 'pit-prison', which is now invariably associated with the word. The form *donjon* is objectionable as a piece of Franglais, of very questionable pronunciation. A straightforward translation of the Latin terms *turris, turris castri* or *magna turris* might seem more practical; but 'tower' and 'tower of the castle' are not sufficiently specific, while 'great tower', though very useful, ought to be reserved for use as a generic term, including other towers besides keeps. It must be pointed out that a number of large towers exist, dominating their castles and containing the quarters of their lord, or of his constable — and so far resembling keeps — but which no-one in his senses would consider suitable for defence after the rest of the castle had fallen. The ambiguous character of the fine tower of Richmond (North Yorkshire) has already been mentioned; alone among great towers, it seems unlikely to have contained the private rooms of its lord; it defensive character is also uncertain. The great tower of Ludlow (Shropshire) seems never to have been capable of independent defence either before or after its gate was blocked. The spendid apsidal tower of Helmsley (North Yorkshire), dated on archaeological grounds to about 1200, has so many entrances — at least in its final form — that it can hardly be thought of as any sort of keep. At Allington (Kent) there is one exceptionally large tower — Solomon's Tower — at the weakest corner of the defences, but there is no sign that it was meant for independent defence. At Whittington (Shropshire) and Newport (Dyfed) are the remains of enormous towers, but each has an undefended doorway at ground level. At Caernarvon the magnificent Eagle Tower was alluded to as *magna turris*, and never was an adjective better deserved, but if there was ever any intention of holding any element of Caernarvon after the fall of the rest of the castle, it was not the Eagle Tower.

Among fourteenth-century work, the Lady Tower at Maxstoke (Warwickshire) is a storey higher than the other angle-towers, but is not arranged as a keep, while the lofty tower at the south-west corner of Beverstone (Gloucestershire) is simply part of the fine domestic accommodation.

Similarly the splendid fifteenth-century brick tower of Tattershall castle (Lincoln) which was called *le Dongeon* in the course of its construction, stands five storeys high with a two-stage parapet, and has polygonal angle-turrets like those of Stafford; nevertheless it communicated directly with the domestic buildings alongside it, and has three unfortified doorways. Another fifteenth-century brick castle, Caister (Norfolk), has a great tower which looks rather fragile for a keep; examination reveals that this appearance is not misleading.

It is clear that there is a class of 'mistress towers' which were never intended for separate defence — a class sufficiently important to be recognised as something different from the defensible towers; I would prefer to use the term 'great tower' to include both categories, and reserve the word 'keep' for those which were intended for defence on their own.

As to the word 'keep' itself, though not medieval, it is of an antiquity scarcely lower. The examples of its use in the *New English Dictionary* are by no means the earliest available, and the compilers have confused matters by their note 'perhaps originally a translation of Italian *tenazza*', relying on a passage from Barret's *Theory of warres*, 1598: 'the Tenaza or Keepe, which stands without the body of the Castell'. Unfortunately, *tenazza* is not a known Italian word; the passage suggests a small outwork. But the dictionary in fact gives a rather earlier example from Sir Philip Sidney: 'He who stood as watch upon the top of the keepe' — exactly where one would expect, by the way; and Leland introduces the word at least seven times in his *Itinerary*,[1] though he prefers 'dungeon'. In two places (Nottingham and Devizes) he equates the two terms: 'Dungeon or Kepe'. It thus appears unlikely that the word 'keep' is of antiquarian origin; and indeed the earliest employment which I have been able to find, in 1523, comes in a purely military document, the report of the Earl of Surrey at Wark-on-Tweed castle (Northumberland). The earl approved of the latter's new donjon, 'which is the strongest thing that I have seen. I would that the keep of Guisnes were like it'. Again in 1541 we find Sir Robert Bowes and Sir Ralph Ellerker in their *View of the castles ... of the east and middle marches* (Survey III) putting forward the suggestion

> And yf yt were the kings majesties pleasure we thinke there might be within the cyrcuyte of the said castelle [Wark-on-Tweed] a stronge towre or kepe devysed and made for the savegarde of such mens lyves as were within the said castell when in extreme nede shoulde chance ...[2]

The suggestion was unacceptable, and probably ill-advised, but at least it shows the purpose a keep was expected to fulfil. Here again the writers are fighting-men, and it seems that 'keep' is initially a soldier's term.

Reverting to our own day and to the company of modern archaeologists, we must touch, if only briefly, upon the most radical theory of all. W. Mackay Mackenzie in his very important work *The mediaeval castle in Scotland*[3] maintained a prolonged argument directed against both the word 'keep', and the conception that keeps form a significant category — an argument carried on with vigour and violence of a kind generally reserved for use in theological discussion (which, after all, concerns matters of more than vital importance). The effect is rather as if a zoologist of repute were to devote a whole chapter on (say) the rhinoceros, to proving that there is no such animal. Perhaps it is not surprising that this theory has never found any serious acceptance. Mackenzie pointed out that the word 'keep' 'has become the normal equivalent with translators for the Latin *turris* or the French *tour* or *donjon*, instead of the quite legitimate word 'tower', as well as the most hardworked term in the vocabulary of writers upon mediaeval castles'.

For all its shortcomings, however, 'keep' fulfils a need felt in other languages; in French the same thing is called *donjon*, in German *Bergfried* or *Wohnturm*, in Italian *mastio*, in Spanish *torre del homenaje*, even in Japanese *ten-shu-kaku*.[4] If 'the quite legitimate word tower' were to be substituted, there would be a loss to our language — unless one is to accept Mackenzie's main contention, which is that there was really no separate category calling for the use of a special term. He argues the point at length, with a perverse brilliance; any occasion of failure to hold out in a keep, or to hold out for long, is made the most of, while if a determined defence is mentioned (and Mackenzie mentions many fewer than he might have been expected to mention) this is treated as merely fortuitous; resolute men will hold out anywhere.

But this is ridiculous; when one finds great towers equipped with every facility for separate defence — solid and lofty walls, small and high windows, crenellations and arrowslits, both within and without the castle; doorways on the first or even the second floor, protected by forebuildings, barbicans, portcullis, drawbridges, and all the contrivances of defence: when one finds such towers sited on mottes, or built where their great strength will have afforded little help to the defence of the castle as a whole — even inside the enclosure — then there can be no argument as to the intentions of their builders; *res ipsa loquitur* — it speaks for itself.[5]

In fairness to Mackenzie, it should be pointed out that the positive side of his argument is far sounder; he will have nothing to do with the notion that great towers were only for emergency occupation.

> The underlying idea that mediaeval nobles disliked living in a tower is wholly beside the mark. A tower was the simplest way of providing a private suite of rooms ... No one in Scotland had so much of the White Knight in him as to maintain an empty house on the chance of its coming into use in the event of a siege.[16]

The author of the next erroneous theory on keeps is not identifiable; it seems to have been evolved in informal discussion or put forward in unpublished lectures. It sprang from a modest and on the whole true statement by the great Clark, that in concentric castles 'the keep, the main feature in a

Norman or an Early English fortress, was dispensed with'.[7] Sir Charles Oman, writing in 1898, was more inclined to play down the importance of the keep: 'By the thirteenth century the feature of the castle which was originally all-important had sunk to a secondary place in the scheme of defence,'[8] but he follows Clark in general; it is in the concentric castles that keeps are dispensed with.

By about 1911, however, matters had gone further, and there seems to have been a general consensus of opinion that at a date early in the thirteenth century the keep had somehow become obsolete. In the words of Harvey,

> The most striking feature of this system was that the keep was boldly abandoned, as it had been proved by experience, especially in the memorable siege and capture of Château-Gaillard, that the main enclosure of a castle once taken, the keep was of little practical utility.[9]

Hamilton Thompson, too, speaks of 'tracing this gradual disappearance of the keep',[10] and again refers — at considerable length — to the siege of Château-Gaillard, ending:

> The prominence of the keep in the plan was, however, an archaic feature; and the history of the siege of 1204 shows very clearly that the great tower was practically a superfluity, and that the last hopes of the defenders were centred in the wall of the inner ward.[11]

It would not be difficult to find a better reason than the suppositiously archaic nature of the keep for this last fact: the donjon of Château-Gaillard is a splendid tower, but by no means capacious; and the garrison were still very numerous when the defences of the mighty inner ward were breached. William le Breton enumerates the prisoners taken as 40 knights, 120 *satellites* (obviously serjeants-at-arms) *et alios multos*.[12] It seems unlikely that there was room for this mass of people in the keep, and the fall of the inner ward was thus the end of any possible resistance. (A small garrison, on the other hand, would have got back into the keep very early in the proceedings, but might have held out there for a long time.)

Of the other early twentieth-century writers, Evans accepts the same narrative: 'The twelfth-century keep, of whatever form, now disappeared, and the bailey ... was abandoned in favour of an enclosure furnished with strong towers at the angles,'[13] but Mrs Armitage entered her *caveat*: 'The new type of keepless castle never entirely displaced the old keep-and-bailey type. We have already seen that keeps of the old sort continued to be built till the end of the Middle Ages.'[14]

It would have been better if more attention had been paid to this warning on the part of the best and most knowledgeable authority of the time. As has been shown, a careful scrutiny will reveal that 'the old keep-and-bailey type' remained in wide — probably predominant — use throughout the thirteenth century, though in the last thirty years of that century an experimental type of gatehouse competed for favour with the traditional tower, and in the fourteenth century a symmetrical type of moated castle with no keep came into considerable vogue. If the keep-and-ward castle fell into partial disfavour, it was probably due to the expense of building both a properly flanked ward *and* a great tower. Even this partial disfavour was peculiar to Southern England — which by the main fourteenth century was well past its best as a theatre for the display of fortification. It did not apply to northern England, which is a country of towers and rectangular keeps, still less to Scotland, and less again to Ireland. France is a country of donjons, and Germany as well; we have no effective narrative of the history of fortifications in medieval Spain or Italy, but in Italy we have been shown that the lords still clung to the *mastio* when they were building bastioned forts;[15] while those spectacular and noble castles in Spain which are all that most of us know anything about include a surprising number of examples from dates well into the fifteenth century, and virtually all of these have a conspicuous *torre del homenaje.*

Perhaps this is hardly relevant, but the Knights of Malta, when they built a fort on Dragut Point in 1792 — Fort Tigné, which was universally considered a very fine and advanced specimen of fortification — gave it a keep which looks very much like a medieval round donjon.

Owing to the relatively advanced state of English castle-studies, there is a danger of generalization from England to foreign countries, which in this particular case would be most unfortunate.[16]

The late Dr W. Douglas Simpson based his theory of 'castles of livery and maintenance'[17] upon this supposition that keeps had fallen out of use in England in the early thirteenth century: but the fairly numerous great towers of the fourteenth and fifteenth centuries did not escape his notice. He was concerned to explain why something so like the supposedly obsolete keep had been reintroduced, and he therefore looked for some new element in the military life of the period to afford a reason. It will be appreciated from what has gone before that this was rather of the nature of Lewis Carroll's suggested enquiry into why the sea is boiling hot and whether pigs have wings: keeps had never become obsolete, so there was no question of their reintroduction.

Nor is the explanation itself very satisfying: Dr Simpson concluded that these later keeps were intended to secure their lords against their own garrisons, because these were now mercenaries, whereas in earlier days they had been feudal subordinates, tenants by castle-guard. These new defenders were so untrustworthy that they had to be guarded against — perhaps so uncouth that they had to be kept entirely away from the household.

In fact, in the later fourteenth century the proportion of new keepless castles in southern England was probably higher than at any other time; the segregation of an undesirable element in the garrison would have been difficult or impossible in the ordinary quadrangular castle[18] — though Simpson made a manful effort to convince himself that Bodiam was designed to give its lord and his family privacy and the tactical mastery of the castle at the expense of his retainers.[19]

Moreover, it is necessary to take a good look at the mercenaries themselves. There had been plenty of these in Norman and Angevin England; the only difference was that by the fourteenth century they would no longer have been foreign troops; English fighting-men by this time enjoyed enormous prestige. Thus we are not dealing with mercenaries in the full sense — soldiers fighting for a nation other than their own, like the Swiss and *Landsknechte* of the fifteenth and sixteenth centuries, or the Hessians of American folk demonology. It is to mercenaries of this sort that most of the suspicion attaches, though a category of men which has included the Varangian Guard of the Byzantine Empire, the Scottish Archers and *Garde Suisse* of the French kings, and the Gurkha Rifles of our own time, can hardly be considered altogether unsatisfactory.

Native mercenaries, serving under their own countrymen, are scarcely more than simply professional soldiers; they may well have been bound to their employers by closer ties than the merely commercial: it would be natural for a magnate to recruit from among his tenantry, a retired banneret from among his old troops. Even swords bought in the open market could prove to be true; one attractive feature of the dismal narrative of the capture of Caister Castle (Norfolk) in 1469 is the conduct of the hireling soldiers engaged for the siege by Sir John Paston — presumably recruited in the London taverns. They were engaged for a particularly hopeless defence, on behalf of a lord in whose service they spent less than a year altogether; but on the testimony of their commander they did everything men could be expected to do, and are last heard of departing, delighted with their wages, to which a well-earned *pourboire* had been added.[20] It is unhappily true that men of this sort could also be used as bully-boys, or as cannon-fodder in the vile little civil wars of the fifteenth century; but there is no evidence that they were, as a class, unreliable.[21] It is very sad that so much of the energy of a notable antiquary should have been expended in formulating a theory of this kind.

As to the parent theory — that keeps became obsolete in the thirteenth century — it has been eroded by so much contrary information that it is no longer widely held; the last statement of it in a work of authority is probably that in Professor Allen Brown's *English mediaeval castles* (1st edn), published in 1954;[22] even this is less categorical than earlier works. The theory perished — as it began — by way of informal discussion and unpublished lectures; it is only fair to Professor Brown to say that he was the first person I ever heard publicly denouncing it, in a lecture at Leeds in 1967. Dr Arnold Taylor's chapter in *Medieval England*, published in 1958,[23] makes no reference to any disappearance of the keep.

The final question concerning keeps is: what is the explanation when there is more than one in the same castle? How can there be two last refuges for the defence, or more than one set of quarters for the lord's family?

Cases in England are happily few; they can mainly be referred to a change in plan. The two mottes at Lewes seem likely to be due to a partial abandonment of the smaller (the Brack Mount) in favour of the larger of the two, which carries the present heavy towers and curtains; but the similar situation at Lincoln appears to owe something to certain obscure manoeuvres of the Countess Lucy of Chester and her son, Earl Rannulf II, which appear to have been aimed at control of the castle in connection with a claim to hereditary constableship.[24]

The mottes of Hastings and Bramber (both in Sussex) both seem to have been superseded by towers on the level. At Chepstow the great oblong Norman keep exists alongside a large and powerful half-round tower of late thirteenth-century date — Marten's Tower — which was both arranged for defence and well-appointed for occupation, standing close to the fine domestic buildings of its period. Clearly this was the tower in which the lord meant to live, and he was also prepared to defend it; but the old keep is in a dominating position; which of the two would be used for a final defence in practice would depend on the circumstances of the attack.

A small group, probably peculiar to England, involves the use of that English hybrid, the keep-gatehouse, alongside some alternative inner position of resistance, and connected to it by a short and massive curtain, so as to present a sort of compound defensive work: at Kidwelly (Carmarthen, now part of Dyfed), where the Great Gatehouse is on the line of the Outer Ward, a compact inner line of defence; at Tonbridge (Kent) a 'shell-keep' on the motte, close to the splendid gatehouse; and at Llangibby (Monmouth, now Gwent) a contemporary keep-tower of complicated plan.

In foreign examples, the duplication of keeps is commonly due to a duality of ownership (*Ganerben*) as in the remarkable set of German castles with two or even three *Bergfriede* set out by Von Cohausen.[25] English law and practice had small room for such divisions; even coparcenary normally ended in the division of the estate between the heiresses, or rather their husbands, in complete shares.

Notes

1. John Leland, *The itinerary of John Leland the antiquary, in or about the years 1535–1545* (ed. Lucy Toulmin Smith, 5 vols., London, 1907–10). At Launceston, i, p. 175; Rockingham, i, p. 12; Nottingham, i, p. 112; Devizes, v, p. 82; Warwick, v, pp. 153-4; Pickering, i, p. 63; Brecon, iii, p. 105.

2. Cadwallader John Bates, *The border holds of Northumberland* (Newcastle-upon-Tyne, 1891), p. 348. This passage is omitted in the transcript of the 1541 survey at p. 30 of the same book.

3. (London, 1927), being the Rhind Lectures for 1926. His argument occurs on pp. 80-4, 230-40.

4. It is fair to admit that, owing to the great difference between European and Japanese styles of building, the *tenshu-kaku* is a strange construction to our eyes, with a towering and ornate timber superstructure above a low stone base, which presumably affords all the military strength of the tower. More unexpectedly, the German *Bergfried* is generally different from other western keep-towers. In mountain-castles in particular it seems commonly to be little more than a watch-tower, with a few small and uncomfortable rooms, a doorway of considerable strength, and generally an abnormally large proportion of the lower part of the tower devoted to providing dungeon accommodation. This fact was noted by Major-General Köhler (*Die Entwicklung des Kriegswesens und der Kriegführung in der Ritterzeit, usw.* (Breslau, 1886–90, 3 vols. in 5) iii, pt. 1, pp. 402, 413).

5. It is the more extraordinary to find such an argument put forward by a Scottish writer, when so many of the keeps of his country are hardly to be distinguished from its numerous isolated towers, which in the nature of things had to be independently defensible.

6. Pp. 83-4. This, of course, is true of England, and other kingdoms, as well.

7. George Thomas Clark, *Mediaeval military architecture*, i, p. 159.

8. *The art of war in the middle ages* (1st edition, London 1898), p. 537.

9. Alfred Harvey, *The castles and walled towns of England* (London, 1911), p. 134.

10. A. Hamilton Thompson, *Military architecture in England during the middle ages* (Oxford, 1912), p. 212.

11. *Ibid.*, p. 216.

12. *Gesta Philippi Augusti*, cap. 129 (ed. Delaborde, Paris, 1882), i, p. 219.

13. Herbert A. Evans, *Castles of England and Wales* (London, 1912). Cf. J.H. Round in *Encyclopedia Britannica* 11th edition, 1910-11, v, pp. 477-8.

14. Mrs Armitage, *Early Norman castles*, p. 377.

15. See J.R. Hale, 'The early development of the bastion' in *Europe in the late middle ages* (London, 1965), pp. 476-7, 481, 483, 488. These examples date from the very end of the fifteenth century and the early years of the sixteenth century.

16. Thus Professor Tuulse, in his wide-ranging *Castles of the western world* (trans. R.P. Girdwood, Vienna and London, 1958) at times expresses himself as if this particular narrative of English castle-history could be applied to France; e.g. p. 65, on Coucy (of all places): 'A donjon still exists, not now alone but as *primus inter pares* of a well organised column of turrets [*sic*]. Admittedly, the master of the castle used the donjon occasionally as a dwelling and as a last refuge, but in time the living rooms were moved out of the dark interior of the tower into the castle yard ...' The theory underlying this very dubious passage is plainly English, and none the better for that.

17. For the development of this theory, see 'Castles of "Livery and Maintenance"' *Journal of the British Archaeological Association*, 3rd Series iv. (1939), pp. 39-54; 'Bastard feudalism and the later castles', *Antiquaries' Journal*, xxvi (1946), pp. 145-71; *Exploring castles* (London, 1957), pp. 115-31.

18. A virtually isolated tower like Nunney would present the same problem in an aggravated form.

19. Dr W. Douglas Simpson, *Antiquaries' Journal*, xxvi (1946), pp. 159-61.

20. *Paston letters* (ed. Gairdner, London, 1904) iv, p. 306; v, pp. 56-7. They would seem to have had much in common with Housman's Mercenaries, who 'saved the sum of things for pay'.

21. Simpson gives none, and his reference to McFarlane in *Trans. Royal Hist. Socy.*, 4th ser. xxvi (1944), pp. 70-2 concerns the independent character of a totally different class of men. His own quotations from Stubbs' *Constitutional history* and Denton's *England in the fifteenth century* appear to describe a type of follower dangerously *loyal* to an unprincipled master.

22. (London, 1953), p. 73. The later edition takes a totally opposite view.

23. Dr. A.J. Taylor, Chapter 3 'Military Architecture' in *Mediaeval England* (ed. Poole, Oxford, 1958), pp. 98-125.

24. D.J.C. King, *Castellarium Anglicanum* (New York, 1983), i, p. 267, n[24] to Lincoln castle; also *History of the King's Works*, ii, p. 704.

25. Von Cohausen, *Die Befestigungsweisen der Vorzeit und des Mittelalters* (Wiesbaden, 1898), p. 155 and plates 22-24.

Index

197